A PRACTICAL APPROACH TO XVA

The Evolution of Derivatives Valuation after the Financial Crisis

A PRACTICAL APPROACH TO XVA

The Evolution of Derivatives Valuation after the Financial Crisis

Osamu Tsuchiya

Simplex Inc., Japan

World Scientific

NEW JERSEY • LONDON • SINGAPORE • BEIJING • SHANGHAI • HONG KONG • TAIPEI • CHENNAI • TOKYO

Published by

World Scientific Publishing Co. Pte. Ltd.
5 Toh Tuck Link, Singapore 596224
USA office: 27 Warren Street, Suite 401-402, Hackensack, NJ 07601
UK office: 57 Shelton Street, Covent Garden, London WC2H 9HE

British Library Cataloguing-in-Publication Data
A catalogue record for this book is available from the British Library.

First published 2019 (Hardcover)
Reprinted 2020 (in paperback edition)
ISBN 978-981-122-142-2 (pbk)
ISBN 978-981-3272-74-3 (ebook for institutions)
ISBN 978-981-3272-75-0 (ebook for individuals)

A PRACTICAL APPROACH TO XVA
The Evolution of Derivatives Valuation after the Financial Crisis

ISBN 978-981-3272-73-6

For any available supplementary material, please visit
https://www.worldscientific.com/worldscibooks/10.1142/11057#t=suppl

Desk Editors: Aanand Jayaraman/Shreya Gopi

Typeset by Stallion Press
Email: enquiries@stallionpress.com

To Maika

Foreword

If all that interests you about finance are the latest trends — machine learning, fintech, algo trading, quantum computing — then look elsewhere. But there is so much more to financial markets — aren't you curious what happened to the derivatives market with notionals in trillions prior to the financial crisis of 2008? In fact, they have not gone away — of course some of the more esoteric products (like CDO squared) have fallen out of favor. But vanilla derivatives like swaps are still very much in demand. The only thing is that, these days there is rightly far greater consciousness of the costs of doing business — including the average cost of counterparty default, the cost of funding the position, the cost of margin, and the cost of capital. This then is the subject matter of this book — the various adjustments (Cross-Valuation Adjustments or XVA) that fully reflect the cost of dealing in derivatives.

There was always a need to bridge academia and industry. For example, information about efficient markets was taught heavily in universities, notwithstanding various examples of market dislocation (e.g. the 1987 stock market crash). So it is worth considering the framework of derivatives valuation with the same amount of cynicism. Simply put, derivatives valuation is based on the cost of constructing a portfolio (possibly dynamically rebalanced) so that it attains the same payoff as the derivative of interest at a future time under any realized market condition — the cost of constructing this portfolio then gives the value of the derivative. (The ability to replicate the payoff removes the need to take account of the true dynamics of the underlying, and this is not premised on rational investors but the existence of liquid markets to execute the transactions necessary to attain the payoff of the derivative.)

Regardless of whether one believes in the ability to replicate the payoff perfectly, there are various externalities not well accounted for by this replication approach in the environment post the 2008 financial crisis. Firstly, the counterparty with which one transacts can default, and if so, the payoff will not be realized. This externality can be incorporated in the valuation by augmenting the payoff to take account of default, and hedging for default via Credit Default Swaps can be undertaken to lock in the cost — this is Credit Valuation Adjustment (or CVA). In a similar vein, with a clear recognition of the fallibility of financial institutions during the 2008 crisis, an institution is not default-free and if its default is to be taken into account, we get Debt Valuation Adjustment (or DVA). This adjustment may be demanded by large corporates (with strong bargaining power) against which a financial institution is attempting to trade.

But this is just the beginning — to replicate a payoff often involves executing transactions in the derivatives or cash market and this must be funded if there is a need to purchase the underlying. Whereas prior to 2008, it was assumed (somewhat justifiably then but no longer so) that AA financial institutions can fund their positions at Libor (i.e. borrow or lend at the same rate), so the theoretical risk-free rate used for derivatives valuation can simply be replaced by the Libor rate and there is no more need to worry about funding costs. But this is no longer true, with banks funding at Overnight Index Swap (OIS) for collateralized positions and Libor potentially being phased out. The forward OIS curve happens to be lower than the government curve even for major developed economies (like USA or Germany), so funding a position (to lend to someone else) now has a cost — not just about credit but an institution's own cost of borrowing. This is a real controversial area since it breaks the law of one price — different institutions have different funding costs. But reality does not have to be elegant — would you lend below your cost of borrowing, just because other institutions would lend at a lower rate?

If that were not enough, the crisis of 2008 has led to regulators seeking to reduce counterparty risk by requiring more derivatives to be cleared on exchanges — i.e. where the exchange (that is backed by initial margin requirements for derivatives, reserve funds and guarantees of clearing members) would be party to both sides of the deal. Or for positions that are not exchange cleared, there is the requirement for both parties to post initial margin to an independent third party to guarantee performance. All well and good to reduce counterparty risk. But the initial margin imposes a huge business cost, i.e. Margin Valuation Adjustment (or MVA).

Finally, regulators have belatedly raised capital requirements massively post 2008 to ensure financial institutions have enough buffer to deal with losses from market risk or counterparty credit risk — this comes in the form of additional components of risk-weighted assets (e.g. stress Value-at-Risk or CVA Value-at-Risk or Incremental Risk Charge), as well as in the form of requirements for higher capital requirements as a percentage of risk-weighted assets. This has severe implications on the long-dated uncollateralized client business, e.g. long-dated cross-currency swaps (typically 30 years) and inflation zero swaps (up to 50 years in UK). There have been product innovations like the advent of mark-to-market cross-currency swaps, or a decline in business for other products (e.g. inflation zero swaps). We can compute the capital implications in an ad hoc manner — after all, is it really P&L? But it is a key driver of business decision, and may be best recognized as such. This is Capital Valuation Adjustment (or KVA).

With the above myriad of valuation adjustments, we just need someone to explain what they are and how to go about computing them in a practical way — there are authors who have been carried away with enthusiasm and come up with grandiose frameworks where everything is interconnected into a coherent whole, but unlikely to be implemented quickly given the patchwork of legacy systems in a typical financial institution. Or what about just doing what is really adding value? That is what this book is about. Enjoy reading.

Chia Chiang Tan
Director and Quantitative Finance Manager at a Leading Global Bank

Preface

After the 2008 financial crisis, derivatives valuation theory has dramatically changed. One of the most important changes is the introduction of XVA. XVA started from Credit Valuation Adjustment (CVA), which is a valuation adjustment which takes into effect the counterparty credit risk. Following CVA, Debit Valuation Adjustment (DVA) and Funding Valuation Adjustment (FVA) are introduced. After the crisis, regulations have been continuously strengthened and from it, Margin Valuation Adjustment (MVA) and Capital Valuation Adjustment (KVA) are introduced. The series of XVA is still increasing.

In this situation, many papers and several books about XVA have been published. Comprehensive books, for example, the one by [Green], have a huge volume. XVA is a combination of many areas of quantitative finance, including hybrid derivatives pricing, credit derivative and exposure calculation for credit limit. Therefore, most of the papers and books are based on their own definition and framework.

The situation is similar to the development of the quantum field theory which is the building block of modern physics, including elementary particle physics and condensed matter physics. Field theory was first introduced as a quantization of classical field theory, especially electro-magnetic field. It is suffering from the divergence which arises because the model has infinitely short distant nature. This divergence was resolved phenomenologically by renormalization, but the real nature of renormalization and quantum field theory was not understood then. The real principle of quantum field theory was understood by the renormalization group of Wilson. Wilson introduced the renormalization group from the statistical model on the lattice. After the renormalization group, the true meaning of field theory is understood as a long-distance effective theory of elementary particle physics and condensed matter physics. Both elementary particle physics and statistical physics (condensed matter physics) are defined in the unified framework via renormalization group (Zinn-Justin, 2002).

I wrote this book to direct readers to the point in XVA which corresponds to the renormalization group in quantum field theory.

I hope this book contributes to the construction of the unified framework in XVA (derivatives valuation theory).

I benefited from a lot of people when I worked as a derivatives and XVA quant. I would like to especially thank the following people who directory contributed to this book.

I would like to thank Chia Chiang Tan for kindly agreeing to review this book and for our extensive discussion about the topic included in this book. I also would like to thank Dr. Assad Bouayoun for reviewing the book carefully and for permitting me to include his materials about IT aspects of XVA in this book. I also would like to thank Dr. Andrew Green for reviewing the core part of this book, which improved this book significantly.

Any errors are my own, however.

About the Author

Osamu Tsuchiya is a Quantitative Analyst at Simplex Inc. He has worked for Dresdner Kleinwort and Citigroup as a rates and hybrid derivatives quant analyst. He has also worked for XVA modeling. Additionally, he has experience working as a financial risk management consultant for Ernst and Young. Before moving to finance, Osamu worked in the field of mathematical physics. He holds a PhD in Theoretical and Mathematical Physics from The University of Tokyo. Part of his research papers were published in *Journal of Mathematical Physics*, *Modern Physics Letters* and *Physical Review B*.

His working papers about finance are available at https://papers.ssrn.com/sol3/cf_dev/AbsByAuth.cfm?per_id=2395992.

Contents

List of Figures

List of Tables

Introduction

Derivatives Valuation Theory Before and After the 2008 Financial Crisis

Following the 2008 financial crisis, the derivatives industry has dramatically changed and is still continuously changing. In terms of focus, the business model has changed from "earning money by taking risk" to "protecting the firm's position by managing risk".

The derivatives business, which was highly profitable for investment banks, has shrunk. Much more regulations now affect the business. From these changes to the business, the emphasis in the valuation of derivatives has also changed.

Traditional derivatives valuation theory before the 2008 financial crisis was based on replication and the existence of an almost risk-free rate (e.g. Libor pre-2008). Here, future cash flows are discounted by the risk-free rate because it is assumed that counterparties are default-free and the bank (which is generally the counterparty pricing the deal) can raise money at the risk-free rate.

In reality, default risk is relevant and would require an adjustment to the values of derivatives. The adjustments from default risk of the counterparty and itself (i.e. the bank) are, respectively, called Credit Valuation Adjustment (CVA) and Debit Valuation Adjustment (DVA).

Before the financial crisis, some global banks started to calculate and manage CVA. JP Morgan started to calculate it in the late 1990s, and most of the global banks started to work in the early 2000s. On the accounting side, FAS 157 introduced CVA in 2006. However, the importance of CVA and DVA was recognized seriously after the crisis.

During the 2008 financial crisis, default risk of major financial institutions was perceived to have increased significantly and most banks suffered losses from actual default of counterparties but even more from changes in CVA due to increased default spreads of counterparties. Further, during the 2008 crisis, all financial institutions tried to retain cash for protection from potential loss from counterparty risk. This led to a shortage of cash and the drying up of funding sources. Due to this liquidity crisis, funding spreads (e.g. the Libor rate vs. Overnight Index Swap rate) rose to hundreds of basis points and the funding cost of derivatives became no longer an afterthought. Following the crisis and in response to lessons learnt, regulators established stricter capital requirements to ensure banks are resilient in the future. Regulators required (or at least strongly incentivized) banks to clear standard derivatives through Central Counterparties (CCP). In CCP cleared trades, banks need to post Initial Margin on top of Variation Margin. Furthermore, since late 2016, regulators require banks to post Variation Margin and Initial Margin with an independent third party for (uncleared) over-the-counter derivatives under SIMM.

Given the substantial changes in the macroeconomic and regulatory environment outlined above, costs of derivatives trading has risen substantially. These costs must be taken into account as adjustments for derivative valuation in order for derivatives trading to remain profitable. Some of these new costs are funding cost of derivatives given by Funding Valuation Adjustment (FVA) and that of Initial Margin given by Margin Valuation Adjustment (MVA). Additionally, given the significant increase in capital in derivatives trading, there is much scrutiny on the capital implications of doing derivatives deals given by Capital Valuation Adjustment (KVA), although it has to be said that capital is not strictly an accounting item and here we are really going into the realm of economic value addition. To complete the picture of accounting for all costs, we would look at other adjustments, even those we deem less relevant. Collectively, these adjustments are referred to as XVA, and derivative

XVA

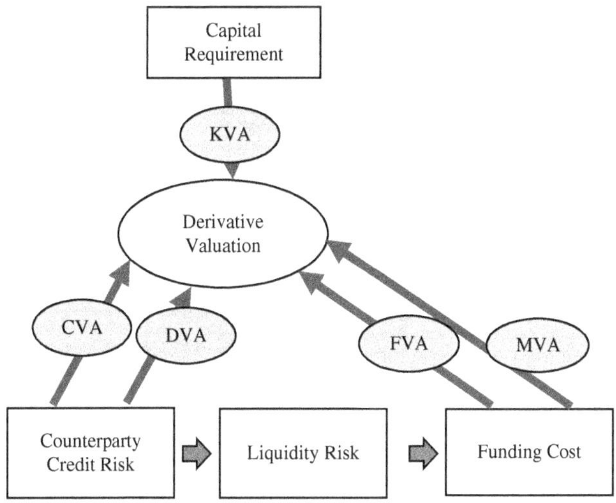

value $\tilde{V}(t)$ is given by

$$\tilde{V}(t) = V(t) + \text{XVA}$$

$$\text{XVA} = \text{CVA}(+\text{DVA}) + \text{FVA} + \text{MVA} + \text{KVA} + \cdots$$

where $V(t)$ is a risk-free value.

CVA is hedgeable theoretically, although there are practical constraints based on the availability (or lack thereof) of CDS referencing the counterparties of interest. CVA is a hedge cost if it is dynamically hedged. (Otherwise, CVA risk is warehoused and a part of the profit needs to be set aside to take account of realized losses from counterparty default.) By hedging CVA, the bank is protected from loss due to counterparty default. The situation is theoretically the same for other XVA components also. After the 2008 financial crisis, most global banks have set up a CVA or XVA desk to manage the above risks. The XVA desk hedges XVA risk or at least calculates adjustments necessary in derivatives valuation to keep in reserve (as shown in the following figure).

As will be explained throughout this book, XVA is calculated at the netting set level (or bank portfolio level for market risk KVA), which is a completely different approach to traditional derivatives

Roles of XVA desk

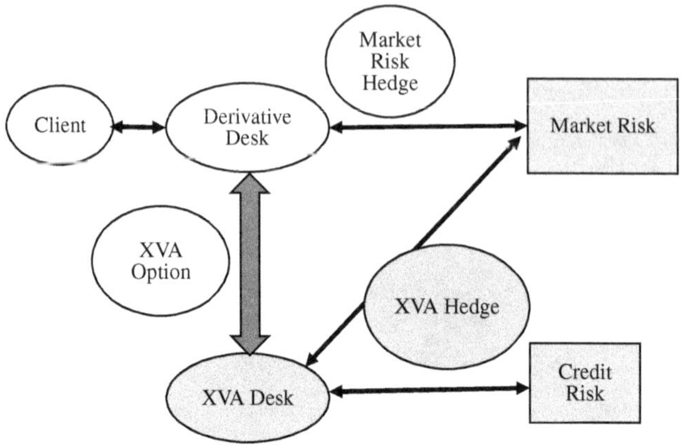

valuation, which is calculated at the individual trade level. In each netting set, there can be trades in many currencies. So an XVA model essentially requires an interest rate and FX hybrid model as backbone.

The most difficult part of the derivatives modeling including XVA model is a calibration of the volatilities.

Fortunately, most global banks have had long experience in valuation of long-dated FX derivatives. This is partly in light of widespread involvement in the market for derivatives, often exotic, e.g. the Powered Reverse Dual Currency (PRDC). So in many banks, the long-dated FX model (or FX hybrid model) can be reused for the calibration of the XVA model. Models of the derivatives in other asset classes such as equities, commodities, inflation, etc. are constructed on top of the FX hybrid model.

In XVA, interest rate derivatives are typically the most important because they are typically the ones with longest maturities. Global banks often have sophisticated interest rate derivative models. On the other hand, computational burden is intense in XVA calculation. For instance, in the CVA component, the calculation of the portfolio (netting set) values on each Monte Carlo path is necessary. In the (market risk) KVA (and CCP-related MVA) component, we may need to calculate VAR of portfolio on each Monte Carlo path.

Therefore, it is difficult to use a sophisticated derivatives pricing model in XVA. Tan (2014) observes that the use of a simplified model for XVA calculation is typical. Actually, most banks use a simple model, such as the Hull–White model, for the interest rate part of the FX hybrid model. This point is also discussed in Green (2016).

The Purpose of this Book

Recently, various books about XVA have been published (Brigo *et al.*, 2013), including the comprehensive one from Green (2016). This book however takes a different approach from existing books.

XVA is a combination of the derivatives valuation theory, accounting, regulation, etc. The field has been developed by many practitioners and academics, and the written material is often based on somewhat different assumptions from author to author. It is one of the reasons for the continued lack of consensus about the key components of XVA (especially FVA) and how to compute it.

XVA has had a relatively short history, but it has developed as a combination of many areas of quantitative finance. When banks started to calculate XVA for purposes of adjusting PV of a trade to go into official P&L, the simulation framework that feeds the derivative prices is typically developed by front office quants. On the other hand, in the calculation of counterparty risk at the portfolio (netting set) level, methodologies developed by risk management quants are used. They include calculation of Potential Future Exposure (PFE)[1] in credit limit management and Effective Expected Positive Exposure (EEPE) in regulatory capital.

The two functions can have rather different approaches for valuation. For example, the front office may prefer to use implied data in calibration to calculate the risk-neutral value (to be locked in by hedging), whereas the risk management function (and finance division) tends to use historical calibration to estimate possible loss that would be reflected by backtesting.

[1]Note that for the calculation of PFE P-measure (real-time measure) is traditionally used while Q-measure (risk-neutral measure) is used for the calculation of XVA.

In these environments, the literature about XVA and counterparty risk is rather complicated. Different texts are based on different assumptions as to risk-neutrality, so they sometimes may seem mutually incompatible.

Now it would be useful to present XVA from one kind of unified practical views. In this book, the value of derivatives (including XVA) is viewed as a cost to hedge (replicate) the position. In the traditional derivatives valuation (arbitrage-free pricing), the value of the derivative is a cost of delta hedging. By taking into account the cost of CDS hedging of the counterparty credit risk, there is a CVA. When we involve the cost and benefit of funding cash flows and/or Variation Margin in the derivative values, there is FVA. When we include the cost of Initial Margin, there is MVA. In the regulation, the banks need to increase capital for the market and counterparty credit risk of the derivatives trade. This increase of the capital is the cost for the bank and it is called KVA. Though it is not discussed in detail in this book, when some of the risks of the derivatives are not hedged (warehoused), the treatment of the cost and benefit can be different to the XVA above (Kenyon and Green, 2016).

The assumptions and the end results of the formulation will be explicitly described when possible.

This book does not intend to describe all of the details about XVA modeling. The focus will be on the basics, which are important for the implementation of any advanced feature of XVA.

Prerequisite

To understand this book completely, undergraduate-level calculus and linear algebra, and basics of stochastic calculus are necessary. Basics of the traditional derivatives valuation theory is assumed, but it is briefly summarized in the book. Knowledge of interest rate and FX derivatives is assumed. For the reader who is less familiar with such material, Tan (2012) or Andersen and Piterbarg (2010) is recommended.

Brief concepts of recognizing P&L in accounts and the main regulations on capital are briefly summarized in the book.

Use Cases

There are three major uses of the adjustment metrics presented in this text: (1) regulatory capital computation, (2) computation of "fair" P&L (and hedging) and (3) efficient allocation of the firm's capital.

For regulatory capital, it is only expected and potential future loss due to counterparty credit deterioration that is taken into account. For this reason, only the material on CVA is relevant.

For "fair" P&L that goes into a firm's accounts, all adjustments that are based on realizable current or future cash flows are applicable, i.e. CVA, DVA,[2] FVA, MVA and potentially other adjustments, but not KVA.[3]

For efficient allocation of the firm's capital, KVA is particularly essential. A firm would be reluctant to do business that does not earn the cost of capital, as it destroys economic value. Note further that KVA is the only part of the text that strays outside counterparty risk but into market risk VAR as well, since market risk and counterparty risk are the two main components of KVA in a derivatives business.

The following roadmap shows the relevant chapters for readers interested in the above use cases.

All readers: Chapter 1.

Readers interested in regulatory capital: Chapters 2, 7, 6 (Section 6.6), 8, 9, 11, 12 and Appendices A and B.

Readers interested in computing "fair" value: Chapters 2, 3, 4, 5, 7, 8, 9, 11 and 12.

Readers interested in capital allocation: Chapters 6, 10 and Appendices A and B.

---

[2]Based on latest accounting concepts, DVA comes under "other comprehensive income" — not quite the same section as CVA. DVA has always been a controversial issue because it works in favor of a firm with deteriorating credit, and hence poses a moral dilemma — especially if there is incentive to manage it.

[3]While there are proponents of recognizing KVA in accounts, there will always be the serious issue of objectivity since it depends on a firm's cost of capital though Green *et al.* (2014) proposed about the proxy of the cost of capital. It will be discussed in detail in Chapter 7.

Part I

Fundamentals

Chapter 1

Underpinnings of Traditional Derivatives Pricing and Implications of Current Environment

XVA is valuation adjustments to the traditional (risk-free) derivative valuation. Therefore before discussing XVA, traditional derivatives valuation theory will be briefly explained in this chapter (Tan, 2012).

1.1. Fundamentals of Derivatives Pricing

Derivatives are instruments whose payoffs depend on some other underlyings, hence the name (from "derived"). An example of such a derivative is a forward contract to buy 1 share of Apple stock in 1 year's time for \$800, where the underlying is Apple stock. A slightly more complex example is a call option giving the investor the right to buy 1 share of Apple for \$800 in 1 year's time. Derivatives are also prevalent in other asset classes (interest rates, FX, credit, commodities). It is thus natural to assume that the pricing of derivatives is related to the pricing of the underlyings.

The explosive growth of the derivatives market over the past decades was driven partly by demands of corporates managing risks (primarily interest rates and FX), and also the ability of financial institutions to "synthesize" these instruments, by effectively hedging (i.e. offsetting) some of their risks using simpler underlyings.

Principle: If two portfolios have exactly the same payout under all circumstances at a future date, then they must have the same value.

It follows that to value a derivative of a certain payoff, the approach is to construct a portfolio of simpler instruments which give exactly the same payoff at a future time. The reason for using simpler instruments is because we assume they are more liquidly traded (i.e. a financial institution can obtain a sufficient supply of them for hedging and without paying too high a bid–offer spread). For example, stocks are readily available, as are interest rate swaps (at least for financial institutions).

The two approaches to construct such a portfolio are as follows:

(1) **Static replication:** Build a portfolio today whose payout at a future date is (at least approximately) equal to the payout of the derivative.
(2) **Dynamic replication:** Implement a self-financing trading strategy to buy and sell simple instruments, so that the final payout of this portfolio equals the payout of the derivative. Here, the cost incurred in the trading strategy gives the value of the derivative. In general, a model is necessary to inform the trading strategy (i.e. how much of the underlying to hold at a given time subject to market moves).

Static replication is the preferred approach where possible, because it is generally model independent,[1] but unfortunately its applicability is limited to a far smaller set of derivatives.

1.1.1. *Assumptions of derivatives pricing*

Derivatives pricing, being predicated on hedging, relies heavily on certain assumptions. Some of them are as follows:

[1]Model independence is of course conditional on the availability of prices of all (simpler) instruments required for the replication.

(1) Dynamics of underlying.
(2) Existence of liquid market for underlying with enough depth such that hedging a reasonable position is achievable quickly and at minimal cost (bid–offer spread).
(3) Existence of a market to fund one's position (i.e. borrow if necessary and invest excess cash).
(4) The bank can fund as necessary to buy the derivative and asset at the risk-free rate $r(t)$.
(5) There is no counterparty risk and future payoff will be paid with certainty.

Traditionally, the approach was to assume (2)–(5), and to focus on (1), i.e. getting the correct dynamics of the underlying. We will however see in Section 1.3 how (2) and (3) are becoming questionable as well.

Here, Black and Scholes established the concept of hedging as follows:

Let us suppose we have a derivative that gives us the option to purchase an underlying. Trade continuously in the underlying in order that the hedged portfolio has zero delta (first mathematical derivative with respect to the underlying). This turns out to get rid of the randomness, leading to the hedged portfolio having only a deterministic component, which grows at the risk-free rate.

Let the value of a derivative with underlying price $S(t)$ be $V(t, S(t))$ and the risk-free short rate be $r(t)$. In the Black–Scholes model, the asset price follows the Geometrical Brownian motion

$$\frac{dS(t)}{S(t)} = \mu(t)dt + \sigma(t)dW(t)$$

The Black–Scholes Partial Differential Equation (PDE) is derived by creating a hedging portfolio with value $\Pi(t)$. The hedging portfolio consists of $\delta(t)$ amount of asset, $\beta_V(t)$ amount of cash to finance the derivative trade and $\beta_S(t)$ amount of cash to finance the asset, that is

$$\Pi(t) = \delta(t)S(t) + \beta_V(t) + \beta_S(t)$$

and $V(t, S(t)) + \Pi(t) = 0$.

For the portfolio value $V(t, S(t)) + \Pi(t)$ to be hedged against asset movements, it is necessary for

$$\delta(t) = -\partial V(t, S(t))/\partial S(t)$$

Because $\beta_V(t)$ is the cash to fund the derivative, we need

$$\beta_V(t) = -V(t)$$

and the amount of cash for funding the asset $\beta_S(t)$ is given by

$$\beta_S(t) = -\delta(t)S(t)$$

In the traditional derivatives pricing theory, the funding rate is assumed to be the risk-free rate $r(t)$, and the following is satisfied:

$$d\beta_V(t) = r(t)\beta_V(t)dt$$

Regarding funding of the money to buy (or sell) underlying stock, there is a dividend yield $\gamma(t)$ on top of the risk-free funding.[2]

$$d\beta_S(t) = (r(t) - \gamma(t))\beta_S(t)dt$$

Using Ito's lemma, by omitting apparent arguments of function, we have

$$dV(t, S(t)) = \frac{\partial V}{\partial t}dt + \frac{\partial V}{\partial S}dS + \frac{1}{2}\frac{\partial^2 V}{\partial S^2}S^2\sigma^2 dt$$

and from the self-financing condition,

$$d\Pi(t) = \delta(t)dS(t) + d\beta_V(t) + d\beta_S(t)$$

Because $d(V(t, S(t)) + \Pi(t)) = 0$, we have the PDE which is called the Black–Scholes equation

$$\frac{\partial V}{\partial t} + \frac{1}{2}\frac{\partial^2 V}{\partial S^2}S^2\sigma^2 + rS\frac{\partial V}{\partial S} - rV = 0$$

[2]Note that the funding for buying assets is done as a repo transaction. However, in the derivation of Black–Scholes formula in this chapter, repo rate is assumed to be the same as the risk-free rate.

From the Feynman–Kac formula, the solution of the Black–Scholes equation is given by the conditional expectation value as

$$V(t) = E^Q\left[\exp\left(-\int_t^T r(u)du\right)V(T)\,|F_t\right]$$

Here, the expectation value $E^Q[\ ]$ is calculated in a probability measure where the asset price process is given by

$$\frac{dS(t)}{S(t)} = (r(t) - \gamma(t))dt + \sigma(t)dW(t)$$

Implications of Black–Scholes Hedging:

> We note that the resultant PDE has a volatility term but not a drift. This immediately leads us to the realization that derivatives pricing is not about predicting the direction in which the underlying will move, since the hedge instruments are supposed to mirror the move.
>
> On the other hand, volatility is relevant because if the underlying is more volatile, hedging has to be conducted more frequently. Roughly, hedging is based on delta, so you buy more when the value of the underlying goes up and sell more when it goes down. Even assuming zero bid–offer spreads, you can only buy when the price has moved from S to $S + dS$ (for an infinitesimal dS), since how would you otherwise know the price is going up? The result of the above is that the hedging strategy costs more when volatility is higher.

But certain limitations of derivatives pricing also stand out given the above details. They are as follows:

(1) **Continuity of underlying:** Given that we are hedging by getting rid of sensitivity to delta (which only exists if the underlying is continuous), we are clearly assuming a continuous distribution for the underlying. In practice, if the underlying moves sharply, a delta hedge will fail to capture such a move. In practice, a limited set of derivatives have risks that very strongly depend on jumps (e.g. gap risk for CPPI or short-dated options on Credit Default Swaps). The pragmatic approach is

often to just add wider margins when in doubt, for cases where dependence is not critical.

(2) **Volatility:** It should be clear from the above that hedging a long position in optionality is more expensive the higher the volatility. Volatility is not an observable, and hedging cost will depend on realized volatility (from date of trade to expiry of option), whereas an option has to be priced before this cost is known. Thus, whether implied volatility (used to price the option and typically what gets charged to the client) is higher than realized volatility will determine whether selling the derivative is profitable in general.

(3) **Funding:** What is however less emphasized in academic texts is that there is a funding rate. Typically, this was conveniently thought of as the "risk-free" rate. But financial institutions could never borrow risk-free (even prior to 2008), so this was conveniently thought of as the Libor rate (for AA borrowing) back then. Post 2008 when funding became a far bigger issue, the exact rate to use has become far more important. This will form the heart of our discussion on FVA subsequently.

1.2. Realities of Derivatives Pricing

Even in classical derivatives pricing, the practice of hedging is far less ideal than the theory. As discussed in Section 1.1, it is not generally the case that one needs to have the correct dynamics of an underlying for hedging to work, and in practice it is rare to have the true dynamics of an underlying.

For instance, stock prices will jump (especially downward when bad news affects a company) and volatility will generally get more elevated under such circumstances. To reflect this accurately, it would be necessary to have jumps in the underlying and even stochastic volatility with jumps in the volatility. Such a framework would be totally computationally intractable and is not used in practice. Similarly, short-term interest rates generally jump as central banks adjust their rates in increments of 25 bp. And the same goes for other assets.

Following a similar theme, it thus must be clear that in general hedging will not be perfect. And at times hedging needs to occur despite a model not recognizing that the risk factor is deterministic. We can consider the following few categories:

(1) **Vega Hedging:** The Black–Scholes model and various other vanilla models assume deterministic volatility, which is in contrast to reality. Financial institutions respond by pricing with volatility skew[3] (i.e. different implied volatilities for different strikes). Sensitivity to vega risk can be computed as a numerical derivative of price with respect to implied volatility. These institutions also generally hedge this first-order risk, typically by trading at-the-money options (if not a wider spectrum of out-of-the-money options). This is an example where model limitations do not constrain practice, as regards hedging.
(2) **Exotic Products:** Calibration tends to be through the hedge instruments, with some other parameters used to "position" the pricing in a desirable way. For example, for Bermudan swaptions, the typical practice is to use a short-rate model where volatility is calibrated to prices of coterminal swaptions (i.e. same maturity date of swap but varying exercise date); this leaves the mean reversion parameter free, and a trader buying Berms who wishes to price conservatively would then choose a low mean reversion (to reduce forward volatility). Typically, mean reversion risk is not hedged.
(3) **Cross-Asset or Curve Shape Products (Correlation products):** Typically, liquid vanilla instruments available are in one asset class (e.g. FX, equities, rates), and typical rates products tend to be generally sensitive only to parallel yield curve moves. A hybrid involving multiple assets is thus sensitive to correlation, but usually no suitable correlation hedge exists.

[3]Some texts use volatility skew to refer to monotonic variation (e.g. decrease) of volatility with strike, and volatility smile to refer to out-of-the-money volatilities being higher than at-the-money volatilities. We do not distinguish smile and skew in this book, and instead use both terms to refer to when volatility is not constant over strike.

Similarly, a Constant Maturity Swap (CMS) spread option involves correlations between CMS rates of different tenors (e.g. 2 year vs 10 year) whereas the underlying swaption hedges do not capture the correlation risk. So to hedge exotic CSM spread products, we should use the CMS spread option market, but there is not enough liquidity in the spread option market.

(4) **Cross-Currency Basis:** If financial institutions can fund at Libor, then the value of a floating leg starting today (together with final notional) must be equal to the notional. Thus, in theory a cross-currency swap (where each leg pays Libor in a different currency and the notional is based on spot FX) should be worth zero at inception. However, this was not the case even prior to 2008 (and the difference was made up by having one leg pay a fixed spread) with the effect very pronounced where one currency is in an emerging market or is the Japanese yen (due to huge supply of yen from a nation of savers with insufficient domestic investment opportunities). Here we see practicalities forcing us to accept that funding in different currencies is not identical. So we cannot consistently assume funding is possible at Libor even prior to 2008.

(5) **Repo:** The concept is one of collateral. You sell a security (e.g. government bond) with a contract to repurchase at a future date. This effectively means you are paid cash now until the date for repurchase, and thus this is a form of collateralized borrowing. Because of the collateral provided (in the form of the security), the rate tends to be lower than Libor.[4] Typically, that is the basis on which many banks deal with government debt (even prior to 2008), as otherwise the yield would not compensate them for their cost of borrowing. And this is the clearest example (even prior to 2008) of how funding is not necessarily at Libor. This concept will be further developed as we discuss FVA subsequently.

[4]Repo rate is a collateralized rate and it should be smaller than OIS rate, which is an uncollateralized rate. However, sometimes RONIA (repo rate) is larger than SONIA (OIS rate). This point will be discussed in detail in Section 5.2.

1.3. Implications of the Current Environment

The 2008 credit crisis led to the collapse of several financial institutions, and further consolidation sometimes initiated by regulators to save failing institutions. A backlash against financial institutions deemed culpable for the crisis also led to a subsequent tightening of regulations on the activities of financial institutions (Volcker rule against prop trading) and their legal structure (e.g. ring-fencing of retail banking from investment banking) and a significant increase in capital requirements (based on higher capital requirements as a function of risk-weighted assets) to reduce the risk of a repeat of this crisis. And the heavy losses from banks due to changes in Credit Valuation Adjustments (CVA) on their positions during the crisis further led to regulators requiring capital to take account of regulatory CVA.

All the above-mentioned events have led to a smaller set of financial institutions being involved actively in financial markets, with most exiting Commodities, some withdrawing from Fixed Income, others withdrawing from Equities, others abandoning the Exotics business and yet others dropping out of long-dated products.[5] This has led to a marked drop in liquidity of products, with exotics becoming the preserve of a few institutions, some previously liquid products now becoming deemed exotic (e.g. market for CMS spread options dried up with available expiries dropping from 30 years to 5 years) and the cost of hedging increasing.

Further, the idea of funding uncollateralized positions at Libor has not survived the crisis, where the spread between 3 m Libor and Overnight Index Swap (OIS) reached 365 bp in USD. Thus, these days funding has become an integral part of derivatives pricing.

An overview of the changes since 2008 is detailed as follows:

(1) **Exotics and bias in pricing:** Financial institutions have tended to be on one side of the market for certain products

[5]The inflation and longevity markets are particularly long dated with 50 year products catering to the needs of pension funds. Even the interest rates market tends to have 30 year products commonly traded. In the US, the 30 year fixed-rate mortgage is actually typical.

due to client demand (e.g. long Bermudan optionality due to corporates issuing callable bonds and swapping their coupons for Libor payments, hence selling callability option to banks). Pricing for these products tends to reflect the lack of demand and difficulty to dispose of position (e.g. switch option value between Bermudan and maximum of underlying Europeans is minimal).

(2) **Hold-to-maturity of long-dated derivatives:** Since there is a limited market to dispose of long-dated derivatives except at fire sale prices, effective hedging with underlyings over the whole life is essential to defend the profit. For unhedgeable parameters (e.g. correlation between rates for CMS spread options), real-world probabilities become much more essential as there is no market to dispose of these positions.

(3) **Drying up of certain hedge instruments:** Capital charges have made it uneconomic to trade certain products for many institutions. For example, most banks have got out of commodities. More importantly, the market for credit protection via single-name Credit Default Swap (CDS) has shrunk so much that single-name CDS are no longer liquid hedge instruments for corporate bonds.[6]

(4) **Collateralization becoming the norm:** Previously, trading between financial institutions tended to involve collateral arrangements as with the more sophisticated clients. Now with the cost of capital and funding for non-collateralized positions and these charges being passed on to clients, the viability of non-collateralized business is seriously threatened and many clients have accepted Credit Support Annex (CSA) agreements on collateral. With this, funding for deals with such counterparties is at the rate applicable to the said collateral. For the highest quality collateral (e.g. government bonds), this OIS rate takes the place of the "risk-free" rate for pricing (Piterbarg, 2010).

[6]Even prior to 2008, single-name CDS tended to be primarily available for large US and Western Europe corporates only, while the coverage of emerging market firms in particular is at best patchy.

(5) **CVA and DVA becoming an integral part of pricing rather than an afterthought:** Whereas previously major financial institutions and high-quality corporates were deemed almost risk-free, now potential credit losses from dealing with them is generally priced in via the CVA. To achieve some symmetry between two counterparties, typically Debit Valuation Adjustment (DVA) is used to reflect the cost of one's own potential credit losses to the counterparty, so that both parties can agree on a price.[7]

(6) **Exchange clearing and uncleared margining and their funding implications:** Regulators are forcing financial institutions to have their bilateral trades with counterparties cleared by central counterparties in the form of exchanges (i.e. the exchange becomes parties to both sides of the deal and will charge a margin since it has to make good the deal if one party becomes insolvent). Similarly, there has to be a margin posted (to a third-party escrow account) for deals not cleared on exchanges. All this is aimed at ensuring financial institutions and their counterparties are adequately protected by collateral in the event of default by one party. But the margin imposes a funding cost, which needs to be accounted for if the deal is to be profitable.

(7) **FVA and funding in general becoming a determinant of profitability of deals:** Funding is now no longer based on Libor for uncollateralized deals, but instead the norm is to fund at the OIS rate between parties with a CSA (collateral) arrangement. If there is no CSA agreement, then the financial institution needs to charge for its own cost of funding the position (FVA) in addition to losses due to potential default of the counterparty (CVA) in order for a deal to be profitable. Note that care is necessary for the calculation of FVA and DVA such that the overlap between them does not happen (see Chapter 4).

[7]There is still some controversy regarding DVA. While accounting bodies have generally required its inclusion to ensure the account "balances" between both parties to a deal, regulators have not allowed its inclusion for calculation of regulatory capital as the inclusion is deemed imprudent.

(8) **Product innovation to mitigate CVA, DVA or FVA:** Various mitigation arrangements have arisen (e.g. mandatory termination where a deal gets settled in cash after say 5 years hence restricting CVA to be based on losses up to 5 years, although in practice the parties are free to extend it on the mandatory termination date), or new types of products have arisen (e.g. mark-to-market cross-currency swaps where in each coupon period, the notionals are returned and the new notional on one leg is based on the new spot FX rate, to ensure exposure of one party to another is limited to one period).

We will explore many of the issues raised in points (4)–(7) throughout this book.

Part II

Pricing Adjustments

Chapter 2

CVA and its Relation to Traditional Bond Pricing

Following the impact of the 2008 financial crisis, the environment of the derivatives trading business has changed dramatically. This change also dramatically affects the practice of derivatives valuation. One of the changes is the adoption of Overnight Index Swap (OIS) discounting of collateralized trades, and the other is a far more comprehensive inclusion of valuation adjustments (XVA — cross-valuation adjustment) in derivatives valuation.

In the OIS discounting framework, the valuation of collateralized (CSA)[1] derivative transactions has changed from the original risk-neutral valuation formula to

$$V(t) = E^C\left[\exp\left(-\int_t^T r^c(u)du\right)V(T)|F_t\right]$$

where $r^c(t)$ is the OIS rate and expectation is taken under the measure with numeraire being an account growing at the rate of collateral, so that $e^{-\int_0^t r^c(u)du}V(t)$ is martingale. The derivation of the equation above is given in Section 2.7.2.

[1]CSA stands for Credit Security Annex, which is an add-on to the ISDA Master Netting Agreement, and serves to regulate collateral arrangements for trades between two counterparties.

The OIS rate is not a risk-free rate but because the risk included in OIS rate is very small (overnight) so in practice, it can be considered as a risk-free rate. (The credit risk of a CSA trade will be discussed in Chapter 6.)

For a non-CSA trade or partially collateralized trade, there is default risk of the counterparty. The valuation adjustment which reflects this is called the Credit Valuation Adjustment (CVA). In this chapter, CVA, which was the first to be introduced as a derivatives valuation adjustment (before the financial crisis) will be discussed.

2.1. Nature of CVA

CVA is a reduction to the value of a derivative to reflect potential losses arising from deterioration in the creditworthiness of the counterparty.

Such losses can occur because of either of the following reasons:

(1) **Potential credit events of the counterparty:** This includes outright default or potential debt restructuring (even if voluntary in the sense of it being imposed on all creditor's following approval by a supermajority,[2] e.g. 75%).
(2) **Changes in the counterparty's credit spread:** Whereas it may be thought that no actual loss is suffered until a counterparty defaults, in practice financial institutions may novate deals (i.e. transfer the contractual obligations of the deal to another financial institution) for various reasons (e.g. when exiting an unprofitable business). If the counterparty's credit is weak and market conditions imply lack of security of expected future cash flows to the financial institution, then this weak credit (as reflected in the counterparty's credit spread) will be reflected in the value obtainable in novation.

As credit spread changes reflect an increased probability of potential default (which causes credit spread to spike sharply), we could focus on credit spread changes in examining CVA losses.

[2]This voluntary restructuring actually happened with the Greek government debt in December 2012.

To better understand CVA for a general derivative, it is perhaps best to look at a simpler instrument with a far longer history of pricing — the corporate bond. A corporate bond is considered as an agreement to pay a series of fixed cash flows from the issuer (counterparty). Therefore, the price of the corporate bond should include CVA with the counterparty as issuer.

2.2. Pricing of a Corporate Bond

A corporate bond effectively entitles the bondholder to a series of cash flows in the future — the coupons $NC\tau$ at future coupon dates T_i for $i = 1, 2, \ldots, n$ (where notional is N, coupon rate is C and accrual fraction is τ) and the notional at maturity date T_n.

If $D(0, T_i)$ represents the discount factor for maturity T_i (as seen at time 0) based on the risk-free rate (typically taken as Libor prior to 2008 but now usually based on the OIS rate), then we have the price of the corporate bond as

$$P = NC\tau \sum_{i=1}^{n} D(0, T_i) \exp(-sT_i) + ND(0, T_n) \exp(-sT_n)$$

where we have introduced the credit z-spread s. Like implied volatility, this could be seen as the number in the formula that gives the market price. More intuitively, this is the additional rate at which we have to discount the cash flows in light of riskiness.

If we assume a recovery rate of R (typically taken as 40% for senior bonds of institutions deemed of good credit, and lower[3] for subordinated bonds) when the bond defaults, then this z-spread is related to the implied (constant) hazard rate λ by

$$\begin{aligned} P = NC\tau \sum_{i=1}^{n} D(0, T_i)(\exp(-\lambda T_i) + R(1 - \exp(-\lambda T_i))) \\ + ND(0, T_n)(\exp(-\lambda T_n) + R(1 - \exp(-\lambda T_n))) \end{aligned}$$

Note however that here we are simplifying things by considering a constant hazard rate λ as implied by the price P of one bond

[3]For example, 25% or even 0%.

with maturity T_n. In practice, we would have multiple corporate bonds, from which we could bootstrap time-dependent probabilities of default given some assumption about the recovery rate R.

The main point to note is that the probability of default is taken into account in the form of the hazard rate λ or the spread s, when pricing a corporate bond. It is this concept that we wish to generalize when we consider CVA.

Specifically, we can consider CVA as $P - \hat{P}$, where

$$\hat{P} = NC\tau \sum_{i=1}^{n} D(0, T_i) + ND(0, T_n)$$

is the idealized price obtained by discounting at the risk-free rate.

Then CVA in this case turns out to be

$$P - \hat{P} = NC\tau \sum_{i=1}^{n} D(0, T_i)(R - 1)(1 - \exp(-\lambda T_i)) + ND(0, T_n)(R - 1)(1 - \exp(-\lambda T_n))$$

Since $R < 1$, we note that the CVA reduces the price as expected. Given that cash flows here are deterministic and always positive, the concept is straightforward in that if a counterparty owes a financial institution money, then the potential reduction in value of the claim is based on the recovery rate and probability of default of the counterparty. This is not necessarily as straightforward for a derivative in general.

2.3. CVA of Swap

In this section, we will analyze the CVA of a derivative, which can be both an asset or a liability (at future times under different market conditions), and derive the CVA formula in general.

Consider a swap where one leg pays Libor and another leg pays a fixed rate K on equidistant tenor dates T_i $(i = 1, \ldots, n + 1)$. For convenience of this example, assume that we can fund at Libor.[4]

[4]These days, banks no longer fund at Libor but rather funding depends on the collateral arrangement, typically OIS in a major currency. There is however no

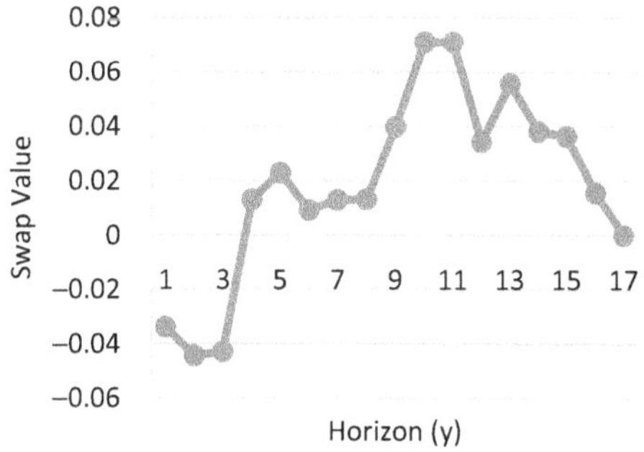

Fig. 2.1: Swap value along a path.

Then the floating leg has value $N\alpha\sum_{i=1}^{n} f(0,T_i,T_{i+1})D(0,T_i) = N\sum_{i=1}^{n}\left(\frac{D(0,T_{i-1})}{D(0,T_i)} - 1\right)D(0,T_i) = N(D(0,T_0) - D(0,T_n))$, where $f(0,T_i,T_{i+1}) = \left(\frac{D(0,T_{i-1})}{D(0,T_i)} - 1\right)/\alpha$ is the Libor rate and $\alpha = T_{j+1} - T_j$. The fixed leg has value $NK\alpha\sum_{i=1}^{n} D(0,T_i)$, so choosing $K = \frac{D(0,T_0)-D(0,T_n)}{\alpha\sum_{i=1}^{n} D(0,T_i)}$ will give the swap a value of zero today.

Whether the swap ends up with the counterparty owing the financial institution money or otherwise depends on future changes in interest rates. It is only if the counterparty owes the financial institution money when it defaults that a loss is incurred. If the financial institution owes the counterparty money, it still has to pay the counterparty's creditors if the counterparty defaults. This asymmetry makes CVA computation for a derivative much like option pricing. Thus, CVA would be based on an expectation of $V^+ = \max(V,0)$, where V is the value of the swap (Fig. 2.1).

Now we will discuss CVA in a general setting. Here, risk-free close out is assumed. Let $C(t,T)$ be the sum of numeraire N rebased cash flows of the derivative from time t to T;[5] the risk-free value of the derivative is given by $V(t) = E^N[C(t,S)|F_t]$, where S is the final maturity of the derivative. In the presence of counterparty default,

point complicating our example here. We will discuss actual funding in more detail in Chapter 7.

[5]This means we ignore any cash flows of the derivative that occur before time t, and have appropriately discounted all future cash flows.

if default time is τ, the value of the derivative $\tilde{V}(t)$ is given by[6]

$$\begin{aligned}\tilde{V}(t) &= E^N[RV^+(\tau)1\{\tau < S\}|F_t] + E^N[V-(\tau)1\{\tau < S\}|F_t]\\ &\quad + E^N[C(\tau,S)1\{\tau \geq S\}|F_t]\\ &= E^N[(R-1)V^+(\tau)1\{\tau < S\}|F_t] + V(t)\end{aligned}$$

Here, tower law of expectation is used. So CVA is given by $(1-R)E^N[V^+(\tau)1\{\tau < S\}|F_t]$.

When hazard rate of the counterparty is $\lambda(t)$,[7] because default intensity is $\gamma(t) = \lambda(t)\exp\left(-\int_0^t \lambda(u)du\right)dt$, CVA is given by

$$(R-1)\int_0^T E^N\left[\frac{\exp\left(-\int_0^t \lambda(u)du\right)\lambda(t)V^+(t)}{N(t)}\right]dt$$

where $V(t)$ is the value of the derivative at time t discounted back to time $0, \lambda(t)$ is the time-dependent hazard rate and $N(t)$ is numeraire.

This formula will be also derived by a partial differential equation (PDE) approach in Section 2.7.

When hazard rate $\lambda(t)$ is independent of market factors, CVA is given by

$$(R-1)\int_0^T \exp\left(-\int_0^t \lambda(u)du\right)\lambda(t)E^N\left[\frac{V^+(t)}{N(t)}\middle|F_0\right]dt$$

If $N(t)$ is a bank account, CVA is given by

$$\begin{aligned}&(R-1)\int_0^T \exp\left(-\int_0^t \lambda(u)du\right)\lambda(t)\\ &\quad\times E^Q\left[\exp\left(-\int_0^t r(u)du\right)\max(V(t),0)\middle|F_0\right]dt\end{aligned}$$

[6]For clarity, we state that in our notation $V^- = \min(V,0)$, whereas some authors use -1 times this quantity.

[7]For the definition of hazard rate and the details of the credit model, see Section A.1 in Appendix A.

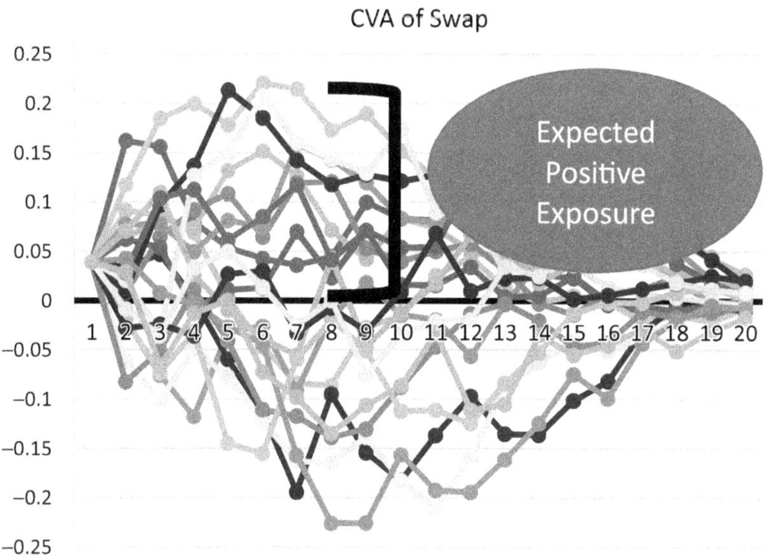

Fig. 2.2: CVA (EPE of swap).

In this case, after the estimation of the hazard rate, the calculation of CVA is reduced mainly to the calculation of the expected positive exposure (EPE) (Fig. 2.2)

$$E(0,t) = E^N \left[\frac{\max(V(t),0)}{N(t)} \middle| F_0 \right]$$

2.4. Complications from Closeout Value on Default

A complication of CVA is the treatment of a derivative in the event of default. Since a derivative is typically priced based on some model, the assumptions in the pricing of such a derivative upon default affects its value. Basically, an important issue is whether upon default at time τ, a derivative's value should be based on risk-free discounting yielding $V(t)$, or on discounting at a rate that takes into account the credit spread of the counterparty and other costs (i.e. CVA, DVA (and FVA) are included in the value) yielding $\tilde{V}(t)$.

Typically, guidance is obtainable by ISDA agreements, but such guidance tends to be vague[8] (perhaps deliberately) and courts have not yet ruled definitively on the issue, and decisions have not necessarily been consistent among major jurisdictions.

The main issues to consider based on these two treatments of default at time τ are as follows:

(1) **Risk-free closeout yielding $V(t)$:** A derivative's value will jump upward upon default (because $V(t) > \tilde{V}(t)$ if $\tilde{V}(t) > 0$) since it would be treated based on risky discounting prior to default (with generally very weak counterparty credit prior to default). Here, it may at times be advantageous (if immoral) to push a weak counterparty into default as the payoff may be higher eventually in bankruptcy, as opposed to novation of such deals with other counterparties.

(2) **Risky closeout yielding $\tilde{V}(t)$:** A derivative's value will not have major moves upon default. However, the severely reduced price (taking account of the defaulted counterparty's credit) will mean that it would be impossible to enter a similar deal with a high-quality counterparty based on what is recovered during default. This could hit the financial institution at a time of crisis, thus leading to contagion (in the form of losses spreading across financial institutions).

For CVA (and FVA) valuation, these two assumptions on close out have important effects on the equations involved. Our earlier definition of CVA is actually based on risk-free closeout.

For risky closeout, the equation is different. We shall develop it further.

Risky closeout value depends on whether the close out value includes not only CVA but also DVA and FVA. Here, when close out price includes only CVA, the value is given as follows. Let us consider the time grids $[T_1, \ldots, T_j, T_{j+1}, \ldots, T_n, \ldots]$ and assume that there are no cash flows before time T_n. When hazard rate $N(t)\lambda$ and recovery rate R are constant and numeraire is included in the value,

[8]The exact wording of ISDA stipulates that upon default, valuation "... may ..." take account of the cost of replacement. The use of "may" leads to ambiguity.

risky closeout value satisfies the relationship

$$\begin{aligned}\tilde{V}(T_j) = {} & R(\exp(-\lambda(T_{j+1}-T_j)) - 1)E^N[\tilde{V}^+(T_{j+1})|F_{T_j}] \\ & + (\exp(-\lambda(T_{j+1}-T_j)))E^N[\tilde{V}^+(T_{j+1})|F_{T_j}] \\ & + E^N[\tilde{V}^-(T_{j+1})|F_{T_j}]\end{aligned}$$

over consecutive points T_j, T_{j+1} in the time grid.

The derivative value and CVA is given by solving the above equation backward.

You can see that in risky closeout, CVA is much more involved than that in risk-free closeout generally.

2.5. Hedging CVA

CVA loss is the result of a counterparty's credit spread deteriorating when it owes a financial institution money as a result of future payoffs due on its derivative positions. The perfect hedge would be a Contingent Credit Default Swap (CDS), i.e. one that pays out an amount tied to the payoff of a derivative on occurrence of a credit event. For example, you could have a Contingent CDS that pays the value of the swap upon counterparty default. However, there is no liquid market for such products, and given the sharp decline in exotics post 2008, there is unlikely to be a growth in the market for such products. Thus, this is not a viable product for use in hedging.

Instead, the practical solution is to hedge CVA by buying protection against default of the counterparty, with a suitable notional (based on the estimated amount that the counterparty will owe the financial institution over the lives of all the positions). There are complications on estimating this quantity, and we shall consider practical treatment of the computations later in this book. For now, we wish to discuss what to do if we assume that we know how much protection to buy.

To buy protection from the default of a counterparty, the following are the typical instruments available:

(1) **Sell corporate bonds in the counterparty:** This is not necessarily feasible as it requires there to be sufficient corporate bonds for the financial institution to borrow, and there is the

danger of a "squeeze" if the supply becomes limited when the financial institution has to deliver on these bonds.

(2) **Buy protection on the counterparty via a CDS:** A CDS is an instrument where the buyer pays periodic (e.g. quarterly) premiums (premium leg) and in return receives compensation (either by delivering physical bonds for par value or by a cash amount assuming a certain recovery rate) for loss on a credit event of the reference name (protection leg). Whereas prior to 2008, the market for CDS was reasonably liquid and hence provided a ready source of hedge instruments for CVA,[9] and higher capital charges for such instruments post 2008 has led to withdrawal by lots of financial institutions from this market, so that hedging CVA of smaller corporates or, in emerging markets, via CDS may not be possible.

(3) **Buy protection on the counterparty by proxying via a CDS on an index:** A CDS index typically contains between 30 and over 100 reference names. Some of the more common CDS indices are CDX (for US), ITraxx Europe, ITraxx Senior Financials, ITraxx Subordinated Financials. Proxy hedging is a well-established approach with similar ideas adopted in equities many decades back: the idea is that risk of an underlying can be represented roughly as a linear combination of systemic risk to an index and idiosyncratic risk (CAPM), or this could be extended to involve multiple indices. So, index hedging is an attempt to get risk of systemic risk, while hopefully the idiosyncratic risk can be diversified away. In this sense, hedging via a CDS index is useful in preventing huge losses from elevated defaults of various counterparties (due to systemic shocks) in a financial crisis, but is unlikely to protect a financial institution if a counterparty defaults due to its own idiosyncratic problems (e.g. bad business decisions). However, in practice, there may not be many other choices available.

[9]We have pointed out earlier that even prior to 2008, single-name CDS largely existed for large corporates in the US and Western Europe.

To illustrate index hedging in practice, consider that the CDS spread s of an illiquid reference name can be represented as

$$s = \beta I + \varepsilon$$

where I is a suitable benchmark index (e.g. ITraxx Europe) and ε is the idiosyncratic part.

If CDS spreads are available (but not liquid enough to use in hedging because of large bid–offer spreads, for example), they could directly be used to estimate β, by directly regressing returns on the CDS spreads vs returns on the reference index. Otherwise, returns on z-spreads implied from bond prices of the reference name might be used instead as a less-ideal alternative (since bond z-spreads are not always closely related to CDS spreads).

Hedging typically is via sensitivities, i.e. compute $\frac{\partial V}{\partial s}$ for the bank's exposure to the counterparty, and then buy CDS on the reference name concerned so that the combined sensitivity after this hedge is zero. For proxy hedging, the idea would instead be to buy a certain quantity of the benchmark index by using the relation $(\partial V/\partial s) = \beta(\partial V/\partial I)$.

Of course, the CDS on the reference name could be proxied by multiple indices, and also hedging could be to the term structure of CDS spreads (i.e. over more than one maturity). But the idea above applies in the same way.

2.6. Dynamic Hedge of Credit and Market Risk of CVA

The role of the CVA desk is to hedge the CVA of derivative transactions. In this section, we will analyze hedging of Interest Rate Swaps (IRSs) to illustrate the principle of CVA hedge (Lee, 2010).[10]

Here we assume there is a liquid market for single-name CDS on the counterparty.

[10]Note that as will be shown in this book, the actual hedging of CVA of the netting set is much more complicated.

Now, assume that the bank has an IRS contract with the counterparty. The swap has interest exchanges at $[T_1, \ldots, T_{n+1}]$ and the bank pays strike rate K to the counterparty and receives Libor. The CVA of the IRS is approximated (assuming independence between interest rates and credit spread of the counterparty) as

$$\mathrm{CVA} = -N(0) \sum_{i=0}^{n} (1-R) \exp\left(- \sum_{j=0}^{i} \lambda(T_j)(T_{j+1} - T_j \right)$$
$$\times \lambda(T_i) E^N \left[\frac{A_i(T_i)(S_i(T_i) - K)^+}{N(T_i)} \middle| F_0 \right] (T_i - T_{i-1})$$

where the annuity is $A_i(T_i) = \sum_{j=i}^{n} \tau D(T_i, T_{j+1})$ and the par swap rate is $S_i(T_i) = (D(T_i, T_{i+1}) - D(T_i, T_{n+1}))/A_i(T_i)$. Now we can see that the CVA of the IRS is a sum of European Swaptions multiplied by credit spread, loss given default (i.e. $1 - R$) and time interval.[11]

Here, $\mathrm{EPE}(T_i) = E^N[A_i(T_i)(S_i(T_i) - K)^+/N(T_i)|F_0]$ is the expected positive exposure.

Hedging of CVA is the same in principle as that of a market risk hedge in derivatives trading. The hedge portfolio consists of Plain Vanilla derivatives such that all the sensitivities are canceled out.

In the above example, the CVA is hedged by the following hedge portfolio at the inception of the trade:

(1) Buy CDS protection such that the CDS sensitivities of the CVA cancel out. The amount of CDS is approximately the EPE of the derivative.
(2) Sell (coterminal) European Swaptions with strike K and exercise dates T_i such that Vega of CVA cancel out. The amount of European Swaption is credit spread $\times$ $(1 - R)$ $\times$ time interval.

[11]Note that this is a simplified example where notional and fixed rate are kept constant over time, and cash flows are regular. Otherwise, we would not have regular European swaptions but the principle is the same: we still have options, just not on standard instruments. It makes hedging more complex in that you cannot just buy liquid swaptions from the market for hedging. But you can still do vega hedging by buying swaptions to cancel out vega.

Note that in this example, if we use European Swaptions with strike K, a delta hedge is not necessary. We can adopt a delta hedge instead of a vega hedge and the situation is almost the same in principle.

Dynamic Hedge: As the market moves, the trader changes the hedge portfolio dynamically such that sensitivities always diminish. For example, when interest rates move and the IRS moves from OTM to ITM, the EPE increases and the trader needs to increase the CDS hedge position. However, he does not need to change the European Swaption position in this case.

On the other hand, when credit spread increases, the trader needs to increase the European Swaption position.

Time Decay: As time passes and the cash flow at time T_i is paid, the CVA decreases correspondingly if the payment is positive for the bank. This decrease of CVA is canceled by the European Swaption hedge which expires at T_i.

Counterparty Default: When the counterparty defaults, total CDS amount is the sum of the future EPEs and it compensates the loss due to the default.

2.7. Partial Differential Equation Approach

As is stated in Chapter 1, the Black–Scholes PDE is derived based on some idealized assumptions. Here, default risk of both the bank and its counterparty is neglected and funding rate is assumed to be the risk-free rate. In this section, we will analyze the PDE when there is counterparty default risk.

2.7.1. *Partial equation with counterparty risk*

In this section, we will extend the PDE approach for the Black–Scholes model in the previous chapter to the case where there is a default risk of client C and bank B. Funding rate is still assumed to be risk-free rate $r(t)$. Here, derivative price $\tilde{V}(t, S(t), J_B, J_C)$ is assumed to depend on asset price $S(t)$, and stochastic variables $J_B(t)$ and $J_C(t)$ which represent the default events of bank B and counterparty C, respectively. Interest rate is assumed to be deterministic, but extension to stochastic interest rate is easy. Here, $J_i(t) = 0$ before the default event and $J_i(t) = 1$ after the default event ($i = B, C$).

Note that when there is no confusion, we write $\tilde{V}(t) = \tilde{V}(t, S(t), J_B, J_C)$.

Asset price $S(t)$ is assumed to follow the stochastic differential equation

$$dS(t) = \mu(t)S(t)dt + \sigma(t)S(t)dW(t)$$

and corporate bonds issued by bank B and client C satisfy the following:

$$dP_B(t) = r_B(t)P_B(t)dt - (1 - R_B)P_B dJ_B(t)$$
$$dP_C(t) = r_C(t)P_C(t)dt - (1 - R_C)P_C dJ_C(t)$$

Here, R_B and R_C are recovery rates of B and C, respectively. We assume only one type of seniority bond is issued by both B and C. We also assume there is no Bond–CDS basis, and evolved future rates of bonds are given by

$$r_B(t) = r(t) + (1 - R_B)\lambda_B(t)$$
$$r_C(t) = r(t) + (1 - R_C)\lambda_C(t)$$

Here, $\lambda_B(t)$ and $\lambda_C(t)$ are hazard rates of B and C, respectively. They are given by

$$\lambda_B(t)dt = E[dJ_B(t)|(J_B(t) = 0)\&F_t]$$
$$\lambda_C(t)dt = E[dJ_C(t)|(J_C(t) = 0)\&F_t]$$

where the conditional expectation value $E[\cdots|(J_B(t) = 0)\&F_t]$ represents expectation value with the condition that $J_B(t) = 0$ (i.e. the bank does not default before t).

The derivative price $\tilde{V}(t)$ depends on three stochastic processes $S(t)$, $J_B(t)$ and $J_C(t)$, and from Ito's lemma, the SDE of $\tilde{V}(t)$ is given by

$$\begin{aligned} d\tilde{V}(t) &= \partial_t \tilde{V}(t)dt + \partial_s \tilde{V}(t)dS + \frac{1}{2}\sigma^2 S^2 \partial_S^2 \tilde{V}(t)dt \\ &\quad + \partial_{J_C}\tilde{V}(t)dJ_C(t) + \partial_{J_B}\tilde{V}(t)dJ_B(t) \end{aligned}$$

Here, partial derivatives of price changes when bank or client default, respectively, are given by

$$\begin{aligned} \partial_{J_B}\tilde{V}(t) &= \tilde{V}(t, S(t), 1, 0) - \tilde{V}(t, S(t), 0, 0) \\ \partial_{J_C}\tilde{V}(t) &= \tilde{V}(t, S(t), 0, 1) - \tilde{V}(t, S(t), 0, 0) \end{aligned}$$

These depend on the closeout term. Under market (risky) closeout, we obtain

$$\begin{aligned} \partial_{J_B}\tilde{V}(t) &= (R_B - 1)\tilde{V}(t) \\ \partial_{J_C}\tilde{V}(t) &= (R_C - 1)\tilde{V}(t) \end{aligned}$$

And under risk-free closeout, we obtain

$$\begin{aligned} \partial_{J_B}\tilde{V}(t) &= (R_C V^+(t) + V^-(t)) - \tilde{V}(t) \\ \partial_{J_C}\tilde{V}(t) &= R_C V^+(t) + V^-(t) - \tilde{V}(t) \end{aligned}$$

Now we will construct the hedge portfolio $\Pi(t)$ which cancels the stochastic behavior of both $S(t)$, and $J_B(t)$ and $J_C(t)$.

$$\begin{aligned} \Pi(t) &= \delta(t)S(t) + \alpha_C(t)P_C(t) + \alpha_B(t)P_B(t) + \beta_S(t) \\ &\quad + \beta_B(t) + \beta_C(t) + \beta_V(t) \end{aligned}$$

Here, the cash amounts required for funding the positions are given as follows:

$$\begin{aligned} \beta_S(t) &= -\delta(t)S(t) \\ \beta_B(t) &= -\alpha_B(t)P_B(t) \\ \beta_C(t) &= -\alpha_C(t)P_C(t) \\ \beta_V(t) &= -\tilde{V}(t) \end{aligned}$$

Under a self-financing trading strategy, the SDE of $\Pi(t)$ is given by

$$\begin{aligned} d\Pi(t) &= \delta(t)dS(t) + \alpha_C(t)dP_C(t) + d\beta_S(t) \\ &\quad + d\beta_B(t) + d\beta_C(t) + d\beta_V(t) \end{aligned}$$

Here, we assume we can obtain all the necessary funding at the risk-free rate. The effect of funding cost will be analyzed in Chapters 3 and 4.

$$d\beta_i(t) = r(t)\beta_i(t)dt, \quad i = S, B, C, V$$

where $r(t)$ is a risk-free rate.

Now we construct a portfolio such that market movement and default of both bank and client are hedged as follows:

$$\begin{aligned} \delta(t) &= -\partial_s \tilde{V}(t) \\ (1 - R_B)P_B(t) &= \partial_{J_B} \tilde{V}(t) \\ (1 - R_C)P_C(t) &= \partial_{J_C} \tilde{V}(t) \end{aligned}$$

The evolution of the total portfolio is given by

$$\begin{aligned} d(\Pi(t) + \tilde{V}(t)) &= \left\{ \partial_t \tilde{V}(t) + \frac{1}{2}\sigma^2(t)S^2(t)\partial_S^2 \tilde{V}(t) + r(t)S(t)\partial_S \tilde{V}(t) \right\} dt \\ &\quad + \left\{ -r(t)\tilde{V}(t) + \lambda_B(t)\partial_{J_B}\tilde{V}(t) + \lambda_C(t)\partial_{J_C}\tilde{V}(t) \right\} dt \end{aligned}$$

and from the condition that evolution of risk-free portfolio is zero, we have the following PDE:

$$\begin{aligned} &\left\{ \partial_t \tilde{V}(t) + \frac{1}{2}\sigma^2(t)S^2(t)\partial_S^2 \tilde{V}(t) + r(t)S(t)\partial_S \tilde{V}(t) \right\} \\ &\quad + \left\{ -r(t)\tilde{V}(t) + \lambda_B(t)\partial_{J_B}\tilde{V}(t) + \lambda_C(t)\partial_{J_C}\tilde{V}(t) \right\} = 0 \end{aligned}$$

Let $V(t)$ be a default risk-free price and satisfy the Black–Scholes equation

$$\partial_t V(t) + \frac{1}{2}\sigma^2(t)S^2(t)\partial_S^2 V(t) + r(t)S(t)\partial_S V(t) - r(t)V(t) = 0$$

If we split $\tilde{V}(t)$ into a component representing risk-free value, and an adjustment component $\tilde{V}(t) = V(t) + U(t)$, under risk-free closeout, the adjustment $U(t)$ satisfies

$$
\begin{aligned}
&\partial_t U(t) + \frac{1}{2}\sigma^2(t)S^2(t)\partial_S^2 U(t) + r(t)S(t)\partial_S U(t) \\
&\quad - [r(t) + \lambda_B(t) + \lambda_C(t)]U(t) + \lambda_B(t)(R_B - 1)V^-(t) \\
&\quad + \lambda_C(T)(R_C - 1)V^+(t) = 0
\end{aligned}
$$

From the Feynman–Kac formula, the adjustment is given by

$$
\begin{aligned}
U(t) = &-\int_t^T \lambda_C(u)(1 - R_C) \\
&\times E^r\left[\exp\left(-\int_0^t (r(v) + \lambda_B(v) + \lambda_C(v))dv\right) V^+(u)\middle| F_t\right] du \\
&-\int_t^T \lambda_B(u)(1 - R_B) \\
&\times E^r\left[\exp\left(-\int_0^t (r(v) + \lambda_B(v) + \lambda_C(v))dv\right) V^-(u)\middle| F_t\right] du
\end{aligned}
$$

where on the right-hand side, first term corresponds to the CVA and the second term corresponds to DVA, which will be discussed in the next chapter. Here, expectation value $E^r[\cdots|F_t]$ is taken under the risk-neutral measure, so asset price follows:

$$dS(t) = r(t)S(t)dt + \sigma(t)S(t)dW(t)$$

2.7.2. *PDE with collateral*

In this section, we investigate the PDE for the completely collateralized trade. The amount of collateral $X(t)$ (posted at each time point t) is assumed to be the same as the value of derivative, i.e. $X(t) = \tilde{V}(t)$. And here we investigate the ideal situation that when the bank or client defaults, all of the loss is compensated by the collateral, so there is no loss upon default, that is

$$
\begin{aligned}
\partial_{J_B}(\tilde{V}(t) - X(t)) = 0 \\
\partial_{J_C}(\tilde{V}(t) - X(t)) = 0
\end{aligned}
$$

Now, the hedge portfolio is given by

$$\Pi(t) = \delta(t)S(t) + \beta_S(t) - X(t)$$

Because there is no loss upon default, $\alpha_C(t) = \alpha_B(t) = 0$, i.e. there is no need to hedge by holding positions of bonds in either the bank or the counterparty.

Note that here all the cash flows needed for derivative transaction come from the collateral and $\beta_V(t)$ is replaced by $-X(t)$. Collateral evolution is given by

$$dX(t) = r_C(t)X(t)dt = r_C(t)\tilde{V}(t)dt$$

where $r_C(t)$ is the collateral rate. We assume $\beta_S(t)$ is funded by the repo transaction of the asset.

$$d\beta_S(t) = (q_s(t) - \gamma_S(t))\beta_S(t)dt = -q_s(t)\delta(t)S(t)dt$$

where $q_s(t)$ is the repo rate and $\gamma_S(t)$ is the dividend yield.

Now, the evolution of the hedged portfolio $\tilde{V}(t) + \Pi(t)$ is given by

$$d(\tilde{V}(t) + \Pi(t)) = \left\{\partial_t\tilde{V}(t) + \frac{1}{2}\sigma^2(t)S^2(t)\partial_S^2\tilde{V}(t) + (q_s(t) - \gamma_S(t))S(t)\partial_S\tilde{V}(t) - r_C(t)\right\}dt$$

Therefore, the derivative price satisfies the following PDE:

$$\partial_t\tilde{V}(t) + \frac{1}{2}\sigma^2(t)S^2(t)\partial_S^2\tilde{V}(t) + (q_s(t) - \gamma_S(t))S(t)\partial_S\tilde{V}(t) - r_C(t)\tilde{V}(t) = 0$$

From the Feynman–Kac equation, $\tilde{V}(t)$ is represented as the conditional expectation value

$$\tilde{V}(t) = E\left[\exp\left(-\int_t^T r_C(u)du\right)\tilde{V}(T)|F_t\right]$$

where the conditional expectation value is calculated in the measure with numeraire being the account which grows at rate $q_s(t)$, where asset price evolves according to

$$dS(t) = (q_s(t) - \gamma_S(t))S(t)dt + \sigma(t)S(t)dW(t)$$

The repo rate depends on the nature of the asset $S(t)$. In a repo transaction, the borrower can suffer a loss when the lender defaults and the asset price decreases. In the (idealized) continuous limit, because the asset value follows a Brownian motion, the possibility of loss is negligible and the repo rate should be close to the risk-free rate irrespective of the asset — this is of course not necessarily true in practice because the rehypothecation value of different collateral varies, which is something that will be discussed in a subsequent chapter on funding.

On the other hand, as is well discussed already (for example in Green, 2016), the OIS rate is the best proxy to the "risk-free" rate. This, in an idealized world, the level of a repo rate is similar to the OIS rate.

Therefore, we assume, at least in the G10 market, that the repo rate $q_s(t)$ and the OIS rate $r_C(t)$ are the same as the "risk-free" rate.

In this situation,

$$\exp\left(-\int_0^t r_C(u)du\right)\tilde{V}(t)$$

is a martingale and the valuation algorithm is nothing but the arbitrage-free valuation theory.

Here, only the single-currency model is treated. The extension to the multicurrency model will be discussed in Chapter 7.

2.7.3. *Exposure profiles for standard derivatives*

As will be discussed afterward, CVA will be calculated at the netting set level, and not the individual trade level. However, before that, we will discuss CVA of some derivative contracts at the individual trade level to reveal the nature of CVA.

First, consider CVA of a plain vanilla swap. The CVA of the swap which is discussed in Section 2.3 is actually represented as a sum of swaptions. If CVA calculation dates are identical to the interest exchange dates of the swap (and the value of the cash flows at the dates is excluded from the CVA), CVA is given by

$$\begin{aligned}\text{CVA} &= \int_0^T (1-R)\gamma(t)E^N\left[\frac{V^+(t)N(0)}{N(t)}\right]dt \\ &\approx \sum_{j=1}^{n}(1-R)\gamma(T_j)E^N \\ &\quad \times \left[\frac{A_j(T_j)(S_j(T_j)-K)^+N(0)}{N(T_j)}\right](T_j - T_{j-1})\end{aligned}$$

where $S_j(t)$ is the swap rate which is based on cash flow exchanges at $[T_{j+1},\ldots,T_{n+1}]$ and $A_j(t)$ is the Present Value of Basis Point (PVBP also known as annuity) of the swap. Exposure $E^N[A_j(T_j)(S_j(T_j) - K)^+N(0)/N(T_j)]$ is nothing but the value of a European swaption, which is liquidly traded and whose price can be observed from the market. In the Black model, the exposures are given similar to that depicted in Fig. 2.3.

CVA of physical-settled swaption: Now we will analyze the CVA of a physical-settled (payer) swaption where the underlying swap has cash flow exchanges on $[T_{m+1},\ldots,T_{n+1}]$, exercise date is T_m and strike is K.

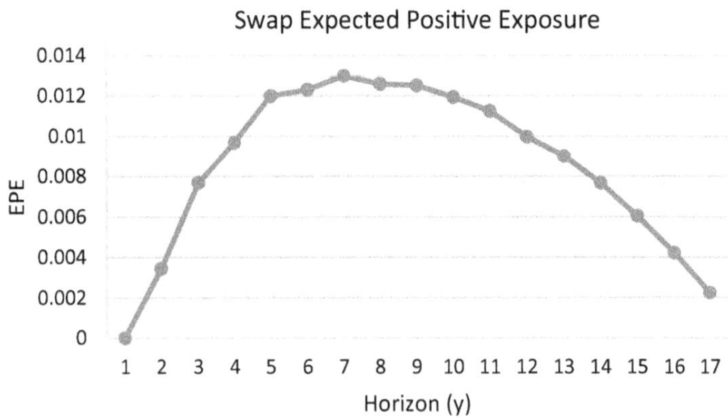

Fig. 2.3: Exposure of swap.

The valuation of physical-settled swaption is given by

$$V(t) = N(t)E^N[A(T)(S(T) - K)^+/N(T)|F_t]$$

where $A(T) = \sum_{i=m}^{n} \tau D(t, T_{i+1})$, with τ being the daycount fraction.

In the Black model, the value can further be computed as

$$V(t) = A(t)(S(t)N(d_1(t)) - KN(d_2(t)))$$

where $d_1(t) = \frac{\left(\ln \frac{S(t)}{K} + \frac{\sigma^2(T-t)}{2}\right)}{\sigma\sqrt{T-t}}$ and $d_2(t) = d_1(t) - \frac{1}{2}\sigma\sqrt{T-t}$, with σ being the implied volatility.

The EPE of the physical-settled swaption $E(t) = E[V^+(t)|F_0]$ is calculated by Monte Carlo simulation as in Fig. 2.4.

Here, the exercise date of swaption is 10 years. After the exercise date, if the option is exercised, then the trade becomes a swap and the exposure continues after the exercise date until the maturity of the swap.

CVA of cash-settled swaption: In a physical-settled swaption, if the option is exercised, the bank enters the swap with the counterparty. On the other hand, in a cash-settled swaption, if exercised the counterparty would pay the value of swap at the exercise date. In the valuation at the exercise date, approximate PVBP $\tilde{A}(T) = \sum_{i=m}^{n} \frac{1}{(1+\tau S(T))^{i/\tau}}$ is used for settlement simplicity

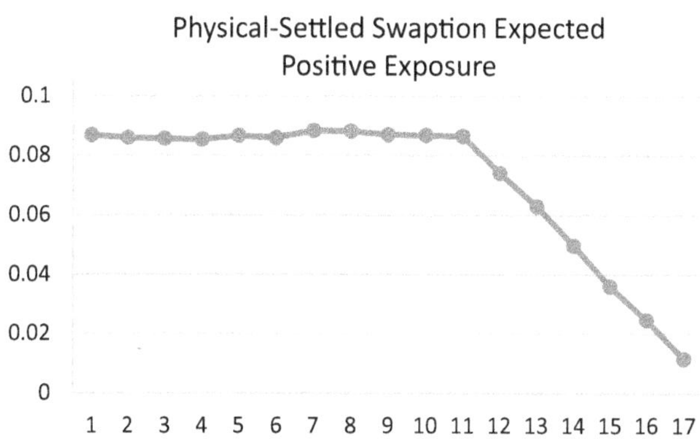

Fig. 2.4: Exposure of physical-settled swaption.

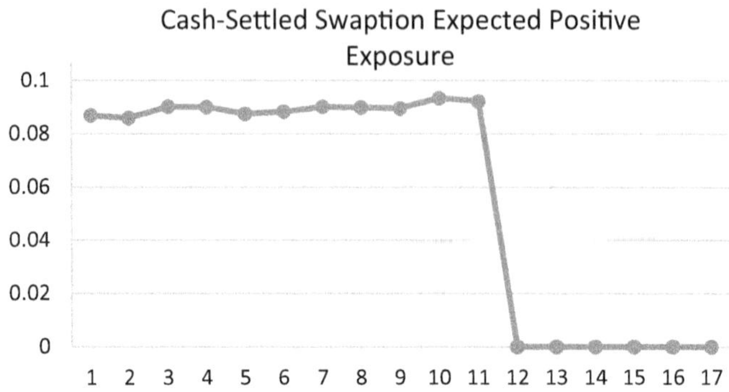

Fig. 2.5: Exposure of cash-settled swaption.

(i.e. only need to fix the swap rate) per the terms of the contract. This is the standard form of swaptions in the EUR market.

Therefore, the valuation of cash-settled payer swaption is represented as

$$V(t) = N(t)E^N\left[\frac{\tilde{A}(T)(S(T)-K)^+}{N(T)}\middle| F_t\right]$$

The difference to the physical-settled swaption is that there is not a simple measure which makes the swap value Martingale. However, in the market, a Black-like valuation formula is used

$$V(t) = \tilde{A}(t)(S(t)N(d_1(t)) - KN(d_2(t)))$$

An example of the exposure profile of a cash-settled swaption is given in Fig. 2.5. The difference to the profile of a physical-settled swaption is that after the exercise date, the exposure drops to zero and CVA is thus smaller than the physical-settled swaption.

Chapter 3

DVA and FVA — Price and Value for Accountants, Regulators and Others

In the previous chapter, valuation adjustment arises from the counterparty default risk of the clients of the bank (Credit Valuation Adjustment or CVA). Whereas the valuation adjustment from the default risk of the clients is necessary, we also need that from the default risk of the bank as a matter of course. The adjustment which corresponds to the default risk of the bank is called the Debit Valuation Adjustment (DVA).

The default risk of the bank is closely related to the funding cost for the bank. The funding cost gives rise to the valuation adjustment called the Funding Valuation Adjustment (FVA).

In this chapter, DVA and FVA will be discussed.

3.1. Debit Valuation Adjustment

DVA, also referred to as Debt Valuation Adjustment, is the natural counterpart to CVA. Prior to 2008, a financial institution would be keen to compute CVA to reflect its expected losses (for its positions with various default-risky counterparties) not reflected by pricing using the "risk-free" (Libor) rate. This would then be a cost factored into when pricing a deal with the client. Further, a bank is likely to attempt to hedge CVA by trading in the Credit Default Swap (CDS) of its client or by proxy-hedging with a CDS index.

However, the natural question is: What about expected losses to a client due to potential default of a financial institution? Prior to 2008, it was generally assumed that the probability of default of the larger (AA-rated) financial institutions was tiny enough to be neglected. However, the default of Lehman Brothers, and near collapse of other financial institutions that were since acquired (Bear Stearns, Merrill Lynch, Wachovia) or bailed out (UBS, RBS, Citi) had permanently debunked the myth of financial institutions as risk-free. Thus, DVA became much more important post 2008.

DVA is simply a reflection of the loss to a counterparty from one's own expected default. DVA thus "adds" value to a derivative. In a sense, this sounds fair, since a counterparty should clearly be compensated for potential losses due to a financial institution's default if it has to compensate the financial institution for its own default.

There are a few problems unfortunately. This largely stems from the concept of price and value. Specifically, DVA represents how much a financial institution's expected default will cost its counterparty since its value depends on how much the financial institution owes the counterparty when it defaults. However, it is assumed that an institution is run for the benefit of its shareholders, whereas shareholders tend to get wiped out upon default, where owing the counterparty upon default means payment of less than the full amount owed (depending on assets) and at best benefits bondholders. Unless DVA can be monetized, i.e. utilized to say decrease the cost of capital or funding, then it is not clear why it should be included when computing the value for a "shareholder" (the difference of value between shareholder and bondholder will be discussed in detail in Section 4.2.3). On the other hand, without DVA, price is asymmetric, and it is questionable if two parties (of equal standing) can agree on such a deal. We explore these and other issues in the following.

3.2. An Accountant's Perspective — Objectivity of Price and the "Balance" Sheet

The balance sheet is the ultimate cornerstone of accounting. It represents assets and liabilities and is meant to be objective, albeit to treat uncertainty and unobservability of value conservatively. But some crucial concepts are the existence of an (objective) value (as opposed to a range), and also the need for a "balance" — for every credit, there must be an equal and opposite debit.

The need for a "balance" suggests that every CVA must have a corresponding DVA, and the need for an objective value works against the idea of different parties recognizing CVA/DVA selectively based on their subjective decisions. This is notwithstanding conservativeness (e.g. applied in real estate being recorded at book value[1]), which would prefer not to recognize DVA.

Ultimately, for corporate accounts, whatever the merits, it is now accepted that DVA has to be included.[2]

3.3. A Regulator's Perspective

It has been explained earlier that DVA really does not benefit a firm pre-default. So it definitely does not reduce the likelihood of default (apart from arguments such as the improvement of capital and credit costs of a financial institution filtering through by taking on higher quality assets). The reality is that there is limited evidence of this filtering effect on credit spreads (via bonds or CDS), short of a transformational change in the business of a bank.

For a regulator interested in macroprudential stability, DVA is therefore not useful in shoring up a financial institution in times of crisis. For purposes of capital calculations (i.e. how much equity a bank has to hold), DVA is generally excluded (i.e. not

[1]Recording real estate at book value however does not breach the "balance" since the value only affects the owner of the real estate.

[2]DVA is however included under "Other Comprehensive Income" — i.e. a different category from CVA.

recognized or considered) as a result (notwithstanding its recognition in accounting) (Basel Committee On Banking Supervision, 2014).

3.4. Perspectives of Stakeholders and Practicalities of Managing DVA

As discussed in Section 3.1, DVA does not seem to benefit shareholders, for whom a company is run in theory. It might however benefit bondholders. While certainly some states (e.g. in Europe) ask for wider consideration of stakeholder interests to be had,[3] it still does not appear that the ultimate goal of a company is anything other than maximizing the shareholder value. To this end, DVA seems to be wrong.

Whereas DVA is argued to be necessary to seal a deal between two equal counterparties, lots of counterparties are not equal (e.g. a corporate entering a derivative for hedging with a bank). Rather than idealize on a perfectly efficient market (where adjustments like CVA, DVA and FVA have debunked the myth), in the real world, price and value need not agree, and a transaction takes place at a price which is of lesser value to the willing seller and greater value to the willing buyer (Green, private communication). As long as we do not confuse these concepts, no tears need be shed for the failure to lead to a unique "value".

The issues about shareholder's value and hedgeability of DVA will be discussed in Chapter 4 with FVA.

3.5. Bilateral and Unilateral DVA

Strictly, the default of a bank and its counterparty are likely to be correlated, and in a large financial crisis, it is likely to be a systemic shock that drives multiple defaults. Thus, it would be a closer reflection of reality for bilateral DVA (i.e. taking account of joint default of bank and counterparty) rather than unilateral DVA to be computed.

[3]In Europe, there is typically the need to represent worker interests with employee representatives on the company's board.

Following Gregory (2009, 2012a, 2012b, 2016), the adjustment for both CVA and bilateral DVA is as follows:

$$V(t) + E^N\left[(1 - R_C)V^+\left(\tau^C\right)1\left\{\tau^C < \tau^B \cap \tau^C < T\right\}|F_t\right]$$
$$+ E^N\left[(1 - R_B)V^-\left(\tau^B\right)1\left\{\tau^B < \tau^C \cap \tau^B < T\right\}|F_t\right] + E^N$$
$$\left[\{\mathrm{V}\left(\tau^B\right) - R_C V^+\left(\tau^C\right) - R_B V^-\left(\tau^B\right)\}1\left\{\tau^B = \tau^C < T\right\}|F_t\right]$$

where the first term is unadjusted PV, the second term represents the adjustment for counterparty default (CVA), the third term represents adjustment for own default (DVA) and the final term avoids double counting by canceling any payout if both counterparty and the bank default at the same time prior to maturity. (Here cash flows are rebased per numeraire N, R stands for recovery, τ for default, maturity is at time T, and subscript/superscript C and B represent the counterparty and bank, respectively. Also, $V^+ = \max(V, 0)$ and $V^- = \min(V, 0)$).

Note that Gregory (2009, 2012a, 2012b, 2016) argues that if one were to hedge the systemic component of own DVA say by a position on CDS index (as discussed in Chapter 2), then it would lock in the second and fourth term, while the third term (with positive value) is unhedgeable and thus may have to be dropped if we wish to be conservative.

To calculate bilateral DVA, the effect of the dependence of default times of the counterparty τ^C and of the bank τ^{B} must be taken into consideration. In the industry, Copula is typically used for the analysis of default time dependence (Green, 2016).

However, in practice, there can be resistance to using the formula for bilateral DVA, because

(1) Of the significant expense of computing the joint probability of default of the bank and many counterparties.
(2) DVA is not allowed for computation of regulatory capital, and there is even controversy in the recognition of DVA (currently treated as "other comprehensive income"), and so lack of consensus on whether or how to manage it.

The default probability of the bank is closely related to its funding cost. Therefore, DVA is inseparable from the funding cost. We will analyze the details of DVA with the valuation adjustment for the funding cost FVA from Section 3.6.

3.6. An Introduction to FVA

If we accept the premise that derivatives pricing is about obtaining the cost of setting up a replicating portfolio, then the cost of funding should be an essential part of the price. FVA should really be the cost of funding a position, as opposed to credit considerations with regard to counterparty default. The derivative trade can both increase and decrease the funding cost. If it reduces the funding cost, it is a benefit for the bank. Funding benefit from the derivative trade is called Funding Benefit Adjustment (FBA), whereas the funding cost from the trade is called Funding Cost Adjustment (FCA). FVA is the sum of FBA and FCA.

3.6.1. *An illustrated example of funding cost*

The best way to illustrate this is via the following example.

Suppose Bank A does a USD interest rate swap with the US government, and say Bank A receives fixed 3% semi-annually and pays Libor quarterly for the next 30 years. Since the bank's business model is likely to be that of an intermediary (i.e. making money from bid–ask spread) rather than prop trading on direction on rates,[4] it is likely to hedge this swap by entering into an offsetting (opposite) swap with another bank B. Typically, the arrangement between both banks would be for collateral to be posted. The arrangement between Bank A and the US government is possibly that no collateral would be posted by the US government (since it is deemed to be risk-free in US dollars),[5] but the bank may have to post collateral if the position

[4]There are various regulations, e.g. Volcker rule, that restrict a bank from proprietary trading.

[5]Whereas a government can theoretically print its own currency and hence is theoretically default-free in debt of its own currency (except the EUR), in practice non-zero CDS spreads for highly rated sovereigns (e.g. US, UK, Germany) suggest

goes against it — this is a one-way Credit Security Annex (CSA), where the bank posts but not the other (higher rated) counterparty.

Case A: Rates rise

Bank B posts collateral worth \$$X$ to Bank A, which posts this to the US Government. Thus, Bank A has no net cash outflow.

Case B: Rates fall

Bank A posts collateral worth \$$Y$ to Bank B, but does not get anything from the US Government. Thus, Bank A needs to borrow to buy this collateral.

To illustrate the situation, let us consider the following two scenarios:

(a) Interest rates rise: The Mark to Market (MTM) of the swap between Bank A and the US government is –\$$X$. MTM of the swap between Bank B and Bank A is however \$$X$. Note that Bank B has to post collateral worth \$$X$ to Bank A, which can then post this collateral to the US government.

(b) Interest rates fall: The MTM of the swap between Bank A and the US government is \$$Y$. MTM of the swap between Bank B and Bank A is however –\$$Y$. Now Bank A has to post \$$Y$ worth of collateral to Bank B. But the US government will not post any collateral to Bank A. It follows that Bank A will have to borrow at its own rate of funding to buy the collateral to post to Bank B.

---

a non-negligible probability of default. However, for convenience, let us ignore this for our discussion.

Effectively, then FVA is the cost of Bank A borrowing at its own rate to buy collateral when necessary to maintain the hedge for this trade. Note that this is more about how much Bank A's cost of funding exceeds the (risk-free) Overnight Index Swap (OIS) rate, since it would be compensated for the collateral at the OIS rate.

Note that FVA is not limited to the situation of one-way CSA. If instead, Bank A had no collateral arrangement with the US government, there would still be FVA. After all, under scenario (b), Bank A will still have to borrow at its own rate of funding. Under scenario (a), Bank A now does not have to post the collateral it receives from the counterparty, so this is different from before. However, there will be non-zero FVA if the benefit (FBA) Bank A receives under scenario (a) does not completely offset the cost (FCA) under scenario (b).[6]

3.7. Controversies of FVA

Notwithstanding the example above, FVA is a controversial topic, which has led to strong academic objections, even though many practitioners have recognized its necessity to make a business viable (Hull and White, 2012a, 2012b).

Objections to FVA can be summarized under the following four categories:

(a) Non-uniqueness of price
(b) Moral issues of charging one's own cost of credit
(c) Non-transparency/independence of pricing with own funding
(d) Breakdown of market efficiency

[6]In practice, for FBA and FCA to cancel out, it is necessary that the institution benefits in reduced funding expense (e.g. since it has to borrow less) from FBA. This is possible since investment banks (or the securities arms of commercial banks tend to be cash poor). Further more, it is necessary that the probability of the deal being in-the-money or out-of-the-money must be the same to the bank, which is not likely in practice.

FVA is the cost of funding required to sustain a position over its life. The reason for the existence of FVA is that financial institutions incur a non-negligible charge in funding their positions. Prior to the financial crisis of 2008, it was wrongly assumed that highly rated (AA) institutions can fund close to the risk-free rate. Traditionally, it was taken that they can fund for uncollateralized borrowing at Libor, and term funding for different periods (e.g. 3 months vs 6 months) did not incur a large spread (typically this was at most 1 bp). Even then, Libor was not the risk-free rate, and there was a small spread of Libor over OIS (used for overnight funding) of under 10 bp. But in the financial crisis of 2008, the spread between Libor and OIS in USD reached 365 bp at its peak, and the myth of almost risk-free funding was forever debunked. This is when FVA finally began its slow journey to gain acceptance.

(a) Non-uniqueness of price

Naturally, each institution is charged a rate of funding in a given currency depending on its own creditworthiness and also the nature of the markets it operates in, e.g. a US bank may have an easier time funding in USD than a local bank in Europe.

This means that by its nature, different institutions will compute a different FVA each for the same position. This is further complicated by the fact that funding has to be done across a portfolio of trades in the same funding set (i.e. collection of trades that are funded together for convenience or due to legal considerations). Specifically, if the MTM at funding set level (net of cash balances) is negative, then an institution will have to borrow to post collateral, but if positive, the same institution may not derive a benefit as the risk-free return only pays the collateral rate.[7] Of course, different institutions have different funding sets in which the same trade lies.

[7] A benefit is derived by a cash-poor institution, which can use the cash to reduce its net borrowing and hence incur a lower borrowing cost. This benefit may not however equal the corresponding cost if it has to borrow to fund the position. (Note this benefit does not apply to a cash-rich institution.)

Non-uniqueness of price grossly complicates finance and pricing theory that has developed over the decades, and leads to quite a few other inconveniences.

(b) Moral issues of charging one's own cost of credit

Naturally, since FVA depends on the creditworthiness of the institution, an institution with a weaker credit will have a higher FVA. If the cost of this FVA is passed on to a client in a transaction, then it appears that the institution has just penalized its clients for its own weak credit. Naturally, there could be moral objections to this.

However, pragmatically, banks are a business, and any business is only viable if it covers its cost. So any regret over the lack of efficiency of charging for a bank's weaker credit should not obscure the fundamental philosophy of a business. Besides, if a bank is weak and hence charges more FVA than its competitors, it would lose business, and hence a natural equilibrium would be reached over time.

(c) Non-transparency/independence of pricing with own funding

A further objection to FVA being dependent on the credit of an institution is the lack of transparency. For accountants, it is not ideal that it is not possible to observe independently the funding cost (or some other benchmark reflecting this) of a bank, and calls into question the objectivity of FVA applied to accounts.

This criticism is not without merits, and a compromise is perhaps to estimate the cost of funding based on borrowing costs of other institutions in a similar credit rating. This can be the FVA used for preparation of accounts.

However, to really address this issue, we need to be clear on the purpose of valuation. Prior to the financial crisis of 2008, it was assumed that valuation was objective and market efficiency allowed for not taking into account funding costs. The real world being a lot less elegant as demonstrated in the crisis, we might have to take account of different valuations — for purpose of accounts, for regulatory purposes or for hedging. If we accept that there need not be just one valuation, then philosophical concerns do not constrain us further, but we indeed have to deal with the more cumbersome task of maintaining the multiple valuations for different uses.

(d) Breakdown of market efficiency

Finally, of course FVA (i.e. having market participants take account of their funding cost) goes against the grain of an efficient market. However, that is probably just a reality we have been slow to recognize.

More practically, it is clear that if a financial institution charges FVA, it is an asymmetric charge to the client. This is likely to cause a drop in the amount of business done. But efficient markets were always an idealization of reality, and perhaps the industry was too optimistic prior to the financial crisis of 2008. These days with higher capital charges and regulatory scrutiny weighing down on business appetite, market efficiency has become a casualty.

We can and should recall that traditional banking was about taking deposits and lending for businesses/mortgages at a profit margin of a few percent. This hyper-efficiency of investment banking coupled with high leverage was probably taken further than it should have been.

3.8. FVA by Discounting via a Spread

In a simplistic setup, FVA could be incorporated by adding a spread to the interest rate used for discounting — the idea being that this spread would compensate for the cost of funding. In practice, this works well only for a counterparty with which a bank has a net lending relation across all trades — i.e. the spread is used to discount cash flows due to the bank, hence decreasing their value. The discounting method in this situation is identical to the bond pricing which was discussed in Chapter 2.

However, given derivatives are such that following inception at par, they can end up being in-the-money to either counterparty, it is necessary to consider the case where the bank owes the counterparty money. (The same could apply across all trades done with a counterparty.) Once the bank owes the counterparty money, using an additional spread for discounting only makes sense if the bank benefits from cash (e.g. if it is cash poor). Further, it is possible that the portfolio may be in-the-money to the bank over one period of time and then out-of-the-money to the bank over a different period. This complicates the case if it is necessary to apply different spreads when in-the-money vs out-of-the-money.

In the current practice, CVA and DVA are included in derivative valuation. If we adopt the discounting approach for FVA, when the exposure of derivative is negative, discount factor with bank funding spread represents FBA (Green, private communication). As will be explained later FBA is a mirror image of DVA, and to account both DVA and FBA is a double counting. Therefore, when we adopt the discounting approach, we should not include DVA.

3.9. Summary

In this chapter, DVA and FVA are introduced and the controversies related to them (especially FVA) are discussed. There are some arguments from academics that FVA should not be included in derivatives valuation. However, FVA is an actual cost inherent to the derivative trade, and we are of the view that FVA exists. When FVA exists, there is still some argument about what is FVA (and DVA). In the next chapter, we will discuss what FVA is. Actually, what FVA is depends on what the valuation is for or ultimately who the stakeholders are.

Chapter 4

Theoretical Framework behind FVA and its Computation

In the previous chapter, Debit-Valuation Adjustment (DVA) and Funding Valuation Adjustment (FVA) were introduced. FVA is sometimes divided into Funding Cost Adjustment (FCA), which has negative value and Funding Benefit Adjustment (FBA), which has positive value. DVA and FVA are closely related to each other. Actually FBA and DVA are mirror images of the same thing. Hereafter, we refer to both FVA and DVA jointly as FVA.

In this chapter, we will show their role in the bank's balance sheet. The difficulty in understanding FVA (DVA) is that it is related to the different valuations from different agents.

Actually, there are three types of FVA + DVA:

(A) FVA from firm's perspective (including bondholders); FVA $= -(1 - R_B) \int \lambda_B(t) E[V^-(t)]dt - \int l_B(t) E[V(t)]dt$

(B) FVA from shareholder's perspective; FVA + DVA $= -(1 - R_B) \int \gamma(u) E[V(u)]du + \int l_B(u) E[V(u)]du$

(C) FVA from regulators' perspective; FVA = FCA = $\int s_B(u) E[V^+(u)]du$

where R_B is the recovery rate of the bank upon default, $\gamma(t)$ is the default intensity of the bank, $l_B(t)$ is the liquidity premium of the bank, and $V(t)$ is the value of a derivative all as seen at time t, with $V^-(t) = \min(V(t), 0)$.

The above three types of FVA are the values from the perspectives of different stakeholders, and further details will be explained in this chapter.

To derive the FVA, three methodologies have currently been discussed in the literature, i.e. an exposure method (cash flow discounting approach), a partial differential equation (PDE) (replication) approach and a discounting approach. Among these, the exposure approach is the most convenient for the analysis of FVA and is gaining popularity. Therefore, the exposure method of FVA will be explained in Section 4.1.

The discounting approach will be described in Chapters 5 and 6, and the PDE approach will be discussed in Section 4.3.

4.1. Exposure Method (Cash Flow Discounting Approach of FVA)

In this section, exposure method for FVA will be discussed. The idea is that we can price a trade based on collateralized funding, and then add adjustments due to potential cash flows from default (CVA and DVA) and from funding. Here, we would have cash flows from margining for collateral arrangements. And in our example of one-way CSA, we have illustrated how in fact we need to consider as a base case the collateral arrangements of our hedge. As such, actually in a non-collateralized arrangement, the cash flows are due to hedging an unsecured trade with a secured trade.

Now we will investigate FVA by analyzing expectation values of cash flows related to derivative transactions with both counterparty and own default.

4.1.1. *Analysis of cash flows of derivative transactions, including funding and collateral margin*

We will analyze FVA of the netting set of derivative trades between bank B and its client A. The notations used in this section is summarized in the following.

Definitions of Terms

Many types of rates and other financial variables are used in this section. We define them here.

In this section, simultaneous default of Bank B and client A is ignored.

$r_C(t_j)$: Interest rate for collateral = risk-free rate
$r_B(t_j)$: Funding rate of bank B
$\lambda_B(t_j)$: Hazard rate of bank B

$\Lambda_B(t_j, t_{j+1}) = P(t_j < \tau_B \leq t_{j+1} | \tau_A > t_j, \tau_B > t_j)$: Probability of bank B defaulting in period $[t_j, t_{j+1}]$ conditional on both the bank and the client surviving until time t_j.

$l_B(t_j) = r_B(t_j) - r_C(t_j) - (1 - R_B)\lambda_B(t_j)$: Liquidity premium of bank B
$\lambda_A(t_j)$: Hazard rate of client A
$\Lambda_A(t_j, t_{j+1}) = P(t_j < \tau_A \leq t_{j+1} | \tau_A > t_j, \tau_B > t_j)$: Probability of client A defaulting in period $[t_j, t_{j+1}]$ conditional on both the bank and the client surviving until time t_j.
R_A: Recovery rate of client A
R_B: Recovery rate of bank B
$P_{AB}(t_j) = \exp(-\int_0^{t_j} (\lambda_A(u) + \lambda_B(u))du)$: Survival probability of both bank B and client A

Here we assume that the collateral rate is stochastic and spreads to other rates are assumed to be deterministic. All of these rates determine the interest rate cost for the period $[t_j, t_{j+1}]$, and are assumed to be fixed at the start of the period t_j. Regarding default intensities, it is assumed that we know them for the period $[t_j, t_{j+1}]$, at the start of the period t_j.

Regarding FVA, there are many controversies in the market. Given the many misconceptions, we reveal here the true nature of FVA. First, we will define FVA clearly.

Definition: FVA of the derivative contract is the difference in the value between a secured trade and an unsecured trade (which excludes CVA and DVA). Here the value of the derivative contract includes costs and benefits of cash flows of funding and the margin procedure.

Let bank B have derivatives trades with client A. Let call margin frequency dates

$$[t_0, t_1, \ldots, t_N]$$

be daily.

Now, we investigate two types of derivatives transactions:

(1) unsecured
(2) completely secured

under the same market scenario.

Key Definition

Let the derivative price (taking into account of netting set) for the unsecured trade be $\tilde{V}(t)$ and for the secured trade be $V(t)$.

Let us assume that for both cases, market risk of the trade is hedged by secured trades. Here because the hedge trade is a secured one, its value is $-V(t)$ (for bank B). We can imagine that bank B has the exactly opposite (secured) transaction as the one with the client to the other bank C (Fig. 4.1). Note that the hedge position is introduced to explain the necessity of daily funding positions in our analysis as will be described below, and it does not affect our result. Also, we could have introduced CDS hedging, but it will not affect our results either.

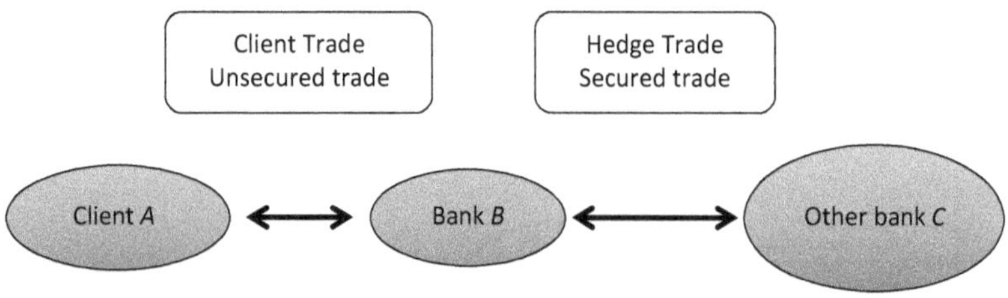

Fig. 4.1: FVA trade and hedge.

Now we assume that changes in value over the period $[t_j, t_{j+1}]$ are the same for both the secured and unsecured trades. That is,

$$\tilde{V}(t_j) - \tilde{V}(t_{j+1}) \sim V(t_j) - V(t_{j+1})$$

We will compare the cash flows of the trade for both the unsecured and secured trades. The analysis is divided into two circumstances: where the value to the bank is positive and negative. We assume when $V(t)$ is positive, $\tilde{V}(t)$ is also positive, and vice versa. This is most often but not always the case.

Here, we will analyze the situation where the bank enters the trade at the start of the period $[t_j, t_{j+1}]$ and exits at the end. From Fig. 4.2, we can see that the sequence of entering and exiting in each period is the equivalent to entering at t_0 and exiting at t_n. We assume also that the collateral interest rate is set at the start of the period $[t_j, t_{j+1}]$ and paid at the end.

At first glance, it seems that for the unsecured trade, after we fund the amount of the money necessary at t_0, we do no need to update the funding amount in each period, but actually considering the cash flows of the hedge trade, an updated funding amount is necessary to compensate for the situation when a market move causes us to be short of cash (Fig. 4.3).

Unsecured Case

For the unsecured case, cash flows related to the derivative transactions are categorized as follows:

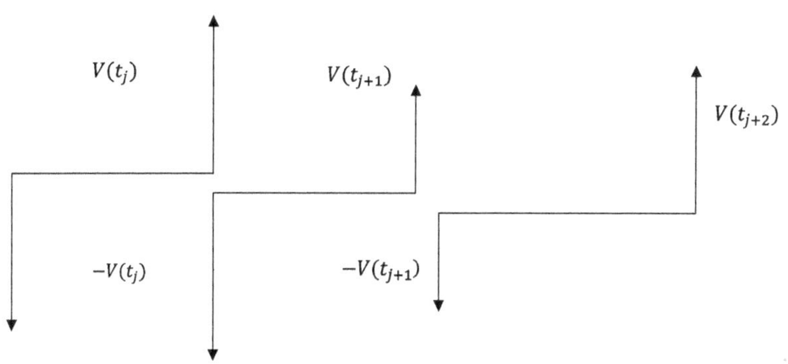

Fig. 4.2: Sequential cash flows.

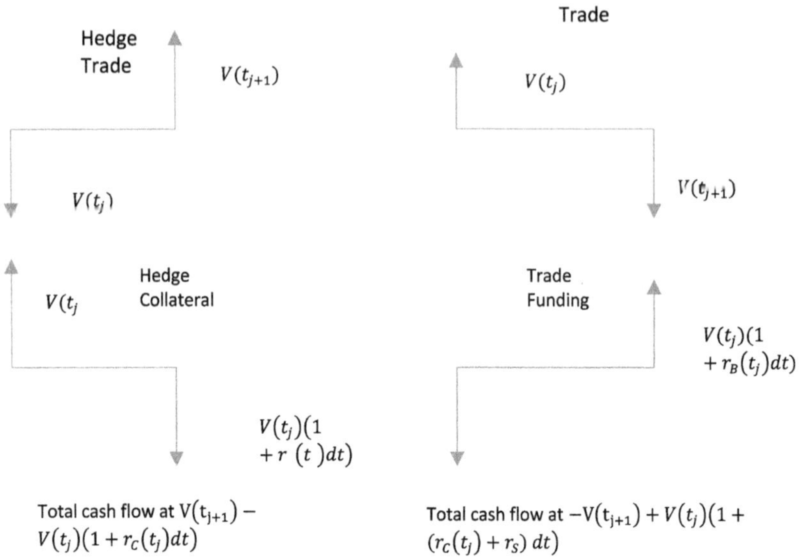

Fig. 4.3: Hedge flow compensates funding.

(a) Cash flows related to buying and selling the derivatives trades and the ones related to the interest exchange of derivatives.
(b) Funding cash flows for the above flows.
(c) Cash flows for the hedge position for market risk.
(d) Cash flows for margin procedures in hedge position.

Secured Case

On the other hand, cash flows for the completely secured case are as follows:

(a) Cash flows related to buying and selling the derivatives trades and the ones related to the interest exchange of derivatives.
(b) Cash flows for the margin procedure for the collateral of the trade.
(c) Cash flows for the hedge position for market risk.
(d) Cash flows for margin procedures in hedge position.

In the above two cases, cash flows for (c) and (d) are the same for both unsecured and secured trades.

Now we will set out an assumption about the funding situation of the whole bank. The assumption is central to our analysis.

Assumption: The (investment) bank is always cash poor. When the bank needs any money for its operation, including its derivatives business, it needs to fund by borrowing at its own funding cost. Similar discussion is given in Albanese and Andersen (2014) and Albanese *et al.* (2014) also.

(Note that this assumption is made only in this section to develop some of the arguments related to funding/liquidity as distinct from credit. In the next section, we will consider the possibility of the bank being cash rich, or where it can switch from being cash poor to cash rich in a netting set dependent on transactions.)

In reality, investment banks (or the securities arms of commercial banks) are usually cash poor and so the assumption is reasonable. Let the amount of the money that a bank needs for its operation at time t_j be $W(t_j)$. The bank lends the amount $W(t_j)$ at time t_j and is repaid the amount of $(1 + r_b(t_j)dt)W(t_j)$ at time t_{j+1} where an interest amount is added ($dt = t_{j+1} - t_j$). The funding and payment of the bank are given in Fig. 4.4.

Note that in this chapter, the up arrow refers to the cash flows that the bank receives, and the down arrow refers to the cash flows that the bank pays.

Before we start our analysis, we will clarify what circumstances and trades we will analyze as follows:

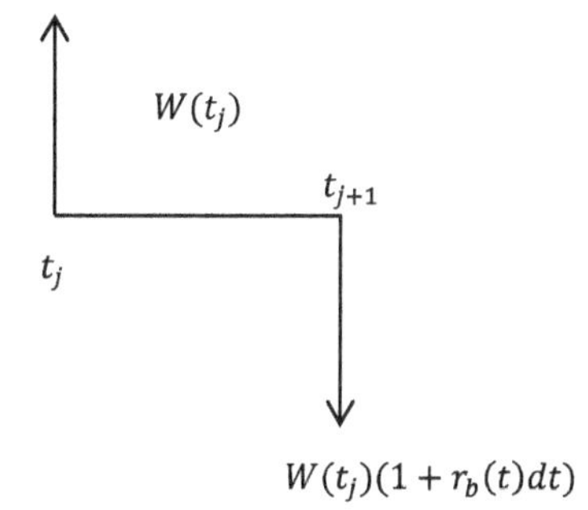

Fig. 4.4: Bank funding.

(A) $V(t_j) > 0$

(1) Unsecured

i. Derivatives Cash flows
ii. Funding Cash flows

(2) Secured

i. Derivatives Cash flows
ii. Collateral margin Cash flows

(B) $V(t_j) < 0$

(1) Unsecured

i. Derivatives Cash flows
ii. Funding Cash flows

(2) Secured

i. Derivatives Cash flows
ii. Collateral margin Cash flows

With this in mind, let us proceed to analyze cash flows related to derivative contracts.

(a) Where Derivative Has a Positive Value

First, we analyze the case where the derivative has a positive value for the bank, i.e. $V(t_j) > 0$.

We will analyze the unsecured trade. Cash flows for the unsecured trade are as follows. The bank enters the trade at time t_j and exits at time t_{j+1}. Because the value of the trade for the bank is positive, the bank needs to pay the amount $\tilde{V}(t_j)$ at t_j to the counterparty and receives the amount $\tilde{V}(t_{j+1})$ at time t_{j+1}. Here if counterparty A defaults in the period $[t_j, t_{j+1}]$, the bank does not receive the value $\tilde{V}(t_{j+1})$ in full but receives the recovery value of $\tilde{V}(t_{j+1})R_A$, where the probability of default in the period (conditional on survival until time t_j) is $\Lambda_A(t_j, t_{j+1})$. Therefore, the value (observed at t_j) of cash flows that the bank receives at t_{j+1} from the derivative contract is $\tilde{V}(t_{j+1})(1 - \Lambda_A(t_j, t_{j+1})) + R_A\tilde{V}(t_{j+1})\Lambda_A(t_j, t_{j+1})$. Here market closeout is assumed. In the case of risk-free closeout, the equation becomes a little bit complicated, but a similar argument can be applied. Note that actually $\tilde{V}(t_{j+1})$ is measurable at time t_{j+1} and our expression should be interpreted as $N(t_j)E[\tilde{V}(t_{j+1})/N(t_{j+1})]$. But to make the notation simpler and more intuitive, we have discarded the explicit use of the expectation operator (Fig. 4.5).

In this unsecured trade, the amount $\tilde{V}(t_j)$ that the bank pays at t_j is raised at the funding cost. The funding cash flows are as follows. At time t_j, the bank gets amount $\tilde{V}(t_j)$. At time t_{j+1}, the bank needs to repay $(1 + r_B(t_j)dt)\tilde{V}(t_j)$. However, if the bank defaults in the period, the bank will repay only its recovery amount $R_B\tilde{V}(t_j)$ and the probability that the bank defaults in this period is $\Lambda_B(t_j, t_{j+1})$. Therefore, the expected cash flows the bank pays at t_{j+1} observed at t_j, is (Fig. 4.6)

$$\begin{aligned}&\tilde{V}(t_j)(1 + r_B(t_j)dt)(1 - \Lambda_B(t_j, t_{j+1}))\\&\quad + \tilde{V}(t_j)(1 + r_B(t_j)dt)R_B\Lambda_B(t_j, t_{j+1})\end{aligned}$$

Here the derivative cash flows and funding cash flows at time t_j cancel each other. On the other hand, the total expected cash flows

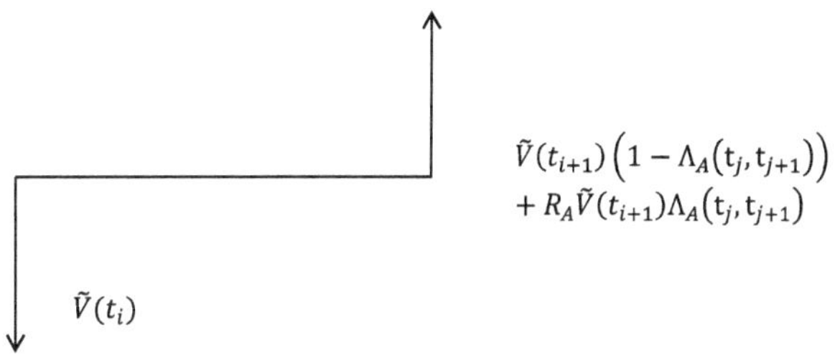

Fig. 4.5: Positive, no CSA derivative.

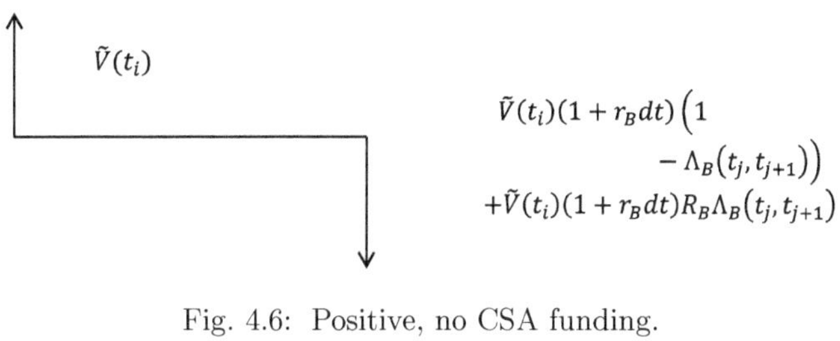

Fig. 4.6: Positive, no CSA funding.

at time t_{j+1} is

$$\tilde{V}(t_{j+1}) - \tilde{V}(t_j) - \Lambda_A(t_j, t_{j+1})(1 - R_A)\tilde{V}(t_{j+1})$$
$$-[r_B(t_j)dt - \Lambda_B(t_j, t_{j+1})(1 - R_B)]\tilde{V}(t_j)$$

where terms of order smaller than $O(dt^2)$ are neglected.

Next we will analyze a secured trade in the same situation. *Now we will make the assumption that for the secured trade with daily margin frequency, there is no default risk. (In reality, market movement can cause default over one day, but we assume the probability is negligible.)*

The derivative cash flows are as follows. At time t_j, the bank pays the derivative price $V(t_j)$ to its counterparty and will receive the amount $V(t_{j+1})$ at time t_{j+1}. Here we assume that there is no default risk and we receive cash flow $V(t_{j+1})$ with certainty (Fig. 4.7).

Next we will analyze the cash flows for the margin procedure. Because the value of the derivative for the bank is positive, at time t_j the counterparty pays amount $V(t_j)$ as cash to the bank. At time t_{j+1}, the bank repays the amount $V(t_j)(1 + r_C(t_j)dt)$ (Fig. 4.8).

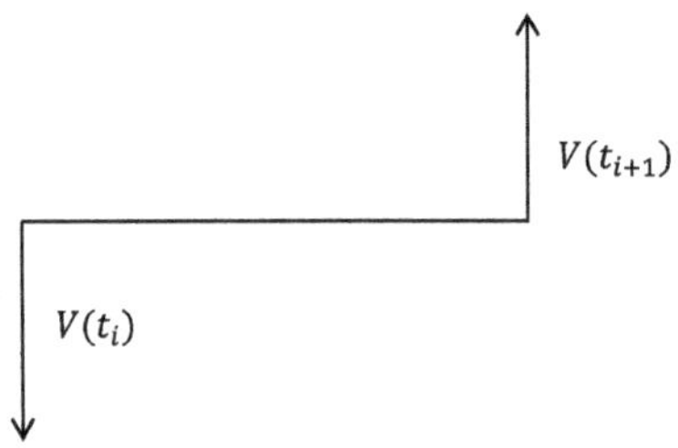

Fig. 4.7: Positive CSA derivative.

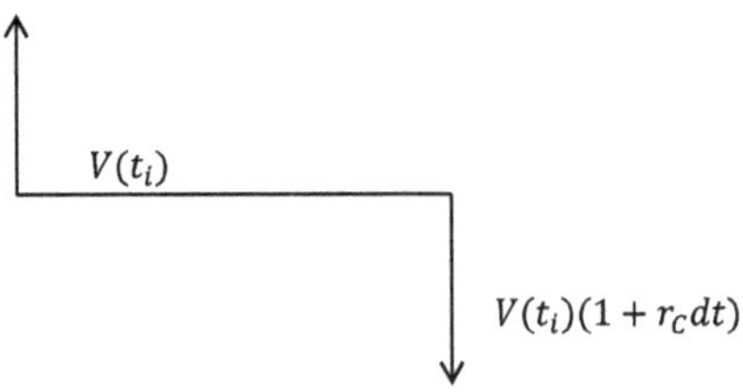

Fig. 4.8: Positive CSA collateral.

For the secured trade, cash flows at t_j cancel each other as well, and at time t_{j+1} total cash flow is

$$V(t_{j+1}) - V(t_j)(1 + r_C(t_j)dt)$$

Now we will compare the cash flows between the secured trade and the unsecured trade. The difference is given by

$$\begin{aligned}
&\tilde{V}(t_{j+1}) - \tilde{V}(t_j) - \Lambda_A(t_j, t_{j+1})(1 - R_A)\tilde{V}(t_{j+1}) \\
&\quad - [r_B(t_j)dt - \Lambda_B(t_j, t_{j+1})(1 - R_B)]\tilde{V}(t_j) \\
&\quad - \{V(t_{j+1}) - V(t_j)(1 + r_C(t_j)dt)\} \\
&= -\Lambda_A(t_j, t_{j+1})(1 - R_A)\tilde{V}(t_{j+1}) \\
&\quad - \{[r_B(t_j)dt - \Lambda_B(t_j, t_{j+1})(1 - R_B)]\tilde{V}(t_j) \\
&\quad - r_C(t_j)V(t_j)dt\}
\end{aligned}$$

where the approximation

$$\tilde{V}(t_{j+1}) - \tilde{V}(t_j) \sim V(t_{j+1}) - V(t_j)$$

is used.

Here the first term $-\Lambda_A(t_j, t_{j+1})(1 - R_A)\tilde{V}(t_{j+1})$ is related to a default event of counterparty A and it is interpreted as CVA. On the other hand, the second term $-\{[r_B(t_j)dt - \Lambda_B(t_j, t_{j+1})(1 - R_B)]\tilde{V}(t_j) - r_C(t_j)V(t_j)dt\}$ is related to the funding cost of the bank and it is related to FCA (FVA). Here if $\tilde{V}(t_{j+1}) \to V(t_{j+1})$, this term is given by

$$\begin{aligned}
&-[r_B(t_j)dt - \Lambda_B(t_j, t_{j+1})(1 - R_B) - r_C(t_j)dt]V(t_j) \\
&= -l_B(t_j)V(t_j)dt
\end{aligned}$$

From this representation, we have a conclusion that *FCA comes from the liquidity spread of the bank.*

(b) Where Derivative Has a Negative Value

Next we will move to the case where the value of the derivative for the bank $V(t_j)$ is negative. First, we will analyze the unsecured trade. Regarding the derivative's cash flows, because the unsecured price

$\tilde{V}(t_j)$ is negative, the bank receives the amount $|\tilde{V}(t_j)|$ and enters the transaction. At time t_{j+1}, the bank needs to pay the amount $|\tilde{V}(t_{j+1})|$ if the bank does not default in the period; but if it defaults, only the recovery amount will be paid. Because default probability in the period is $\pi_B(t_j)dt$, the expected cash flow is given by

$$\tilde{V}(t_{j+1})(1-\Lambda_B(t_j,t_{j+1}))+\tilde{V}(t_{j+1})R_B\Lambda_B(t_j,t_{j+1})$$

Note that here $\tilde{V}(t_{j+1})$ is negative and this cash flow is payment from the bank (Fig. 4.9).

Regarding the amount of money $\tilde{V}(t_j)$ which the bank receives at t_j, because the bank is assumed to be cash poor, this amount is not used for investment, but used to reduce the total amount of the money that the bank needs to fund its operation. That is, if the amount of the money the bank needs at time t_j is $W(t_j)$, it would be reduced to $W(t_j)-\tilde{V}(t_j)$ because of the cash flows of this derivative. Therefore, we can interpret the reduction of funding cost from the derivative as a benefit and we will investigate the opposite of the cash flows of this reduced funding. The cash flow from this reduced funding at time t_j cancels with the cash flow from the derivative. The cash flow from

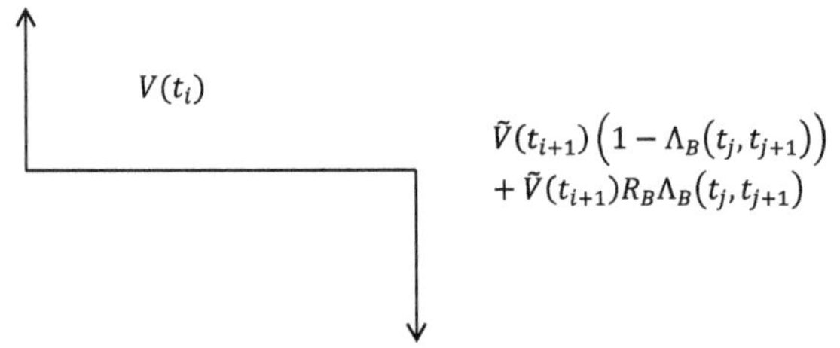

Fig. 4.9: Negative non-CSA derivative.

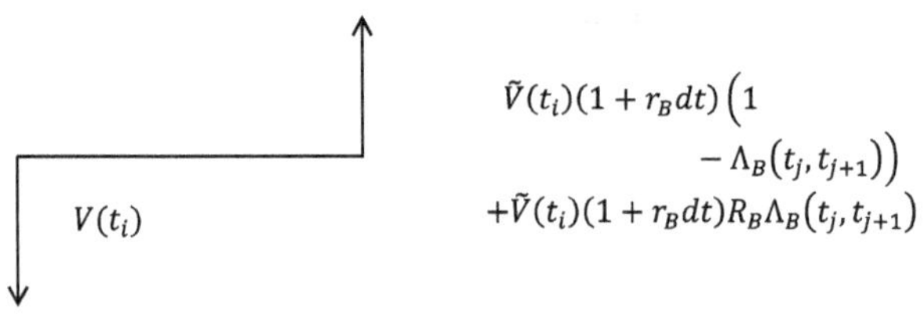

Fig. 4.10: Negative non-CSA funding.

the reduced funding at t_{j+1} is given by (Fig. 4.10)

$$\begin{aligned}&\tilde{V}(t_j)(1+r_B(t_j)dt)(1-\Lambda_B(t_j,t_{j+1}))\\&\quad+\tilde{V}(t_j)(1+r_B(t_j)dt)R_B\Lambda_B(t_j,t_{j+1})\end{aligned}$$

The sum of cash flows of the derivative and funding of the unsecured trade at t_{j+1} is therefore given by

$$\begin{aligned}&\tilde{V}(t_{j+1})-\tilde{V}(t_j)-\Lambda_B(t_j,t_{j+1})(1-R_B)\tilde{V}(t_{j+1})\\&\quad-[r_B(t_j)dt-\Lambda_B(t_j,t_{j+1})(1-R_B)]\tilde{V}(t_j)\end{aligned}$$

Now we will analyze the secured trade. The cash flows from the secured trade are the same as when $V(t_j)>0$ except for the direction. The total flow at t_{j+1} is given by

$$V(t_{j+1})-V(t_j)(1+r_C(t_j)dt)$$

Therefore, when $V(t_j)>0$, the difference of cash flow between the unsecured and the secured trade is given by

$$\begin{aligned}&-\Lambda_B(t_j,t_{j+1})(1-R_B)\tilde{V}(t_{j+1})\\&\quad-\{[r_B(t_j)dt-\Lambda_B(t_j,t_{j+1})(1-R_B)]\tilde{V}(t_j)-r_C(t_j)V(t_j)dt\}\end{aligned}$$

Here the first term $-\Lambda_B(t_j,t_{j+1})(1-R_B)\tilde{V}(t_{j+1})$ is related to the bank's default and should correspond to DVA. On the other hand, the second term

$$-\{[r_B(t_j)dt-\Lambda_B(t_j,t_{j+1})(1-R_B)]\tilde{V}(t_j)-r_C(t_j)V(t_j)dt\}$$

is related to the funding of the bank and should correspond to FBA (FVA).

If we can assume $\tilde{V}(t_j)\to V(t_j)$, FBA becomes

$$\begin{aligned}&-\{[r_B(t_j)dt-\Lambda_B(t_j,t_{j+1})(1-R_B)-r_C(t_j)dt]V(t_j)\}\\&=-l_B(t_j)V(t_j)dt\end{aligned}$$

From this argument, we can understand that FBA is related to the liquidity spread of the bank and is clearly distinguished from DVA. *We would like to emphasize that the concept that there is duplication between DVA and FBA is wrong.* And this Linear FBA is similar to the one given by Hull and White (2014c).

4.1.2. FVA via linear approximation

Here, we will present the FVA result under the approximation $\tilde{V}(t_j) \to V(t_j)$. When this approximation can be applied, the adjustment to the value of the secured derivative trade from the value of the unsecured trade is

$$-\Lambda_A(t_j, t_{j+1})(1 - R_A)V(t_j) - l_B(t_j)V(t_j)dt$$

when $V(t_j) > 0$, and

$$-\Lambda_B(t_j, t_{j+1})(1 - R_B)V(t_j) - l_B(t_j)V(t_j)dt$$

when $V(t_j) < 0$.

Combining them, the conditional expected value of the adjustment at valuation time 0 is given by

$$\begin{aligned} P_{A;B}(t_j)\Bigg\{ & E^N\left[\frac{\Lambda_A(t_j, t_{j+1})(1 - R_A)V^+(t_j)}{N(t_j)}\middle| F_0\right] \\ & - E^N\left[\frac{\Lambda_B(t_j, t_{j+1})(1 - R_B)V^-(t_j)}{N(t_j)}\middle| F_0\right] \\ & - E^N\left[\frac{l_B(t_j)V(t_j)}{N(t_j)}\middle| F_0\right]\Bigg\} dt \end{aligned}$$

Here, the first term is the well-known representation of CVA and the second term is DVA. The last term is FVA, which is a sum of FBA and FCA. Note that FVA is additive, and FVA of the netting set (or bank portfolio) is a sum of individual FVAs.

Here we use the fact that the adjustments are only present when both A and B have not defaulted before time t_j.

Because in the limit $dt \to 0$, there is a relationship $P_{AB}(t)\Lambda_A(t_j, t_{j+1}) \to \exp(-\int_0^t (\lambda_A(u) + \lambda_B(u))du)\lambda_A(t_j)$ and $P_{AB}(t)\Lambda_B(t_j, t_{j+1}) \to \exp(-\int_0^t (\lambda_A(u) + \lambda_B(u))du)\lambda_B(t_j)$, the overall adjustments including CVA and DVA for derivatives trade is given by

$$\int_0^S P_{AB}(t)\lambda_A(t)(R_A - 1)E[V^+(t)]dt$$
$$- \int_0^S P_{AB}(t)\lambda_B(t)(R_B - 1)E[V^-(t)]dt$$
$$+ \int_0^S P_{AB}(t)l_B(t)E[V(t)]dt$$

and FVA is given by $\int_0^S P_{AB}(t)l_B(t)E[V(t)]dt$.

For the calculation of FVA without linear approximation (nonlinear FVA), we need least-squares Monte Carlo. It is discussed in Tan and Tsuchiya (2016).

4.2. FVA in the Bank's Balance Sheet

Funding cost of the bank should be analyzed on the bank's balance sheet. Therefore, in this section, we analyze the effect of the derivative transactions on the bank's balance sheet and on the funding cost of the bank. By analyzing the bank's balance sheet, the value of the derivatives to the shareholders, to the bank as a whole, and from the perspective of regulators, will be revealed.

We analyze the cash flows by separating the cases when the derivative value is negative vs when it is positive. Here the derivatives are assumed to be uncollateralized.

4.2.1. *FVA when the derivative is liability (FBA and DVA)*

Here we will analyze the balance sheet when value of the derivative is negative (derivative is a liability).

4.2.1.1. *Cash flows are invested in risk-free asset*

When the value of the derivative is negative, the bank receives cash when it enters a derivative contract. In this section, we analyze the case when the cash is invested in a risk-free asset (e.g. treasury). Now liability is increased by the amount of $|V(t)|$, asset is also increased

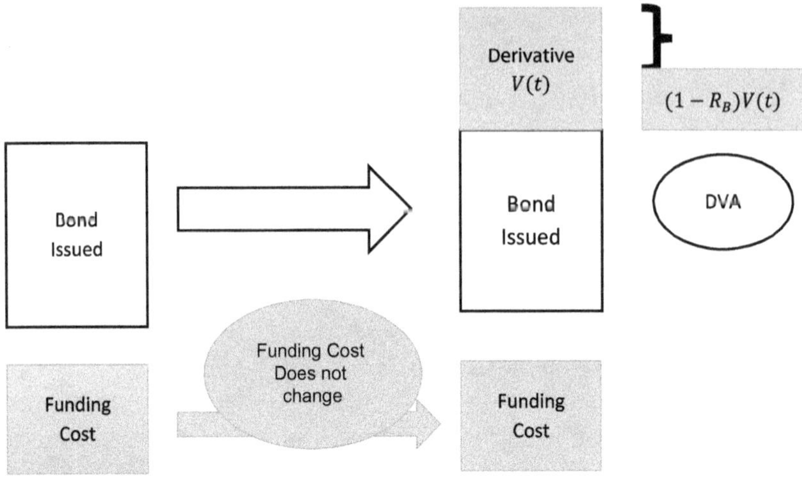

Fig. 4.11: Derivatives value is negative. Cash is invested with risk-free rate.

by the same amount and the balance sheet is expanded. Here, the amount of the bond issued does not change and funding cost does not change. On the other hand, total liability is increased, and when the bank defaults the loss to debtholders (the benefit to the bank) increases by the amount $(1 - R_B)|V(t)|$. The value of this is the DVA (see Fig. 4.11).

4.2.1.2. *Cash flows are used to reduce the bond issued*

Regarding cash flows the bank receives when the derivative value is negative, we can adopt the other assumption. As is stated in Section 4.1, the investment bank is usually cash poor. Therefore, if it has cash flows from the derivative trade, it is reasonable to assume that they are used to reduce the bond issued.[1] Under this assumption, part of the liability ($|V(t)|$) is transformed from the bond to the derivative. Because the amount of total liability does not change, the total loss that the debtors suffer (or extent of bank's benefit) when the bank defaults does not change.

[1]The details about the operation of reducing the bond issued using the collateral received is discussed in Albanese and Andersen (2014) and Albanese *et al.* (2014).

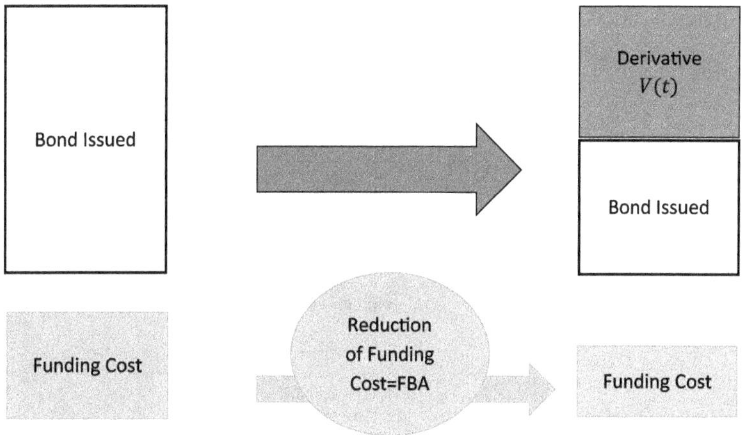

Fig. 4.12: Derivatives value is negative. Cash is used to reduce the bond position.

On the other hand, with this assumption, the bond issued is decreased by the amount of $|V(t)|$ and funding cost is reduced by $|V(t)|s_B(t)dt$ for the period $t \sim t + dt$. This decrease of funding cost is FBA. Observe how DVA in the previous assumption has changed to FBA. *That is, FBA is a mirror image of DVA.* FVA and DVA should be always analyzed together (Fig. 4.12).

Note that here funding spread $s_B(t)$ comes from credit risk and liquidity premium of the bank

$$s_B(t) = \Lambda_B(t, t + dt)(1 - R_B)/dt + l_B(t)$$

Therefore, FBA is different from DVA by the amount of the liquidity premium.

Note that actually regulators restrict banks from trading their own bonds actively and DVA cannot be assumed to become FBA free. The actual situation is that part of the debt contributes to DVA and part of it contributes to FBA.

4.2.2. *FVA when the derivative is an asset (FCA)*

In this section, we will investigate the case when the derivative is an asset, i.e. $V(t) > 0$. If $V(t) > 0$. To enter a derivative transaction, the bank needs to finance $V(t)$ amount of money by issuing bonds. The balance sheet is expanded. Because the bond issued is increased by

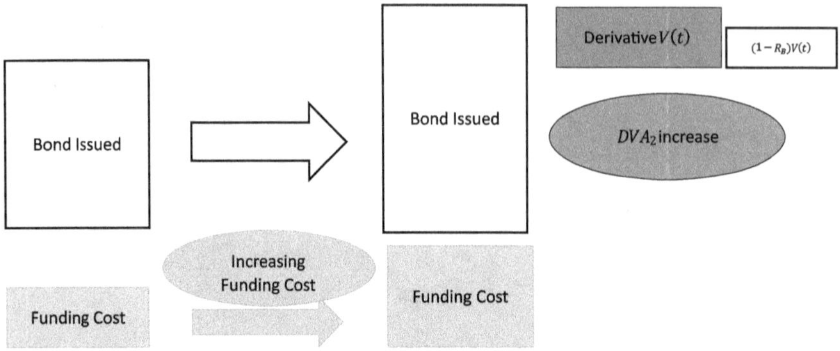

Fig. 4.13: Derivatives value is positive.

the amount of $V(t)$, funding cost for the period $t \sim t + dt$ increases by $V(t)s_B(t)dt$. This increase in cost is FCA (Fig. 4.13).

Here, because total liability is increased, the loss to the debtor (benefit to the bank) when the bank defaults is increased. The value of this benefit for the bank is $V(t)(1 - R_B)\Lambda_B(t, t + dt)dt$. This value is called DVA_2.

The DVA_2 cancels the credit risk part of FCA, and if DVA_2 is included in derivative value, FCA comes only from liquidity premium, i.e.

$$\text{FCA} = \int l_B(t)E[V^+(t)]dt$$

Here note that realizing the benefit of DVA_2 is really difficult and whether the benefit is included in the value is a controversial topic. This point will be discussed in the following sections.

4.2.3. *Value for creditors and shareholders*

In the previous section, we showed that the credit spread part of FCA is canceled by DVA_2. DVA_2 is the value to bondholders rather than to shareholders. That is DVA_2 is realized basically only when the bank defaults. When the bank defaults, the value of the bank to shareholder is 0 and DVA_2 is not a benefit to shareholders. On the other hand, DVA_2 from the derivative transaction increases the recovery rate of the liability and it is a benefit to bondholders

(Burgard and Kjaer, 2011a, 2011b, 2013). Therefore, for the valuation for both shareholders bondholders (whole balance sheet), DVA_2 and DVA should be included in the derivative value. On the other hand, for the valuation for shareholders, DVA_2 and (unhedged) DVA should not be included in the derivative value.

Note that the increase in recovery rate should decrease the funding spread. Burgard and Kjaer showed that this reduction of the funding spread removes FCA. However, they also claimed that the effect to funding spread from the derivative trade will take quite a long time and this removal of FCA is not efficient.

The above arguments about DVA_2 are completely parallel to the one in DVA. Therefore, under the assumption that DVA is not hedged by buying back the bond issued by the bank, DVA is also to the benefit of bondholders.

4.2.4. *Metrics of FVA*

Based on the discussion in the previous sections, we will summarize three metrics about FVA and DVA which are common in the market.

(A) FVA + DVA is given by

$$\begin{aligned}\mathrm{FVA} + \mathrm{DVA} &= \mathrm{FBA} + \mathrm{FCA}\\ &= -\int s_B(t)E[V^-(t)]dt - \int l_B(t)E[V^+(t)]dt\\ &= -(1-R_B)\int \lambda_B(t)E[V^-(t)]dt\\ &\quad - \int l_B(t)E[V(t)]dt\end{aligned}$$

Here, we assume that DVA is fully hedged and converted to FBA. We also assume that DVA_2, which cancels out FCA, is fully accounted for. In the right-hand side, the first term is identical to DVA. This value is the value in the whole balance sheet and the value for both shareholders and creditors. This metric is derived by Tan and Tsuchiya in the exposure method and matches the one given by

Hull and White.[2]

(B) FVA + DVA is given by

$$\begin{aligned}\text{FVA} + \text{DVA} &= \text{FBA} + \text{FCA}\\ &= -\int s_B(t)E[V^-(t)]dt - \int s_B(t)E[V^+(t)]dt\\ &= -\int s_B(t)E[V(t)]dt\end{aligned}$$

Here DVA is converted to FBA, but DVA_2 is not included in the value. This value is given in the exposure method, if DVA_2 is not included in the value. The replication method with hedge error also gives this value. If we interpret the trading value as the hedge cost in a theoretically hedged strategy, this value is reasonable. Burgard and Kjaer derived this adjustment by the replication method, but they also showed that with some assumption, (A) can be possible. *If we do not include DVA, the discounting method gives this FVA. Thus, when we adopt the discounting method, we should not include DVA.*

(C) FVA + DVA is given by

$$\text{FVA} + \text{DVA} = \text{FCA} = -\int s_B(t)E[V^+(t)]dt$$

In Basel Committee on Banking Supervision (2012), the Basel committee requires banks not to account for value which increases when the bank's credit deteriorates in relation to the effect on Common Equity Tier 1 capital (CET_1). That is, the banks cannot include DVA or DVA_2 in derivatives valuation. Albanese and Andersen (2014) and Albanese *et al.* (2014) introduced a regulatory valuation which includes only FCA as FVA. This metric is a shareholder's value with the assumption that DVA is not hedged by the bond buyback.

---

[2]Kjaer also analyzed FVA in firm value based on PDE (Kjaer, 2017a, 2017b).

4.3. PDE Approach to FVA

In this section, we will study FVA by the PDE (Replication) approach. PDE approach to FVA is the mathematical formulation of the bank balance sheet analysis in Section 4.2 (Burgard and Kjaer, 2011a, 2011b, and 2013).

In the replication method, we create a portfolio which hedges all risks from derivatives trading. To incorporate XVA in the replication method, we need to treat the default risk of both the counterparty and the bank and the funding strategy on top of market risk. Counterparty default risk is hedged by trading bonds issued by it.

Here, we assume that the bank issues a bond (or buys back the bond) to finance derivative transactions. *Note that default of the bank is not hedged in this assumption because the amount of the bond the bank issues does not necessarily match the amount necessary to hedge the bank's default.* Actually, if the value of the derivative $V(t)$ is positive, then the bank defaults the value $V(t)$ is returned in full by the counterparty, but the bond issued to finance the amount $V(t)$ is not returned to the bondholder. This benefit is a hedge error. This hedge error is not favorable. Here the trading (front office) value of a derivative is a hedging cost of derivative transaction. In traditional derivatives valuation theory, all of the costs of trading a derivative can be hedged, but in post-crisis derivatives valuation theory, some hedge errors cannot be removed with reasonable assumptions.

Trading valuation of a derivative is the hedging cost of the derivative trade. However, in this situation, there are risks which cannot be hedged. Hedge error is a profit which is realized when the bank defaults. On the other hand, when the bank defaults, the value of trading desk (book) is zero for the shareholder. Therefore, the value of trading book should not include the value of hedge error and the PDE is constructed by excluding the profit from the hedge error.

Note that by trading a CDS index which has a high correlation with the CDS of the bank, we can at least partially hedge the bank's default without affecting the funding strategy.

Burgard and Kjaer pointed out that if we can dynamically trade senior and subordinated bonds, we can hedge a bank's default with financing cash flows necessary for the derivative transactions. However, they also claimed that this dynamic trading is not realistic. Note also that regulations restrict frequent trading of a bank's own bond and dynamic hedging of funding and/or a bank's default is therefore not realistic.

In this section, we will study the valuation of a derivative when there is default risk of both the client C and the bank B, and there is a funding cost. Here the derivative price $\tilde{V}(t, S(t), J_B, J_C)$ depends on the asset underlying price $S(t)$, and stochastic variables $J_B(t)$ and $J_C(t)$ as in Chapter 2.

Consider a derivative transaction between the bank B (us) and a counterparty C. The risk-free price of the derivative seen from B is $V(t)$, and it depends on the asset price $S(t)$. The counterparty C has issued a discount bond P_C which has the recovery rate R_C and the bank B has issued a bond P_B with the recovery rate R_B. The stochastic differential equations of the assets are given by

$$\begin{aligned} dS(t) &= \mu(t)dt + \sigma(t)S(t)dW(t) \\ dP_C(t) &= r_C(t)P_C(t)dt - (1 - R_C)P_C(t)dJ_C(t) \\ dP_B(t) &= r_B(t)P_B(t)dt - (1 - R_B)P_B(t)dJ_B(t) \end{aligned}$$

Here, J_B and J_C represent default event of B and C and move from 0 to 1 upon their default. Default probabilities of B and C are, respectively, given by

$$\begin{aligned} \lambda_B(t)dt &= E[dJ_B(t)|F_t] \\ \lambda_C(t)dt &= E[dJ_C(t)|F_t] \end{aligned}$$

Deterministic rates are assumed to be given by

$$\begin{aligned} r_B(t) &= r(t) + (1 - R_B)\lambda_B(t) + l_B(t) \\ r_C(t) &= r(t) + (1 - R_C)\lambda_C(t) + l_C(t) \end{aligned}$$

where $r(t)$ is the risk-free rate and $l_B(t)$ and $l_C(t)$ are liquidity premium of issuers B and C, respectively.

Now let $V(t)$ be the risk-free price of the derivative, $\hat{V}(t)$ be the adjusted price which includes the bilateral counterparty risk and $\Pi(t)$ be the price of a portfolio which replicates $\hat{V}(t)$. When either B or C defaults, the price $\hat{V}(t)$ jumps to the closeout price and it is a function of time t, asset price $S(t)$, J_B and J_C. That is,

$$\hat{V}(t) = \hat{V}(t, S, J_B, J_C)$$

Now we assume risk-free closeout, where

$$\hat{V}(t, S, 1, 0) = g_B(V)$$
$$\hat{V}(t, S, 0, 1) = g_C(V)$$

Here when there is no collateral arrangement, $g_B(V) = V^+ + R_B V^-$ and $g_C(V) = R_C V^+ + V^-$.

The replication portfolio $\Pi(t)$ is given by

$$\Pi(t) = \delta(t)S(t) + \alpha_C(t)P_C(t) + \alpha_B(t)P_B(t) + \beta_S(t) + \beta_C(t)$$

where $\delta(t)$, $\alpha_C(t)$, $\alpha_1(t)$ and $\alpha_2(t)$ should be chosen such that $\Pi(t)$ hedges $\hat{V}$, while $\beta_S(t)$ and $\beta_C(t)$ are cash amounts which are given by

$$\beta_S(t) = -\delta(t)S(t)$$
$$\beta_C(t) = -\alpha_C(t)P_C(t)$$

Here, bonds issued by the bank are used to fund the cost of entering the derivative and the relationship

$$-\hat{V}(t) = \alpha_B(t)P_B(t)$$

is satisfied. Because the replicating portfolio is self-financing,

$$d\Pi(t) = \delta(t)dS(t) + \alpha_C(t)dP_C(t) + \alpha_B(t)dP_B(t) + d\beta_S(t) + d\beta_C(t)$$

Both the asset and the bond issued by the counterparty are financed by repo transactions. We assume the repo rate for bond $P_C(t)$ to be the risk-free rate $r(t)$ and for the asset $S(t)$ to be $q(t)$ (where the difference is to take account of potential dividends), so

$$d\beta_S(t) = -q(t)\delta(t)S(t)dt$$
$$d\beta_C(t) = -r(t)\alpha_C(t)P_C(t)dt$$

On the other hand, by Ito's lemma, the adjusted price has the following dynamics:

$$d\hat{V}(t) = \partial_t\hat{V}(t)dt + \partial_S\hat{V}(t)dS(t) + \frac{1}{2}S^2(t)\sigma^2(t)\partial_S^2\hat{V}(t) + \partial_{J_B}\hat{V}(t)dJ_B(t) + \partial_{J_C}\hat{V}(t)dJ_C(t)$$

Here,

$$\partial_{J_B}\hat{V}(t) = \hat{V}(t, S, 1, 0) - \hat{V}(t, S, 0, 0)$$
$$\partial_{J_C}\hat{V}(t) = \hat{V}(t, S, 0, 1) - \hat{V}(t, S, 0, 0)$$

Now the amount of the asset S and the bond P_C are chosen as follows:

$$\delta(t) = -\partial_S\hat{V}(t)$$
$$(1 - R_C)\alpha_C(t)P_C(t) = \partial_{J_C}\hat{V}(t)$$

the risk from asset dynamics and default of counterparty C is hedged. On the other hand, the risk from the bank's default is not hedged.

In this situation, the sum of the prices of the derivative and the replicating portfolio has the following dynamics:

$$\begin{aligned} d(\hat{V}(t) + \Pi(t)) &= (\partial_t\hat{V}(t)dt + \frac{1}{2}S^2(t)\sigma^2(t)\partial_S^2\hat{V}(t) \\ &\quad + q(t)S(t)\partial_S\hat{V}(t))dt \\ &\quad - \left(r + \lambda_B + \lambda_C + l_B + \frac{l_C}{1 - R_C}\right)\hat{V}(t)dt + \left(\lambda_C + \frac{l_C}{1 - R_C}\right)g_C dt \\ &\quad + (g_B - \epsilon_B)\lambda_B + \epsilon_B dJ_B \end{aligned}$$

where

$$\epsilon_B = \partial_{J_B}\tilde{V} + (1 - R_B)\tilde{V} = g_B - R_B\tilde{V}$$

Here, ϵ_B is the hedge error when loss or profit due to default of bond B does not completely compensate those of the derivative position.

Because of this hedge error, $d(\hat{V}(t)+\Pi(t))$ cannot be 0, which is different to the Black–Scholes model (Chapter 1) and the situation where risk-free funding is possible (Chapter 2). How this hedge error is handled is related to the different stakeholders' perspective in the valuation of derivatives, as will be discussed in detail afterward. Here we will consider the trading valuation. We define the trading value (front office value) as the hedging cost of the derivative. If we do not take into account the funding of the derivative transaction, all of the risks are (theoretically) completely hedged. On the other hand, if funding of the trade is taken into account, there will inevitably be hedge errors (e.g. if only one seniority of bond is issued by the bank). If the derivative valuation $\hat{V}(t)$ is positive, a positive amount of bond is issued by the bank to finance the position. When the bank defaults, the value of the derivative position does not change except for the closeout difference of $V(t) - \hat{V}(t)$. However, the issued bond will not be returned, creating a positive value for the whole bank's balance sheet, which is a hedge error.

Hedging error is a profit to the bank as a whole, but it is not a profit to shareholders of the bank. Therefore, if we do not account for the value which arises from the hedging error, we can establish the PDE (Burgard and Kjaer (2011a), (2011b) and (2013)).

$$\begin{aligned}&\left(\partial_t\hat{V}(t)dt+\frac{1}{2}S^2(t)\sigma^2(t)\partial_S^2\hat{V}(t)+q(t)S(t)\partial_S\hat{V}(t)\right)\\&\quad-\left(r+(1-R_B)\lambda_B+\lambda_C+l_B+\frac{l_C}{1-R_C}\right)\hat{V}(t)\\&\quad+\left(\lambda_C+\frac{l_C}{1-R_C}\right)g_C=0\end{aligned}$$

If we split the adjusted price $\hat{V}(t)$ into the risk-free price and the adjustment

$$\hat{V}(t)=V(t)+U(t)$$

then using the condition that $V(t)$ satisfies the Black–Scholes equation, the adjustment term $U(t)$ satisfies the following equation:

$$\begin{aligned}
&\partial_t U(t) + \frac{1}{2}S^2(t)\sigma^2(t)\partial_S^2 U(t) - q(t)S(t)\partial_S U(t) \\
&\quad - \left[r + \lambda_B + \lambda_C + l_B + \frac{l_C}{1-R_C}\right]U(t) \\
&= \lambda_B(g_B - V(t)) - \lambda_B\epsilon_B + \left(\lambda_C + \frac{l_C}{1-R_C}\right)(g_C - V(t)) + l_B V(t)
\end{aligned}$$

From this equation, using the Feynman–Kac formula, we see that there is an FVA term on top of CVA and DVA terms, i.e.

$$\begin{aligned}
\text{FVA} = &\int_0^T l_B(t)\exp\left(-\int_0^t \left(r(u) + \lambda_B(u) + \lambda_C(u)\right.\right. \\
&\left.\left. + l_B(u) + \frac{l_C(u)}{1-R_C}\right)du\right)\{E[\epsilon_B(t)] + l_B(t)E[V(t)]\}dt
\end{aligned}$$

Here, because $\epsilon_B(t) = g_B(t) - R_B V(t) = (1 - R_B)V^+(t)$, there is an FCA from default risk of the bank and FVA from liquidity premium.

If there is extra cash, it is assumed that it will be used to buy back bonds issued by the bank. Active trading of a bank's own bonds is usually prohibited, but if we assume that the (investment) bank is cash poor and extra money is used to reduce the money the bank needs in other businesses, the assumption above turns out to be reasonable in practice.

In the above arguments, it is assumed that funding is done at the netting set level. However, actually the bank can fund in the funding sets between which collateral can be freely rehypothecated.

Chapter 5

Ingredients of the Modern Yield Curve and Overlaps with XVA

Ultimately, XVA can be thought of as a set of adjustments to the price of an instrument to fully take into account costs (and benefits) pertaining to various activities needed to maintain and risk manage the position (i.e. funding, potential default, margining, etc.). But what is the base (e.g. potentially but not necessarily "risk-free") case to which these adjustments are made? This naturally needs us to consider the construction of the modern yield curve, post 2008 (Bianchetti, 2010).

5.1. Forecasting and Discounting

Prior to 2008, it was assumed that investment banks (typically AA rated) could fund at Libor, and thus the Libor rate was typically used in place of the theoretical "risk-free" rate for valuing derivatives. Even then, it was clear that some higher rated (e.g. AAA) banks could borrow at less than Libor and in cases when their Treasury departments charged the bank's borrowing costs to the derivatives desks, it indirectly encouraged those desks to pursue deals that yielded even less than Libor since they would still register a profit.

With the spread between Libor and Overnight Index Swap (OIS) exploding in the 2008 crisis (to 365 bp for USD at its maximum) and settling at a far wider equilibrium thereafter (e.g. OIS vs 3 m

Libor has hovered around 20 bp for USD), it is now clear that banks can no longer use the (uncollateralized) Libor rate to reflect their funding costs since they generally engage in collateralized funding (reflected by the OIS rate). Further, the costly nature of uncollateralized borrowing (in addition to higher capital charges for counterparty risks) has proven to be a sufficient incentive for a huge swath of the larger market participants to adopt CSA[1] (i.e. collateral) arrangements in their dealings with the banks.

In this situation, as market practice after the 2008 crisis, the curve for discounting is constructed from the OIS rate.

However, Libor has remained relevant because the vast majority of contracts in the swap market refers to Libor (or its cousins Euribor and Tibor) to determine the rate of a floating coupon. In that sense, Libor will remain the curve used for "forecasting"[2] future cash flows, whereas it will no longer be used for "discounting". The construction of the curves which generate Libor rates and discount factors is explained as follows.

Market Instruments

If we consider a swap, we can write the Present Value (PV) as a combination of

$$\text{(a) the fixed leg PV} = R\sum_{i=1}^{N} \tau_i D\left(T_i\right)$$

$$\text{minus (b) the floating leg PV} - \sum_{i=1}^{M} \tau_i^* f^\tau\left(T_{i-1}^*, T_i^*\right) D\left(T_i^*\right)$$

where R is the fixed (swap) rate, $\{T_i\}_{i=1}^N$ are fixed payment dates, $\{\tau_i\}_{i=1}^N$ are fixed accrual periods, $\{T_i^*\}_{i=1}^M$ are float payment dates, $\{\tau_i^*\}_{i=1}^M$ are float accrual periods and $D(T)= D(0,T)$ is the discount factor from OIS discounting up to time Tobserved at item 0.

[1]CSA stands for Credit Security Annex and is the part of the ISDA agreement that deals with collateral arrangements.

[2]"Forecasting" is not used with the traditional meaning of prediction of a future outcome. It merely refers to risk-neutral cash flow projection, where we can lock in the value via hedging. Sometimes, the term "projecting" is used as an alternative.

Crucially, there is the term $f^{\tau}(t,T) = f^{\tau}(0,t,T)$ which represents the forward rate over the period t to T (where $T - t \approx \tau$) observed at time 0. This can be defined as

$$f^{\tau}(t,T) = \frac{\left(\frac{D^{\tau}(t)}{D^{\tau}(T)} - 1\right)}{(T-t)}$$

where we are working off a discount curve $D^{\tau}(T) = D^{\tau}(0,T)$ constructed to represent Libor rates of tenor τ. Here, τ can be thought of as 1 month, 3 months, 6 months, 12 months or whatever tenor our Libor periods are.

Note that we have two unknowns $D(T)$ and $D^{\tau}(T)$, and only the quoted swap rate R. To complete the system, we need one more instrument: the OIS. One leg pays the OIS rate, while the other pays Libor plus a spread. The PV is then a combination of[3]

$$\text{(a) the OIS leg PV} = \sum_{i=1}^{N} \tau_i f(T_{i-1}, T_i) D(T_i) = D(T_0) - D(T_N)$$

minus (b) the floating leg

$$\text{PV} = \sum_{i=1}^{M} \tau_i^* \left(f^{\tau}\left(T_{i-1}^*, T_i^*\right) + s\right) D\left(T_i^*\right)$$

where s is a spread.

Thus, to bootstrap an interest rate curve, we need to simultaneously solve to match the prices of standard (fixed vs Libor) swaps and OIS.

[3]Here, we get the simplification because the forecasting rate is based on the same OIS curve used for discounting. Strictly, OIS by daily compounding (e.g. EUR) involves the payoff $\prod_0^{n-1}(1 + f(T_{i-1}^j, T_{i-1}^j + \tau_b)\tau_b)$ where τ_b is 1 business day, $T_{i-1}^0 = T_{i-1}$, $T_{i-1}^{n-1} + \tau_b = T_i$ and $f(t, t+\tau_b) = \frac{1}{\tau_b}\left(\frac{D(t+\tau_b)}{D(t)} - 1\right)$. However, note that in some markets (the most important being USD), the OIS rate for a period is based on the sum $\sum_0^{n-1}(1+f(T_{i-1}^j, T_{i-1}^j+\tau_b)\tau_b)$ rather than the earlier product. Strictly, we no longer get the difference of two discount factors $D(T_0) - D(T_N)$ in this case. However, the approximation is close enough conceptually.

Note that to build the discount curves for different Libor tenors τ, we work with basis swaps, i.e. one leg pays Libor of tenor $\hat{\tau}$ (e.g. 6 m), and another pays Libor of tenor τ (e.g. 3 m) and a spread s.[4]

5.1.1. *Stochastic funding spreads*

Given that OIS and Libor rates are not the same, there is a spread between them. Naturally, we can observe this spread historically and will realize that it is stochastic and correlated to the Libor rate. We remark that the above equation for forecasting with Libor and discounting with OIS holds only in the case where the spread has zero correlation with Libor (note that a deterministic spread will automatically satisfy this condition).

Otherwise, there is a quanto-style adjustment when pricing a standard swap, due to the correlation between the spread and Libor as pointed out by Piterbarg (2012). It is not common for institutions to take this into account in general, partly because the correlation of the spread and Libor is not easily observed and not generally stable. More importantly, since we are using market swap rates as inputs to the curve, provided we stick to swaps of standard collateral, then whether we take account quanto adjustment really only affects the internally generated forecasting and discounting curves and hence the prices of standard swaps outside the terms for which our quotes exist (i.e. this is a matter affecting interpolation and extrapolation of swap rates mostly).

Consider a cash flow based on the floating rate $f^{\tau}(T,T,T+\tau)$ set at T and payable at time $T+\tau$. Its value at time t is given by $B_t^O \tau E_t^O \left[\frac{f^{\tau}(T,T,T+\tau)}{B_{T+\tau}^O}\right]$ where the money market account is $B_t^O = \exp(-\int_0^t r_s ds)$ and grows at the OIS rate, whereas the floating rate depends on discount bonds constructed with tenor τ as follows:

$$f^{\tau}(T,T,T+\tau) = \frac{\left(\frac{D^{\tau}(T,T)}{D^{\tau}(T,T+\tau)} - 1\right)}{\tau}$$

[4]Note that to construct a curve in practice, we need to consider more subtle points. Here, only the theory to construct a curve is explained.

When funding spread is stochastic and correlated with rates,

$$\tau E_t^O \left[\frac{f(T, T, T+\tau)\, B_t^O}{B_{T+\tau}^O} \right] \neq f(t, T, T+\tau)\, D(t, T+\tau)$$

does not hold and there is a quant-type adjustment. This point will be discussed in Section 5.7.1.

5.2. OIS and Collateral

At this stage, it is perhaps fitting to revisit the "risk-free" rate, which forms the theoretical underpinning of much of derivatives pricing.

In particular, recall how in Section 2.7.2, we derived the equation for derivatives valuation in the presence of collateral, but also showed how the hedged portfolio grows at the repo rate, which replaces the risk-free rate in the PDE. We can also think back to Section 1.1.1 and immediately see that we can make the same argument replacing the "risk-free" rate with the collateral rate, since any (collateralized) funding is at this rate.

Alternatively, we could show by the following analysis how actually it is the funding rate as opposed to the risk-free rate that is used for derivatives pricing.

The main thing to note is that this "(collateralized) funding rate" is the rate associated with the collateral in question. Naturally, one could surmise that a different quality or arrangement of collateral (e.g. if mortgage-backed securities were permissible collateral as opposed to government bonds, or if collateral is not posted daily or subject to a Minimum Transfer Amount) would lead to a different funding rate. Whereas this analysis sounds new to someone schooled in traditional derivatives pricing, the concept has been long employed in the pricing of repo (forward) on government bonds prior to 2008.

A repo is a transaction where a party sells an instrument (e.g. government bond) and agrees to repurchase it at a future date. This is effectively collateralized borrowing, since the seller receives cash now which is repayable at a future date with the instrument serving as collateral for what is effectively a loan. Since Libor is uncollateralized, the value of the high-quality collateral serves as

Fig. 5.1: Illustrative diagram of pricing a government bond forward.

additional security for repayment, and so the repo rate is typically lower than Libor. Thus, the repo allows market participants to more efficiently fund a forward in a government bond, which now has a higher price than implied by forward valuing at Libor. This is traditionally how trading in government bonds takes place, since the lower yields on government bonds would otherwise not be worthwhile for banks assuming Libor funding before 2008 (Fig. 5.1).

At time 0, party A sells the bond to party B for N. At time T, party A buys back the bond for N^* from B. The repo rate is then $\left(r = \left(\frac{N^*}{N}\right)^{1/T} - 1\right)$. This was typically less than Libor being secured by the bond. And this explains a major reason for banks to hold government bonds, which can be used for borrowing under repo, rather than just to earn much lower interest than the swap market.

Importantly, we should note that OISs are based on CSA arrangements which require posting of collateral daily based on cash or very high-quality instruments (i.e. government bonds) in the currency of the swap. This makes the OIS curve a proxy[5] to the "risk-free" rate in the currency concerned.

[5]Describing OIS as a proxy to the risk-free rate is realistic since there is still a one business day risk of default even in the best case, while in practice it can be worse since counterparties may dispute valuations, sometimes even as a tactical delay to posting collateral. But these days, even governments are not considered risk-free in their own currency and the Euro is a major currency where strictly no sovereign state is risk-free. The concept of a risk-free rate is useful in terms of having a base case to compute CVA off, but otherwise whether OIS is risk-free or not is not particularly important.

5.3. Different Collateral and Funding Implications

In Section 5.1, bootstrapping of Libor curves and the OIS curve in the single-currency economy is explained.

But realistically, financial institutions operate in multiple economies globally, and naturally collateral is likely to exist in multiple currencies. For example, a US (non-financial) company would probably much rather post collateral in US dollars even if it was doing an EUR swap to fix the cost of borrowing in euros. Similarly, this is applicable for companies in other regions wanting to post collateral in their own currency. More vexing is that FX deals involve more than one currency (e.g. a forward to sell USD and buy JPY) and the collateral would naturally only be posted in one currency. As discussed in the previous section, different collateral implies different funding rate. Therefore, we need discount factors for the collateralization of different currencies than trade currencies.

In the next section, we discuss the construction of discount factors and Libor curves in the multicurrencies economy. We need the cross-currency swap on top of the IRS and the OIS as base instruments (Tan, 2013).

5.3.1. *The cross-currency swap*

The practical approach of a financial institution dealing with a counterparty that wishes to post collateral in a different currency is to hedge via a cross-currency swap. Here, one party pays Libor in USD and the other pays Libor plus a spread in a different currency. Further, for a traditional cross-currency swap, there is exchange of notional at the start and end of the period.

For a simple illustration (Fig. 5.2), Client C posts an EUR security to Bank A and seeks USD collateral for its value. Bank A hedges by posting the security to Bank B but receives EUR collateral (since security is in EUR). The missing piece is the cross-currency swap, which Bank A does with Bank D, where it pays Euribor + spread and receives USD Libor.

In a cross-currency swap, Libor in the domestic currency (USD) is exchanged for Libor in a foreign currency plus a basis spread. In

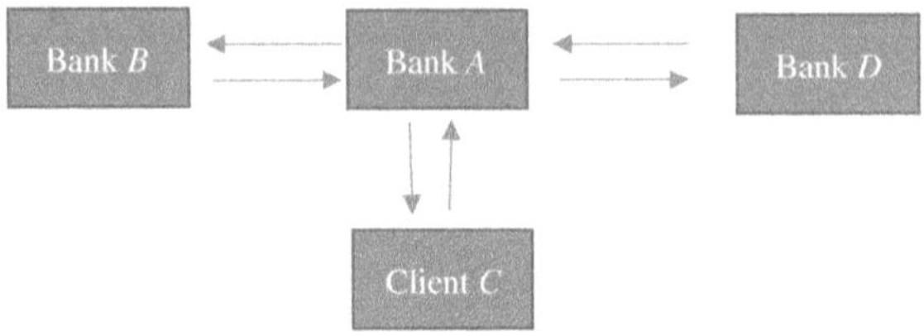

Fig. 5.2: Collateral in different currencies and CCS swap.

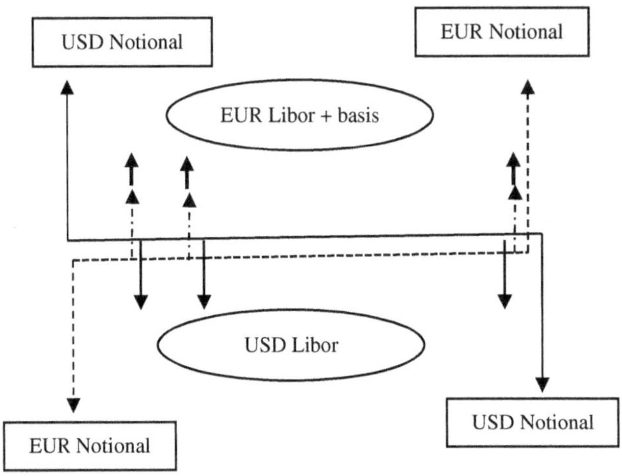

Fig. 5.3: Cross-currency swap cash flows (USD vs EUR).

such a swap, the notional of the domestic currency is exchanged for that of the foreign currency at the beginning of the trade and the notionals are repaid at the end of the trade also (Fig. 5.3).

Typically collateral is in USD for both legs. From our earlier discussion on how collateral affects discounting, this implies that the foreign leg would have a different discount factor than a standard swap in the foreign currency (namely USD collateralized foreign discount factor). Specifically, the value of the foreign leg would be

$$\mathrm{PV} = \sum_{i=1}^{M} \tau_i^* \left\{ f^{\tau;f}\left(T_{i-1}^*, T_i^*\right) + s^{\mathrm{CCY}} \right\} D_{\mathrm{USD}}^{f}\left(T_i^*\right) + D_{\mathrm{USD}}^{f}\left(T_M^*\right)$$

where $D^f_{\text{USD}}(T)$ refers to the discount factor in the foreign currency under USD CSA and $f^{\tau;f}(T_{i-1},T_i) = \left(\frac{D^{\tau;f}(T_{i-1})}{D^{\tau;f}(T_i)} - 1\right)$ is a foreign Libor rate.

The value of the USD leg would be as before, with the addition of the notional repayable at maturity, i.e. USD leg PV =

$$X_0 \sum_{i=1}^{M} \tau_i^* f^\tau\left(T_{i-1}^*, T_i^*\right) D\left(T_i^*\right) + X_0 D\left(T_M^*\right)$$

where X_0 is the spot exchange rate, the USD discount factor under USD CSA is $D(T)$ and the USD Libor rate is $f^\tau(T_{i-1},T_i)$ as before.

Note that we now need to build our curve by simultaneously solving for $D^f_{\text{USD}}(T)$, $D^{\tau;f}(T)$, $D(T)$ and $D^\tau(T)$ to match the prices of cross-currency swaps, OIS and standard (fixed vs Libor) swaps in both the domestic and foreign currencies.

These days, the market standard is for mark-to-market (MtM) cross-currency swap. Here the notional is repaid at the end of each period and the notional of the USD leg is reset based on prevailing FX rates at that time (Fig. 5.4). This is to avoid the large potential exposure from a traditional cross-currency swap, where the future FX rate (applied to the notional set at inception T_0) can mean the swap ends up very much in-the-money for one party over a period of time.

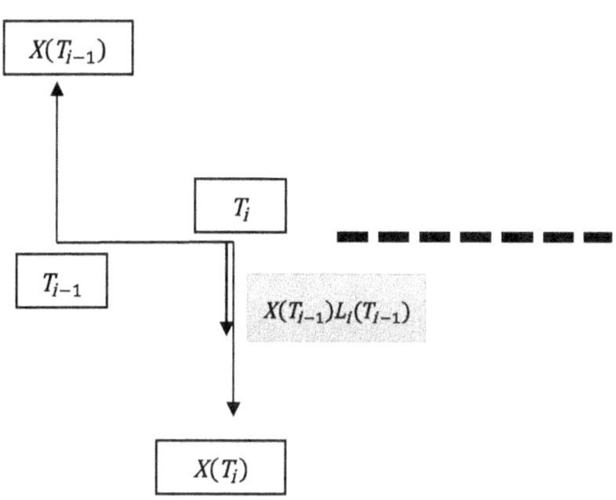

Fig. 5.4: MtM cross-currency swap USD leg cash flows.

The USD leg PV of an MtM cross-currency swap is given by

$$\begin{aligned}\mathrm{PV} &= N(0)\sum_{i}^{M} E^{N}\left[X\left(T_{i-1}\right)\left\{-1+\left(1+\tau_i^* f^{\tau}\left(T_{i-1}^*, T_i^*\right)\right)\right.\right.\\ &\quad \left.\left.\times D\left(T_{i-1}, T_i\right)\right\}/N(T_{i-1})|F_0\right]\\ &= \sum_{i=1}^{M} X_{i-1}\left\{-D\left(T_i^*\right)+\left(1+\tau_i^* f^{\tau}\left(T_{i-1}^*, T_i^*\right)\right) D\left(T_i^*\right)\right\}\end{aligned}$$

where X_i is the forward FX rate as seen at time T_i^*, i.e. $X_i = X_0 \frac{D(T_i^*)}{D^{\mathrm{USD,CCY}}(T_i^*)}$.

5.4. Implications of Stochastic Funding

In Section 5.1.1, we had considered the more realistic situation where the spread between Libor and OIS is stochastic, and had concluded that the implications are limited when pricing standard swaps. However, this is because our concern there is where input market instruments are in the same collateral and the only deviation in our instrument is the maturity.

Having used cross-currency swaps, OIS and standard swaps to bootstrap our discount curve, if we now seek to use this curve to price a fixed EUR cash flow under USD CSA, the choice of stochastic funding spreads will however affect this discount factor. It is beyond the scope of this book to discuss in detail the implications of stochastic funding spreads. However, it should be noted that, as in the case of a quanto in interest rates, the effect grows more than linearly with time, and is relevant only when correlation is non-zero.

This is particularly relevant for assets that have long-dated cash flows payable at maturity. Examples are the final notional repayment of traditional cross-currency swaps, and asset swaps, and especially the inflation-linked notional repayment of inflation zero swaps or asset swaps. Note that cross-currency swaps and asset swaps can have maturities of 30 years and inflation swaps can even have maturities of 50 years.

USD OIS Spread Vol	0.30%	0.30%	0.30%	0.30%	0.30%	0.30%	0.30%	0.30%
USD OIS Spread Mean Rev	10%	10%	10%	10%	10%	10%	10%	10%
EUR OIS Spread Vol	0.25%	0.25%	0.25%	0.25%	0.25%	0.25%	0.25%	0.25%
EUR OIS Spread Mean Rev	10%	10%	10%	10%	10%	10%	10%	10%
EUR USD–CSA Spr Vol / EUR OIS Spr Vol	2.0	2.0	2.0	2.0	2.0	2.0	1.2	1.2
USD OIS Spread Corr vs USD Libor	30%	−30%	−30%	30%	0%	0%	25%	−25%
EUR OIS Spread Corr vs EUR Libor	20%	−20%	−20%	20%	0%	0%	20%	−20%
EUR USD–CSA Spread Corr vs EUR Libor	17%	−17%	−17%	17%	0%	0%	24%	−24%
EUR/USD FX vs USD Libor Corr	−20%	20%	0%	0%	−20%	20%	−10%	10%

100 EUR Notional under USD CSA

Maturity	Deterministic	Stoch 1	Stoch 2	Stoch 3	Stoch 4	Stoch 5	Stoch 6	Stoch 7	Stoch 8
1 year	100.15	100.15	100.15	100.15	100.15	100.15	100.15	100.15	100.15
5 year	98.16	98.22	98.10	98.15	98.16	98.21	98.10	98.19	98.13
10 year	87.97	88.19	87.75	87.95	88.00	88.17	87.78	88.09	87.86
20 year	66.94	67.60	66.28	66.81	67.06	67.48	66.40	67.28	66.59
30 year	53.41	54.56	52.28	53.15	53.67	54.30	52.54	54.02	52.81

Fig. 5.5: Effect of stochastic funding spread to discounting (Tan, 2014).

Tan (2014) has shown in the context of stochastic funding spreads, correlated to interest rates, that the impact on discount factors of long-dated cash flows under a foreign CSA can be non-negligible if horizons are long, e.g. 30 years. Figure 5.5 shows an abstract from the table in his paper.

Figure 5.5 is the result of jointly bootstrapping a curve to fit vanilla swaps and OIS in the domestic market and MtM cross-currency swaps. We note that (1) domestic swaps are based on discounting under domestic CSA, while (2) cross-currency swaps are based on discounting under USD CSA. Thus, they are both subject to different quanto adjustments.

For details, please see Section 5.7.

5.5. Choice of Collateral

Looking into practical CSA arrangements, there is often the provision for posting collateral in a set of currencies at the discretion of the poster (counterparty with negative MtM). The logic is to allow convenience for the counterparty in obtaining collateral. Sadly, the additional complexities in valuation or potential value of this optionality were not understood by all the parties involved when most such agreements were concluded, since many such arrangements were made in the days prior to financial institutions becoming fully aware of the cost implications of collateral arrangements toward 2011.

Based on bootstrapping the multicurrency curve to match the prices of cross-currency swaps, we should obtain the discount factor of any currency (of the trade), based on collateral posted in currency i; thus, we can obtain the funding rates for different collaterals between periods $[t_{j-1}, t_j]$ as

$$r^i\left(t_{j-1}, t_j\right) = \frac{\left(\frac{D^i(t_{j-1})}{D^i(t_j)} - 1\right)}{(t_j - t_{j-1})}$$

Then it would be optimal for a counterparty with the choice of collateral to post collateral for each period $[t_{j-1}, t_j]$ in the currency that attracts the highest funding rate $\max_i r^i(t_{j-1}, t_j)$. (The optimal currency for the collateral can and indeed does vary over different time periods.)

More realistically, one would have to take account of stochastic funding spreads, and assuming non-zero correlation, then really the "quanto" adjustment in bootstrapping the curve needs to be accounted for. This is extremely cumbersome, and many of the quantities involved (namely the correlation of funding spreads) are not observable; so, in practice a full-fledged model is unlikely to be used in production across all portfolios, although it might be used to value certain important deals which cause significant concern.

One saving grace of collateral choice is that under English law, collateral substitution is only allowed when new collateral needs to be posted because consent of the recipient to a substitution is otherwise required. (No such consent is required under New York law.) So if a counterparty has posted collateral in USD and subsequently it turns out to be more optimal to post in GBP, it may not recall its USD collateral and post GBP collateral instead. It can only decide to post GBP collateral in the future for subsequent collateral demands. This significantly restricts the value of collateral choice. Piterbarg (2010) and (2012) has a rather interesting approach on how to value collateral choice where substitution is not allowed, but this is really outside the scope of this book. This is an area that is likely to benefit from more research in the days ahead.

5.6. A Base Case for XVA

Following our exposition above as to the various circumstances of collateral arrangements and our discussion of building curves under the circumstances, it leads us to the natural question of a base case for XVA. That is, what collateralized discount rate is the risk-free rate? After all, XVAs are the adjustments that are made to fully account for costs and benefits pertaining to maintaining the position, and these adjustments have to be made with respect to some base case (risk-free rate).

As is pointed out by Brace (2013) and Fujii *et al.* (2010), if we assume that the collateral rate in the base currency is the same as the risk-free rate, we can also interpret the discount factor of other currencies with base currency collateral as risk-free discount factors.

For example, if we assume USD collateral rate in USD is a risk-free rate, we can consistently assume that the EUR cash flows with USD collateral is discounted by the risk-free rate. So to determine the base case, all we need to do is find in what currency the collateral rate is the same as the risk-free rate. Typically, USD CSA or the CSA in which the bank operates is the base case.

Of course, the closer the base case is to reflecting the "risk-free" rate, i.e. some form of OIS curve, the easier it is for us to have sensible treatment of credit concepts like CVA and DVA in the limit of dealing with very high credit counterparties — after all, we cannot have a negative implied probability of default, which would happen if a rate is below our "risk-free" rate. However, there is no strict requirement as to what the base case should be: e.g. USD CSA for all currencies or CSA in the respective currency are both sensible alternatives.[6] The most important thing is to be consistent and to ensure that XVA is computed taking this base case into account.

---

[6]There is also no issue if say our base case is CSA in the currency concerned for developed economies but USD or EUR CSA for emerging markets. This is logical since foreign funding for emerging markets tend to be in USD mostly (or potentially in EUR where Eastern Europe is concerned).

Specifically, if our base case is CSA in the respective currency, then we really need an FVA for USD CSA (for non-USD currencies) and also for choice of collateral. It is otherwise possible to end up double counting or losing some important adjustments along the way. Note that this "FVA" can really just be computed by discounting based on the relevant CSA or a choice of collateral, as opposed to the more typical formula seen in Chapter 4. However, it is nevertheless an FVA, and thinking of it as such is helpful in understanding the concept of FVA.

5.6.1. *Illustration*

Consider the following three choices of base curves, and the implications for FVA on various deals in Table 5.1.

We emphasize that all other adjustments (i.e. CVA, DVA, other FVA, MVA, KVA) must be computed with the same base curve, in order to avoid double counting or omitting material risk factors.

We note that some authors (e.g. Kenyon or Brace) have referred to choice of collateral and similar topics as other adjustments Collateral Valuation Adjustment (ColVA). We have preferred to simply consider this as another aspect of funding and hence treat it under FVA in our attempt to limit the proliferation of different types of adjustments but rather focus on drawing out their similarities.

5.7. OIS and MtM CCY Swap with Stochastic Basis Spread

In this section, the OIS and MtM cross-currency swap will be analyzed when basis spread is stochastic and is correlated with the FX and IR processes. In this section, risk-neutral measure is adopted (Tan, private communication).

5.7.1. *OIS spread*

Here, the issue is what implications a stochastic funding spread correlated with the underlying Libor rate has on values of the underlying.

Table 5.1: Choices of base case and FVA.

	Choice 1 USD CSA as base	Choice 2 Domestic CSA as base for domestic EUR, CHF, GBP, JPY and USD CSA as base for everything else	Choice 3 Domestic Libor 3 m as base
A: GBP deal under USD CSA	Base Curve: GBP under USD OIS. There is no FVA.	Base Curve: GBP OIS. There is collateral-induced FVA.	Base Curve: GBP 3 m Libor. There is collateral-induced FVA.
B: JPY deal under JPY CSA	Base Curve: JPY under USD OIS. There is collateral-induced FVA.	Base Curve: JPY OIS. There is no FVA.	Base Curve: JPY 3 m Libor. There is collateral-induced FVA.
C: KRW deal under EUR CSA	Base Curve: KRW under USD OIS. There is collateral-induced FVA.	Base Curve: KRW under USD OIS. There is collateral-induced FVA.	Base Curve: KRW 3 m Libor. There is collateral-induced FVA.
D: BRL deal under USD CSA	Base Curve: BRL under USD OIS. There is no FVA.	Base Curve: BRL under USD OIS. There is no FVA.	Base Curve: BRL 3 m Libor. There is collateral-induced FVA.
E: EUR CHF cross-currency swap under EUR CSA	Base Curves: EUR and CHF under USD OIS. There is collateral-induced FVA.	Base Curves: EUR and CHF under USD OIS. There is collateral-induced FVA.	Base Curves: EUR and CHF 3 m Libor. There is collateral-induced FVA.
F: EUR CHF cross-currency swap under USD CSA	Base Curves: EUR and CHF under USD OIS. There is no FVA.	Base Curves: EUR and CHF under USD OIS. There is no FVA.	Base Curves: EUR and CHF 3 m Libor. There is collateral-induced FVA.
G: USD deal with choice of collateral	Base Curve: USD OIS. There is collateral-induced FVA.	Base Curve: USD OIS. There is collateral-induced FVA.	Base Curve: USD 3 m Libor. There is collateral-induced FVA.

Let $r_t = \phi_t + x_t$ be the short rate corresponding to the discount curve for Libor rate with tenor $f^{\tau}(t, T, T+\tau)\tau$ with $dx_t = \lambda dW_t$ and $r_t + s_t$ be the short rate corresponding to the OIS discounting, where $s_t = \varphi_t + y_t$ and $dy_t = \eta dV_t$ with $dW_t dV_t = \rho dt$, $B_t^{\tau} = \exp(-\int_0^t (r_u) du)$ and $B_t^O = \exp(-\int_0^t (r_u + s_t) du)$. Let $D^O(t,T)$ be a discount factor in base currency collateral

Define

$$
\begin{aligned}
D^{\tau}(t,T) &= E_t^O\left[\frac{B_t^{\tau}}{B_T^{\tau}}\right] \\
&= \exp\left(-\int_t^T \phi_u du - x_t(T-t) + \frac{\lambda^2}{6}(T-t)^3\right)
\end{aligned}
$$

where

$$
\int_t^T \phi_u du = -\log D^L(t,T) - x_t(T-t) + \frac{\lambda^2}{6}(T-t)^3 .
$$

From no-arbitrage, we have

$$
\begin{aligned}
D^O(t,T) &= E_t^O\left[\frac{B_t^O}{B_T^O}\right] \\
&= \exp\left(-\int_t^T (\phi_u + \varphi_u) du - x_t(T-t) - y_t(T-t)\right. \\
&\quad \left. + \frac{\lambda^2}{6}(T-t)^3 + \frac{\rho\lambda\eta}{3}(T-t)^3 + \frac{\eta^2}{6}(T-t)^3\right)
\end{aligned}
$$

giving

$$
\begin{aligned}
\int_t^T \varphi_u du &= -\log D^O(t,T) - \int_t^T \phi_u du - x_t(T-t) - y_t(T-t) \\
&\quad + \frac{\lambda^2}{6}(T-t)^3 + \frac{\rho\lambda\eta}{3}(T-t)^3 + \frac{\eta^2}{6}(T-t)^3 \\
&= \log\frac{D^L(t,T)}{D^O(t,T)} - y_t(T-t) + \frac{\rho\lambda\eta}{3}(T-t)^3 \\
&\quad + \frac{\eta^2}{6}(T-t)^3
\end{aligned}
$$

We seek to evaluate the payoff

$$\tau E_t^O\left[\frac{f^\tau(T,T,T+\tau)\,B_t^O}{B_{T+\tau}^O}\right]$$
$$= D^O(t,T+\tau)$$
$$\times\left[\frac{D^\tau(t,T)}{D^\tau(t,T+\tau)}\exp\left(-\frac{\rho\lambda\eta\tau(T-t)^2}{2}+\rho\lambda\eta(T-t)\tau^2\right)-1\right]$$

Note that when the funding spread is not stochastic (i.e. $\eta = 0$), the payoff is given by

$$\tau E_t^O\left[\frac{f^\tau(T,T,T+\tau)\,B_t^O}{B_{T+\tau}^O}\right] = D^O(t,T+\tau)\,f^\tau(t,T,T+\tau)$$

and reproduce the non-stochastic funding spread case in Section 5.1.

Because OIS has payoff

$$\sum_{i=1}^N \tau E_t^O\left[\frac{f^\tau(T_{i-1},T_{i-1},T_i)\,B_t^O}{B_{T_i}^O}\right]$$
$$+s\sum_i^N \tau D^O(t,T_i) = D^O(t,T_0) - D^O(t,T_n)$$

Thus, the fair OIS spread is given by

$$s\sum_{i=1}^N \tau D^O(t,T_i) = D^O(t,T_0) - D^O(t,T_n)$$
$$-\sum_{i=1}^N D^O(t,T_i)$$
$$\left[\frac{D^\tau(t,T_i)}{D^\tau(t,T_i+\tau)}\exp\left(-\frac{\rho\lambda\eta\tau(T_{i-1}-t)^2}{2}+\rho\lambda\eta(T_{i-1}-t)\tau^2\right)-1\right]$$

5.7.2. *MtM cross-currency spread*

In this section, we will study the effect of stochastic funding spread to the MtM cross-currency swap (see Section 5.3.1) with base currency collateral.

Let M_t be the spot FX rate (i.e. number of units of base currency per unit of foreign currency) at time t. Then no-arbitrage requires

$$E_t^T\left[M_T\right]=E_t^T\left[M_T\frac{D^f\left(T,T\right)}{D^O\left(T,T\right)}\right]=\frac{M_tD^f\left(t,T\right)}{D^O\left(t,T\right)}\equiv M_{tT}$$

where $D^f(t,T)$ is the value at time t of a foreign discount bond with maturity T based on collateral under base CSA (USD) and we have defined M_{tT} as the forward FX rate with maturity T as seen at time t. Note $M_{TT}=M_T$.

The base currency rebalancing leg is given by

$$E_t^O\left[-\sum_i^{N-1}\frac{M_{T_i}B_t^O}{B_{T_i}^O}+\sum_{i=1}^{N}\frac{M_{T_{i-1}}\left(1+f^\tau\left(T_{i-1},T_{i-1},T_i\right)\tau\right)B_t^O}{B_{T_i}^O}\right]$$

$$=-\sum_i^{N}D^O\left(t,T_i\right)M_{tT_i}+\sum_{i=1}^{N}E_t^O\left[\frac{M_{T_{i-1}}D^O\left(T_{i-1},T_i\right)B_t^O}{D^\tau\left(T_{i-1},T_i\right)B_{T_{i-1}}^O}\right]$$

We posit the process $dM_{tT}=\sigma_TM_{tT}dZ_t^T$ for the FX forward under the T-forward measure with $dW_tdZ_t^T=\rho_rdt$ and $dV_tdZ_t^T=\rho_sdt$.

We want the process for M_{tT} under the risk-neutral measure with numeraire B_t^O. The Radon–Nikodym derivative for change of measure is $R=\frac{dQ^O}{dQ^T}=\frac{B_T^OD^O(t,T)}{B_t^OD^O(T,T)}=\frac{B_T^OD^O(t,T)}{B_t^O}$ with $dR_t/R_t=-\left(T-t\right)\left(\lambda dW_t^T+\eta dV_t^T\right)$. So Girsanov's Theorem says that a change of measure will lead to the FX forward following the process given as follows under the risk-neutral measure:

$$dM_{tT}=\left(T-t\right)\left(\rho_r\lambda+\rho_s\eta\right)\sigma_TM_{tT}dt+\sigma_TM_{tT}dZ_t$$

We thus evaluate terms like

$$E_t^O\left[\frac{M_TD^O\left(T,T+\tau\right)}{D^L\left(T,T+\tau\right)}\frac{B_t^O}{B_T^O}\right]$$

$$=D^O\left(t,T+\tau\right)\frac{D^\tau\left(t,T\right)}{D^\tau\left(t,T+\tau\right)}M_{tT}\exp(-\rho_s\sigma_T\eta\tau\left(T-t\right)$$

$$-\frac{\rho\lambda\eta\tau}{2}\left(T-t\right)^2+\rho\lambda\eta\left(T-t\right)\tau^2)$$

This gives the value of the base currency rebalancing leg as

$$E_t^O\left[-\sum_{i=0}^{N-1}\frac{M_T B_t^O}{B_{T_i}^O}+\frac{\sum_i^N M_{T_{i-1}}\left(1+\tau f^\tau\left(T_{i-1},T_{i-1},T_i\right)\right)B_t^O}{B_{T_i}^O}\right]$$

$$=-\sum_{i=0}^{N-1}D^O\left(t,T_i\right)M_{tT_i}+\frac{\sum_i^N D^O\left(t,T_i\right)D^\tau\left(t,T_{i-1}\right)M_{tT_i}}{\mathrm{D}^\tau\left(t,T_i\right)}$$

$$\times\exp\left(-\sigma_T\tau\left(T_{i-1}-t\right)-\frac{\lambda\tau}{2}\left(T_{i-1}-t\right)^2+\lambda\tau^2\left(T_{i-1}-t\right)\right)$$

Thus, our rebalancing notional USD leg has value

$$E_t^{O;\mathrm{USD}}\left[-\sum_{i=0}^{N-1}\frac{M_{T_i}B_t^O}{B_{T_i}^O}+\sum_{i=1}^{N}\frac{M_{T_{i-1}}\left(1+f^\tau\left(T_{i-1},T_{i-1},T_i\right)\tau\right)B_t^O}{B_{T_i}^O}\right]$$

$$=-\sum_{i=0}^{N-1}D^O\left(t,T_i\right)M_{tT_i}+\frac{\sum_{i=1}^N M_{tT_{i-1}}D^O\left(t,T_i\right)D^L\left(t,T_{i-1}\right)}{D^\tau\left(t,T_i\right)}$$

$$\times\exp\left(-\rho_s^{\mathrm{USD}}\sigma_T\eta^{\mathrm{USD}}\tau_i\left(T_{i-1}-t\right)-\frac{\rho^{\mathrm{USD}}\lambda\eta^{\mathrm{USD}}\tau_i\left(T_{i-1}-t\right)^2}{2}\right.$$
$$\left.+\rho^{\mathrm{USD}}\lambda\eta^{\mathrm{USD}}\left(T_{i-1}-t\right)\tau_i^2\right)$$

Here for the parameters in USD, superfix of USD is added.

Note that when the basis spread is not stochastic (i.e. $\eta=0$), the value of the USD leg is represented by the forward FX and forward Libor rate (see Section 5.3.1).

Now let us investigate foreign leg, which pays Libor of the foreign currency but under USD CSA.

From our discussion on the single-currency case, the value of the leg is given by foreign currency

$$\sum_{i=1}^{N} \tau_i E_t^{O;f}\left[\frac{f^{f;\tau}\left(T_{i-1}, T_{i-1}, T_i\right) B_{t;\mathrm{USD}}^{f}}{B_{T_i;\mathrm{USD}}^{f}}\right] + D_{\mathrm{USD}}^{f}\left(t, T_N\right) + s^{\mathrm{CCY}}$$

$$\sum_{i=1}^{N} \tau_i D_{\mathrm{USD}}^{f}\left(t, T_i\right) = D_{\mathrm{USD}}^{f}\left(t, T+\tau\right)\left[\frac{D^{f;\tau}\left(t, T\right)}{D^{f;\tau}\left(t, T+\tau\right)} \times \exp\left(-\frac{\rho\lambda\eta^{\mathrm{CCY}}\tau}{2}\left(T-t\right)^2 + \rho\lambda\eta^{\mathrm{CCY}}\left(T-t\right)\tau^2\right) - 1\right] + D_{\mathrm{USD}}^{f}\left(t, T_N\right) + \sum_{i=1}^{N} \tau_i D_{\mathrm{USD}}^{f}\left(t, T_i\right)$$

where η^{CCY} is the vol for the spread of USD CSA vs Libor for the foreign curve, $E_t^{O;f}[\quad]$ is the conditional expectation value in foreign risk-neutral measure, $D_{\mathrm{USD}}^{f}(t, T)$ is a discount factor of foreign currency with USD collateral, $B_{t;\mathrm{USD}}^{f}$ is a bank account corresponding to it and $f^{f;\tau}(t, T, S)$ is a forward Libor in foreign currency and $f^{f;\tau}(t, T, T+\tau) = (\frac{1}{\tau})(\frac{D^{f;L}(t,T)}{D^{f;L}(t,T+\tau)} - 1)$.

Combing the two legs of the cross-currency swap, we have

$$E_t^{O}\left[-\sum_{i=0}^{N-1} \frac{M_{T_i} B_t^{O}}{B_{T_i}^{O}} + \sum_{i=1}^{N} \frac{M_{T_{i-1}}\left(1 + f^{\tau}\left(T_{i-1}, T_{i-1}, T_i\right)\left(T_i - T_{i-1}\right)\right) B_t^{O}}{B_{T_i}^{O}}\right] = M_t \sum_{i} \tau_i E_t^{O;f}\left[\frac{f^{f;\tau}\left(T_{i-1}, T_{i-1}, T_i\right) B_t^{f;\mathrm{USD}}}{B_{T_i}^{f;\mathrm{USD}}}\right] + M_t D_{\mathrm{USD}}^{f}\left(t, T_N\right) + M_t s_t^{\mathrm{CCY}} \sum_{i=1}^{N} \tau_i D_{\mathrm{USD}}^{f}\left(t, T_i\right)$$

So, the cross-currency swap spread is given by

$$s_t^{\mathrm{CCY}} = \left\{ -\sum_{i=0}^{N-1} \frac{D^O(t,T_i)\, M_{tT_i}}{M_t} + \sum_{i=1}^{N} \frac{D^f(t,T_i)\, D^\tau(t,T_{i-1})}{D^\tau(t,T_i)} \frac{M_{tT_{i-1}}}{M_t} \right.$$

$$\times \exp\left(\eta^{\mathrm{USD}} \tau \sigma \rho_S^{\mathrm{USD}} (T_{i-1}-t) - \frac{\rho_S^{\mathrm{USD}} \lambda \eta^{\mathrm{USD}} \tau}{2} (T_{i-1}-t)^2 \right.$$

$$\left. + \rho \lambda \eta^{\mathrm{CCY}} (T_{i-1}-t)\, \tau^2 \right) - \sum_{i=1}^{N} D^f_{\mathrm{USD}}(t,T_i) \left[\frac{D^{f;\tau}(t,T_{i-1})}{D^{f;\tau}(t,T_i)} \right.$$

$$\left. \times \exp\left(-\frac{\rho\lambda\eta^{\mathrm{CCY}}\tau}{2} (T_{i-1}-t)^2 + \rho\lambda\eta^{\mathrm{CCY}} (T_{i-1}-t)\,\tau^2 \right) - 1 \right].$$

$$\left. + D^f_{\mathrm{USD}}(t,T_N) \right\} \% \sum_{i} \tau D^f_{\mathrm{USD}}(t,T_i)$$

$$s_t^{\mathrm{CCY}} = \left\{ -\sum_{i=0}^{N-1} D^O(t,T_i) \frac{M_{tT_i}}{M_t} + \sum_{i=1}^{N} D^D(t,T_i) \frac{D^{\tau,\mathrm{USD}}(t,T_{i-1})}{D^{\tau,\mathrm{USD}}(t,T_i)} \right.$$

$$\times \frac{M_{tT_{i-1}}}{M_t} \bullet \exp\left(-\rho_S^{\mathrm{USD}} \sigma_T \eta^{\mathrm{USD}} \tau_i (T_{i-1}-t) - \frac{\rho^{\mathrm{USD}} \lambda \eta^{\mathrm{USD}} \tau_i}{2} \right.$$

$$\left. \times (T_{i-1}-t)^2 + \rho^{\mathrm{USD}} \lambda \eta^{\mathrm{USD}} (T_{i-1}-t)\, \tau_i^2 \right) - \sum_{i=1}^{N} D^{f;O}(t,T_i)$$

$$\left[\frac{D^{f;\tau}(t,T_{i-1})}{D^{f;\tau}(t,T_i)} \exp\left(-\frac{\rho\lambda\eta^{\mathrm{ccy}}\tau_i}{2} (T_{i-1}-t)^2 \right. \right.$$

$$\left. \left. \left. + \rho\lambda\eta^{\mathrm{ccy}} (T_{i-1}-t)\, \tau_i^2 \right) - 1 \right] + D^{f;O}(t,T_N) \right\}$$

$$\div \sum_{i=1}^{N} \tau_i D^{f;O}(t,T_i).$$

Chapter 6

Margin Valuation Adjustment (MVA)

In Chapters 3 and 4, we have discussed about FVA. FVA is the funding cost related to derivatives trading. Here, funding is necessary for collateral margin and/or cash flows from derivatives. Collateral margin here is (a function of) exposure of derivatives. This collateral margin is called Variation Margin (VM). In addition, there are certain important circumstances where Initial Margin (IM) is posted on top of VM in derivative trading. VM protects derivative counterparties from loss with the amount of positive exposure when the opposite counterparty defaults. On the other hand, IM protects counterparties from potential losses from market movements in the Margin Period of Risk (MPOR) (i.e. the short period of time required for margin to be posted in response to market moves). MPOR is well captured by VAR, SVAR or Expected Shortfall.

IM is posted in two very important types of transactions: one is Central Counterparty (CCP) trades (i.e. trades done or cleared on recognized exchanges) and the other is bilateral trades subject to the requirements of Standard Initial Margin Model (SIMM). In CCP trades, the amount of IM is calculated using the CCP's internal model. Typically, the amount is related to VAR of the transactions. Regarding bilateral trades, the Basel Committee requires major dealers to post (to an escrow account with a third party) IM on top of VM (Basel Committee on Banking Supervision, 2013b) when conducting bilateral deals to avoid the situation of these dealers opting to avoid exchange clearing of trades to save IM. To remove the possibility of dispute between two counterparties, ISDA established the standard model, namely SIMM. The SIMM is based on a sensitivity approach to VAR, which is then subject to simplified assumptions of distributions of risk factors based on historical observations.

While the cost of IM in trades can be seen as a special case of FVA, it is important enough (affecting a sufficiently large set of trades and counterparties) that it deserves a separation classification as Margin Valuation Adjustment (MVA), and we treat it in this chapter.

6.1. The Concept of Initial Margin

The typical idea of collateral agreements is that the parties to a deal would agree to post collateral to cover any changes in P&L. Specifically, if the net value of all position of counterparty A with respect to counterparty B is $V(t)$ at time t, then counterparty B must post a net amount of collateral worth $V(t)$ to counterparty A. In that case, upon default of either party, the other does not lose out.

However, in practice, the arrangement for collateral posting is not perfect. First, the process of posting collateral is not instantaneous. If at time t, counterparty A seeks collateral from counterparty B, there will be a time lag δ before counterparty B responds to the collateral call.

Then really at time t, the true exposure of counterparty A to counterparty B is $\max(V(t) - V(t-\delta), 0)$, where the period $[t-\delta, t]$ is referred to as the MPOR.

In Figs. 6.1 and 6.2, we show the portfolio values along two sample paths, together with the exposure over the MPOR (taken as 1 week).

The lag δ can be contractually specified to be a given number of days, but that could also be subject to delays from disputes on valuation. However, even if collateral is to be posted intraday, and with the best of intentions, a delay of hours is typically inevitable.

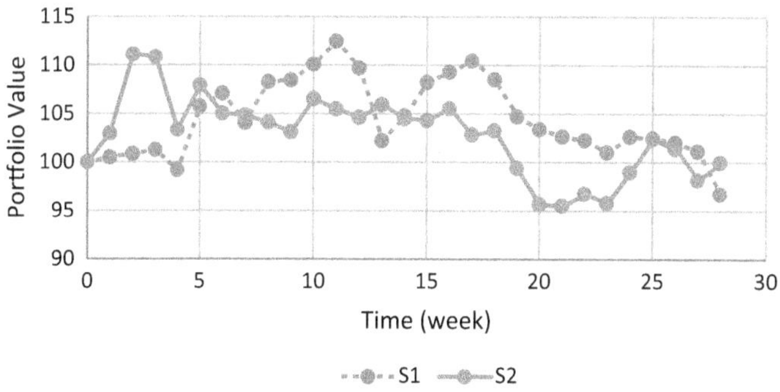

Fig. 6.1: Portfolio values.

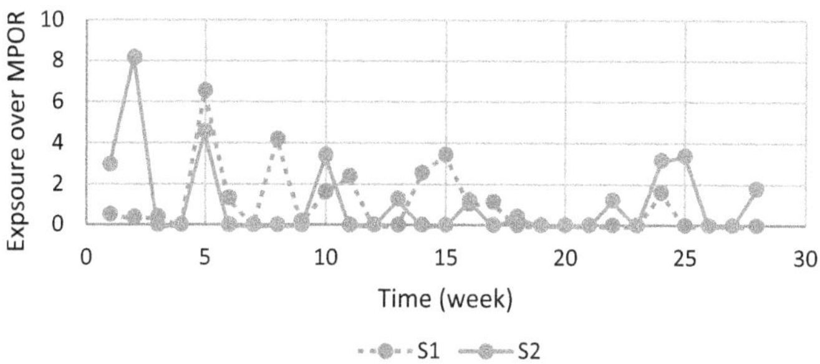

Fig. 6.2: Exposure based on changes in portfolio value over MPOR.

Some deals however (e.g. selling CDS protection) can be subject to jumps (e.g. reference name experiences imminent default), and even a short delay can lead to a meaningful non-continuous P&L change.

Thus, initial margin is intended to protect both parties from unexpected but not catastrophic change in exposure during the MPOR. For this to work, it needs to be posted by both counterparties to a third party. The typical arrangement is for initial margin to be posted to a central derivatives exchange under exchange clearing or to a third party to hold in an escrow (trust) account under the uncleared margining rules.

Exchange Clearing: The idea of exchange clearing is that after two parties have done a deal, they novate this so that the exchange steps in between them and is the counterparty to both sides. For all intents and purposes, the identities of the two counterparties

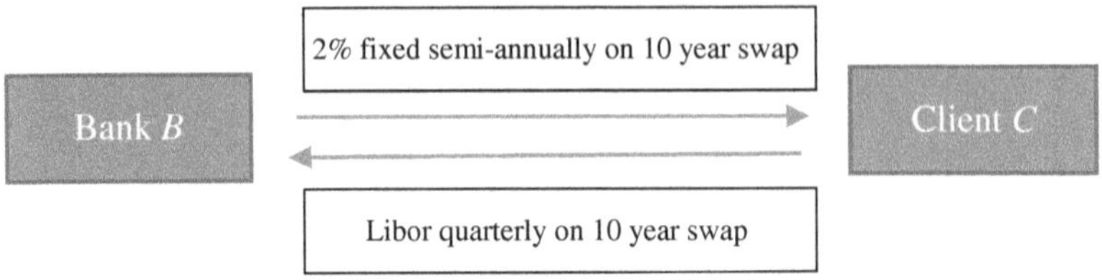

Fig. 6.3. Originally, Bank B and Client C do a 10-year swap, where the bank pays 2% fixed coupons semi-annually, while the client pays Libor quarterly.

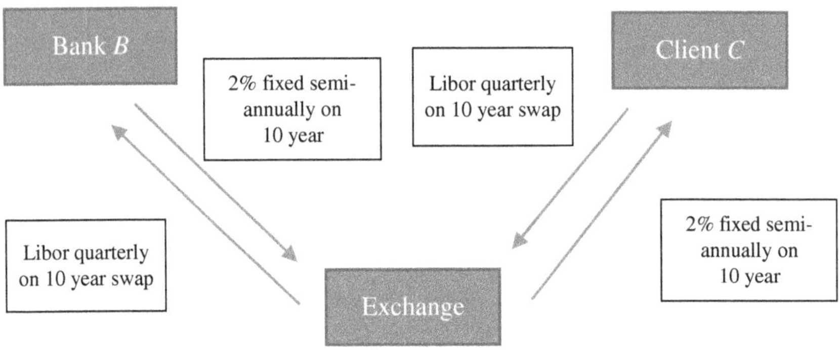

Fig. 6.4: Following exchange clearing, the deal is novated, i.e. transferred. Instead, the Bank B pays 2% fixed coupons semi-annually to the exchange and receives Libor quarterly from the exchange. Client C pays Libor quarterly to the exchange and receives 2% fixed coupons semi-annually. The bank and client do not have direct exposure to each other, but instead all exposures are between the exchange and the parties directly.

vis-à-vis each other no longer matters. This is very much in line with the treatment of exchange traded contracts (e.g. futures), where the exchange takes both sides and the parties actually do not even know who takes the other side (Figs. 6.3 and 6.4). Naturally, the exchange will seek initial margin from both sides to protect itself from exposure to both parties during the MPOR. And it would seek VM (i.e. collateral based on market moves at the end of each day), but this would really be transferred from one party to the other.

Uncleared Margining: Given that exchange clearing is typically only possible for vanilla deals (that the exchange is comfortable being a party to), regulators have nevertheless sought for all other deals to be subject to margining arrangements to protect against counterparty loss and to stop banks trying to avoid the funding cost of initial margin of exchange clearing. The idea is that based on the net position values that both parties have with respect to each other, both parties have to post initial margin to a third party to hold on escrow.

Initial margin clearly leads to a cost on each counterparty. Thus, the value of a derivative needs to take account of this cost, MVA, defined as

$$\int_0^T M(t)D(t)\phi(t)dt$$

where $M(t)$ is the initial margin due at time t, $D(t)$ is the discount factor up to maturity t and $\phi(t)$ is the survival probability. (Note that if we consider an exchange to be default-free, then $\phi(t) = 1$.)

The methodology for initial margin is meant to protect against unexpected but not catastrophic change, i.e. the initial margin should be adequate to cover losses over a high degree of confidence.[1]

The details of the calculation methodology for $M(t)$ differ. For exchange clearing, it is proprietary to the exchange. For uncleared margining, there is a methodology under SIMM.

Both however are based on a concept from market risk, i.e. value-at-risk (VAR) (at $\alpha\%$, typically 99%) — the amount such that losses will only exceed this figure by a probability of $1-\alpha\%$ (e.g. 1%) over the horizon of interest (e.g. 1 business day or maybe 10 business days to be conservative[2]). Thus, we explore this in the following section.

6.2. MVA from SIMM

The Basel committee requires posting VM and IM for non-centrally cleared derivatives. Therefore, the cost for IM (MVA) needs to be included in derivatives valuation. ISDA introduced SIMM for the

[1]It would be prohibitively expensive and impractical to have 0% probability of loss.

[2]The choice of a longer horizon can be justified in that it may require time to unwind a large illiquid position if the counterparty is unable to post the margin required when P&L drops significantly due to huge market moves during a period of shock.

calculation of the IM amount of bilateral trades so as to avoid disputes about the IM amount between counterparties. SIMM is calculated using the sensitivity-based VAR, assuming a parametric returns distribution as well as parametric forms for the risk factors. In fact, the distribution parameters (mean, variance, correlations) are kept constant based on some historical analysis. In this way, for any derivative, SIMM gives a formula for VAR of the portfolio as a function of deltas, gammas and vegas of all relevant risk factors.

Therefore, to compute MVA due to IM under SIMM, we need to calculate deltas and vegas (in addition to PV) at each future point in time in the Monte Carlo simulation (Tsuchiya, 2019b).

In SIMM, the number of buckets is 12 for Interest Rates (IRs) and if we do not use less granular bucketing, we need to calculate greeks (PV) at least 24 times for all of the paths and time grid (12 for IR delta and 12 for IR vega).

SIMM is based on the same methodology as the Standardized Approach of Market Risk Capital in FRTB (Base Committee on Banking Supervision, 2016a). Therefore, the calculation methodology of SIMM MVA is applied to that of Market Risk KVA in the standardized approach, which will be discussed in Chapters 9 and 10.

6.3. More General Computation of MVA for SIMM

To compute sensitivities, as will be discussed in Chapter 7, we can use Green–Kenyon Shocked-States Augmentation (GKSSA).[3] However, to be clear, it would likely be a lot faster if we use something like Adjoint Algorithmic Differentiation (AAD) (discussed later in this book) so that we can have a single computation for many sensitivities (e.g. all $\frac{\partial V}{\partial R_i}$, $\frac{\partial^2 V}{\partial R_i^2}$ and $\frac{\partial V}{\partial \sigma_j}$ where V is value, R_i is rate bucket and σ_j is vol bucket) at the same time. (This can more generically apply to risk factors in other asset classes too.) This comes at the expense of more memory requirements.

[3] GKSSA can be unstable when expiration of option is short (in SIMM, the shortest bucket is 2 weeks). Therefore, though GKSSA is faster than closed-form formulae, closed-form formulae can be a preferred option to calculate MVA.

We should be willing to make compromises. For example, SIMM will specify using market vol, but it would be a lot faster to use model vols (to avoid recalibration or use of expensive matrix inversions going from model to market vol). Also, maybe we should use fewer buckets for both rates and vols for both stability and to cut memory footprint. The justification is that this is just MVA and there is already a lot of inaccuracy from assumptions as to distribution of underlying risk factors. Further, compromise in vols is reasonable because by far exposure will largely come from linear instruments, so at the portfolio level, the effect is not so bad.

6.4. MVA for CCP Trades

In CCP trades, IM is computed by the CCP. This is typically based on 99% VAR over a 1-day horizon. While the exact methodology used for IM can vary between CCP and is not disclosed, we can presume that IM is calculated based on 99th percentile of Historical VAR. To evaluate the funding cost of initial margin, we need to generate historical VAR shock for each scenario generated by the Monte Carlo simulation. If the number of swaps in a portfolio is $N_{\text{Portfolio}}$, number of scenarios to calculate VAR is N_{Scenario} and the number of paths in Monte Carlo simulation is N_{Paths}, we need to calculate swap values $N_{\text{Portfolio}} \times N_{\text{Scenario}} \times N_{\text{Paths}}$ times for each time grid. Here the CVA calculation takes only $N_{\text{Portfolio}} \times N_{\text{Paths}}$ and N_{Scenario} is typically 260 under historical simulation VAR (or 10,000 under parametric VAR). That is, if we use a brute-force approach, calculation burden for MVA is at least 260 times larger than that of CVA. Though calculation of swap value is very fast in most of the models, the calculation burden is huge and can be infeasible.

Finally, this brings us to the point about exotics. Neither VAR nor SIMM in general captures exotics risk too well. Again, at the portfolio level, this is not too important because linear products dominate. And further, this is a calculation for MVA, so we should again keep the accuracy concerns in perspective, especially given that the exact method for IM calculation by exchanges is not even fully known and would differ across exchanges.

6.5. Inefficiencies of Initial Margin

It should be noted that initial margin is calculated by an exchange based on the net position between a counterparty and this exchange. Thus, if a counterparty has similar deals done with multiple exchanges (e.g. if it pays fixed on a 10-year swap with Exchange A and receives fixed on the same 10-year swap with Exchange B), then it will have to post initial margin with both exchanges. This means it is inefficient for a counterparty to have the same types of deals cleared by multiple exchanges.

Similarly, if a deal is too exotic to be exchange cleared and hence subject to SIMM (e.g. a callable zero coupon swap) but is hedged by the bank with a vanilla product (e.g. a standard swap) which is exchange cleared, then the initial margin will have to be posted twice rather than netted. This seems punitive. However, the profit margin of an exotic product almost certainly should factor in such costs going forward (if not previously).

However, if we consider that there is a limited set of CCPs that perform exchange clearing of derivatives and there tend to be preferred CCPs for certain products in certain markets, and given the large volume of trades done by financial institutions, the net positions that these institutions have with these exchanges are likely to be much smaller than the outright positions, so this inefficiency is likely to be more limited in practice. Also, while dealing with a big client, a financial institution is likely to have both long and short positions, so that the net exposure subject to SIMM is again likely to be more limited.

6.6. Calculation of VAR

As is explained in this chapter, the amount of IM depends on market risk VAR. It is also the vital part of the market risk capital, which will be discussed in Chapter 7.

In this section, the calculation methodologies of (market risk) VAR is summarized (JP Morgan, 1996). VAR of CVA which compose CVA capital is also based on the same idea.

Formally, if A is the $\alpha\%$ VAR over horizon t, then

$$P\left(V\left(t\right)-V\left(0\right)<-A\right)=1-\alpha\%$$

where $V(t)$ is the value of the portfolio at time t.

Typically, VAR is computed based on one of the following methodologies.

First, the VAR is categorized as follows based on the assumption about distributions of risk factors:

(1) Historical Simulation (Non-Parametric) VAR: Assume that risk factor returns follow historically observed values and generate scenarios from the historical time series. Let t_j $(j = 1, \cdot, N_{\text{Scen}})$ be the dates time series are observed and $R(t_i)$ be the risk factor of the date for the normal model. For the 1-day time horizon, the return is given by $r(t_j) = R(t_i) - R(t_{j-1})$. The scenario for the VAR is generated as $R(0) + t(t_j)$. For the log-normal model, the log-normal return $r(t_j) = \ln(R(t_i)/R(t_{j-1}))$ is adopted and scenario is generated as $R(0)\exp(r(t_j))$. Historical simulation has a benefit to take into account stressed market movement.

(2) Parametric VAR: Assume a parametric distribution for underlying risk factors $R_i(i = 1, \ldots, N_{\text{fac}})$ as well as vol risk factors $\sigma_i(i = 1, \ldots, N_{\text{fac}})$, then simulate them and revalue the portfolio. In parametric VAR, distribution for risk factors are typically based on normal (or log-normal) distribution.

Second, let us consider the following valuation of portfolio given risk factors at the horizon:

(1) Full Revaluation: Here the value $V(t)$ is obtained by repricing based on the new set of state variables $R_i(i = 1, \ldots, N_{\text{fac}})$ and $\sigma_i(i = 1, \ldots, N_{\text{fac}})$. Both Historical VAR and Monte Carlo VAR can be based on full revaluation. The main concern is the computational expense. Typically for parametric VAR, 10,000 paths are used, so this means 10,000 calls of the pricing function. But for historical simulation, only 260 paths are used (corresponding to 1 year worth of data), which is more feasible.

(2) Sensitivities-Based (Taylor Expansion): Sensitivities-Based VAR is based on the sensitivities (greeks) of the portfolio. Here, we compute the future portfolio value via a Taylor Expansion over the current portfolio value and change in values of risk factors

$$
\begin{aligned}
V(t) &\approx V(0) + \sum_{i=1}^{N} \frac{\partial V}{\partial R_i}(0)\left(R_i(t) - R_i(0)\right) \\
&\quad + \frac{1}{2}\sum_{i=1}^{N}\sum_{j=1}^{N} \frac{\partial^2 V}{\partial R_i R_j}(0)\left(R_i(t) - R_i(0)\right)\left(R_j(t) - R_j(0)\right) \\
&\quad + \sum_{i=1}^{M} \frac{\partial V}{\partial \sigma_i}(0)\left(\sigma_i(t) - \sigma_i(0)\right) \\
&= V(0) + \sum_{i=1}^{N} \Delta_i(0)\left(R_i(t) - R_i(0)\right) \\
&\quad + \frac{1}{2}\sum_{i=1}^{N}\sum_{j=1}^{N} \Gamma_{i,j}(0)\left(R_i(t) - R_i(0)\right)\left(R_j(t) - R_j(0)\right) \\
&\quad + \sum_{i=1}^{M} v_i(0)\left(\sigma_i(t) - \sigma_i(0)\right)
\end{aligned}
$$

Typically, the first- and second-order derivatives delta $\Delta_i = \frac{\partial V}{\partial R_i}$ and gamma $\Gamma_{i,j} = \frac{\partial^2 V}{\partial R_i R_j}$ in underlying risk factors (e.g. rates, FX, equities) are used, but only the first derivative in vol vega $\nu_i = \frac{\partial V}{\partial \sigma_i}$ is used. Unless we have very good-quality data or sensitivity to cross risk is strong, it may only be decided to omit cross gammas, i.e. only keep $\Gamma_{i,i}$. The advantage of this approach is that you avoid the computational expense of full revaluation and only need as many computations as needed for obtaining the sensitivities. Typically, these are done by finite difference methods, i.e. $\frac{\partial V}{\partial R_i} \approx \frac{V(R_i+\delta)-V(R_i)}{\delta}$ and $\frac{\partial^2 V}{\partial R_i^2} \approx \frac{V(R_i+\delta)-2V(R_i)+V(R_i-\delta)}{\delta^2}$, so a first-order derivative needs at least one additional evaluation for the bumped state, while a second-order derivative needs at least two additional evaluations for the bumped state. In sensitivities approach, if we assume (multidimensional) normal distribution of the riskfactors, VAR is given analytically.

One problem with the sensitivities-based approach is that it assumes small change in the underlying risk factors (somewhat justifiable due to a short time horizon) and works less well for exotics with nonlinear payoff.

(3) Parametric Returns Distribution: Here we assume the distribution of portfolio returns is normal, parametrized completely by mean μ and standard deviation Σ. For a normal distribution, the $\alpha\%$ VAR is then given by $N^{-1}(1 - \alpha\%)\Sigma$, where $N(z) = \frac{1}{\sqrt{2\pi}} \exp(-\frac{z^2}{2})$ is the cumulative normal distribution function. The justification for the above is the Central Limit Theorem, which states that the normalized sum of a large number of independent returns tends toward a normal distribution even if the individual returns are not normal. This is then applied to a large well-diversified portfolio to approximate "independent" returns. We thus have to compute the standard deviation Σ. Assuming some parametric distribution for our risk factors (and some correlation structure), we typically do this by matching the second moment. But the point to emphasize is that this approach relies on a large well-diversified portfolio (with hopefully normal returns for major components), and would not work if our portfolio contains a concentration of a few highly non-normal returns distributions (e.g. out-of-the-money options).

Chapter 7

KVA and Other Adjustments and Costs

Whereas prior to 2008, derivatives pricing was very much based on the concept of efficient markets (i.e. ability to borrow and lend large amounts at the same rate, existence of deep markets which allows one to trade in size without affecting market prices) and costs were seen as an afterthought; it has now been well established that pricing must reflect a lot of the costs associated with maintaining the position (i.e. CVA, DVA, FVA and MVA). Indeed, markets have become less efficient since 2008 (i.e. scarcity of capital leading to a high cost in funding, reduction in market depth as players exit unprofitable businesses and higher capital charges take hold), so that such adjustments become more significant.

We seek to address some of the remaining costs, explore their nature and relevance and also provide ways to potentially treat them in the sections below.

7.1. Capital Valuation Adjustment (KVA)

The 2008 financial crisis has established that capital is a scarce resource. Capital is needed to conduct a business and absorb any losses in the process. Regulators have an interest to ensure that financial institutions are well capitalized, and have greatly increased the capital requirements of financial institutions post 2008 with the

Table 7.1: Diagram of capital charge as a percentage of RWA (Basel Committee on Banking Supervision, 2010, Annex 1).

	Common Equity Tier 1	Tier 1	Total
Minimum	4.5%	6%	8%
Conservation buffer	2.5%	—	—
Minimum plus conservation buffer	7.0%	8.5%	10.5%
Countercyclical buffer	0–2.5%	—	—

aim of ensuring that they are more resilient to future financial crises to avoid any contagion from the failure of systemically important institutions (Table 7.1).

Roughly, the capital in a firm is deemed to be based on the money raised when issuing shares, as well as the money kept from retained earnings. Regulators require financial institutions to maintain a certain amount of capital, related to their assets and the nature of their business. The losses related to the derivatives business can be divided into three types: losses from the movement of market risk factors (market risk), losses arising from counterparty default and/or from deterioration of counterparty creditworthiness (credit risk), and losses due to operational and legal matters (operational risk).

7.1.1. *Outline of regulatory capital*

Specifically, the Basel accords (currently Basel 2.5) define the capital requirements for market risk, credit risk and operational risk. Basel III will come into effect from January 2022. Capital requirement is defined as a percentage of risk-weighted assets (RWAs). Conceptually, RWAs attempt to convert exposures of financial institutions into standardized units of notional by taking the risk of loss when deriving the amount. This is in accordance with the fractional reserve banking system, where banks hold less than 100% of the assets they lend in reserve. The higher the capital requirement as a percentage of RWAs, the tighter the constraint on financial activity of banks.

National regulators define the exact percentage, typically taking account of the importance of the institution and a countercyclical buffer (to dampen market activity in a boom).

$$\text{RWA} = \text{Market Risk RWA} + \text{Credit Risk RWA} + \text{Operational Risk RWA}$$

7.1.1.1. *Basel 2.5*

Market risk RWA itself is typically either calculated via internal models (where approved by the financial institution's regulator) or the more punitive standardized models otherwise. Under Basel 2.5, the internal model effectively calculates capital based on the 99% value-at-risk (VAR) and stressed value-at-risk (SVAR) over a 10-day horizon (and a few other measures detailed below).

$$\text{Market Risk RWA} = \text{Multiplier} \times (\text{VAR} + \text{SVAR} + \text{IRC} + \text{CRM})$$

Here, $\alpha\%$ VAR is the amount, by which an institution's losses are expected to exceed $(100 - \alpha)\%$ of the time. SVAR is simply VAR over a period of stress — the rolling historical period of 12 months that would lead to the largest losses for the bank.

Incremental Risk Charge (IRC) is the loss at the 99.9% level over a 1-year horizon due to default or change in credit spread and applies only to instruments subject to credit risk. Comprehensive Risk Measure (CRM) is the loss at 99.9% level over a 1-year horizon for credit correlation and other securitized products (e.g. tranches of CDOs).

Counterparty Credit Risk (CCR) is a part of credit risk, i.e. being an allowance for unexpected losses due to counterparty default over a 1-year horizon. For banks with approval to use the Internal Models Method from their supervisor, the capital is based on a regulatory formula below that takes account of EAD (Exposure At Default), M (effective maturity), LGD (loss given default) and PD (probability of default). LGD and PD are attributes related to the counterparty, while M and EAD are attributes related to the derivative, with EAD conceptually similar to EPE discussed in Chapter 2. The exact formula of CCR capital and EAD under the internal model will be given in Appendix B.

7.1.1.2. *Basel III*

Basel III further requires a market risk charge on CVA to be computed, and this is by taking account of variability of counterparty credit spreads and other market risk drivers (e.g. interest rates, FX rates, equity values) that affect the value of CVA. More details of the calculations are covered in Section 7.4.

Going forward, the Basel rules will instead be replaced by Expected Shortfall (ES) at the 97.5% level under Fundamental Review of the Trading Book (FRTB) (Basel Committee on Banking Supervision, 2013), where liquidity horizon varies depending on the asset. ES is the average conditional on exceeding the threshold. They also proposed to use the model calibrated to market data of the stressed period. Also, IRC is due to be replaced by DRC (Default Risk Charge) under FRTB, where only default is considered but the scope is extended to equity products as well.

And CRM will be replaced by a new securitization framework, with much less scope for use of internal models.

The calculation for CCR capital under the Internal Models Method is largely unchanged, even though the scope of application and governance is tightened. However, the CEM and SM will be replaced by a new standardized approach (SA-CCR).

Given that Basel III will be the new framework which is imminently due (from January 2022), and capital considerations for derivatives can be over very long horizons (e.g. 30y), we present a detailed discussion of the Basel III framework so that the reader can appreciate the computations required. (However, it is beyond the scope of this book to present precise minutiae for implementing the Basel III requirements to satisfy regulators.)

In BCBS (2017), finalization of Basel III is given.

The details of the finalized Basel III is summarized in Appendix B.

7.1.1.3. *Conclusion*

It follows from the above that to sustain various trades, capital is required. The exact amount depends on whether internal models (and which regime applies: i.e. pre or post Basel III) or the standard model is used. However, in principle it could be argued that a KVA could exist. To state it simply, KVA is the cost of raising money from a shareholder where FVA (including MVA) is the cost of raising money from a debtor.

7.1.2. *Relevance of KVA and controversies*

Given the scarcity of capital (since increasing capital is only possible by issuing more shares in the absence of increased profits), it is clear why it might be sensible to take account of the cost of capital. Indeed, many financial institutions will seriously take the cost of capital into account in deciding whether to do a new deal or would consider unwinding legacy deals if they prove too capital-expensive in the new regime post 2008.

However, it should be recognized that whereas there is an objective cost of borrowing, there is no comparable cost of capital. Naturally, a financial institution will only want to do business if the return on equity is acceptable to shareholders. But this is more like a question of economic value added or destroyed. In short, it may be silly to do a deal if it consumes too much capital and makes a miniscule profit, but we should avoid confusing valuation from a subjective judgement call such as whether a deal is worth doing. After all, the appropriate cost of capital is somewhat a business decision, even if it can be proxied by the return on equity.[1] This is not to say KVA is not important (indeed capital considerations can be the main reason to exit some businesses), but just to realize that it is a crucial metric which is not necessarily a part of the valuation itself.

There are some advocates of recognizing KVA as part of P&L. The supporting argument is that shareholders would not benefit from economic activities of a firm that do not return a threshold of capital and should be free to write off (i.e. deduct from P&L) activities

[1] Note that proxying the cost of capital on the return on equity may require using the target return, as the actual return may fluctuate too much over time and can even be negative in some periods. So this involves significant judgement call.

that are destructive of economic value. Two possible concerns are: (1) Whether this approach can be assured to always be conservative, and (2) the subjectivity regarding the choice of threshold.

The first concern of conservatism can be satisfied if we only recognize KVA as a cost when entering into an activity that consumes capital, and then eliminate the associated KVA when the capital is returned following exit of such activity, i.e. as long as KVA can never lead to an increase in value.

The second concern of subjectivity cannot be easily addressed. However, as an analogy, we should refer to the practice of taking reserves when pricing exotic derivatives. This is where the uncertainty due to not easily hedgeable and subjective model-dependent price and lack of liquidity attracts an amount reserved (set aside from P&L) as a provision for losses. In the event that the deal matures or is terminated early (due to client instructions or by some contractual event, e.g. knockout barriers), the reserve (or part of it not consumed by realized losses) gets returned as P&L. The process of reserving has a certain element of subjectivity since typically conservatism is applied in the face of uncertainty. Thus, to reserve for KVA (despite its subjectivity) is not exactly going against the spirit of derivatives valuation.

Whether ultimately KVA becomes recognized as part of P&L or the subjectivity is too much for Finance and Auditors to accept is a matter that only time will resolve. A further complication is whether writing off KVA will lead to a tax benefit and hence attract scrutiny on its reasonableness.

It is also crucial to bear in mind that KVA does not apply to just the derivatives business, but indeed to all investments be they in the trading book or banking book. What would be dangerous is for KVA to be added to OTC derivatives just because of a bunch of other adjustments, and then for profitability to be compared against other business lines (e.g. exchange-traded or spot products) where KVA may be ignored.

However, we should be cognizant of some derivatives whose future capital requirements may be very different to today's. For example, consider a swap done at the par swap rate today with zero net value.

If it goes in the bank's favor in the future due to interest rate moves, then it will have a higher CVA-related capital at that point. For this reason, some measure of capital cost (be it by an adjustment or otherwise) at the counterparty level is very useful.

7.1.3. *Modeling KVA*

KVA is given by

$$\mathrm{KVA} = \int_0^T \lambda_{\mathrm{capital}}(u)\phi(u)E[K(u)]du$$

where $K(u)$ is the capital observed at time u, $\phi(u)$ is the bank's survival probability and $\lambda_{\mathrm{capital}}(u)$ is the cost of capital.

Capital $K(u)$ is defined in Basel documents as will be stated in Appendix B. The calculation of future profile of capital is computationally intense and it will be described in Chapter 10.

Regarding this KVA formula, Green *et al.* (2014) pointed the following two points:

(1) The money raised as capital can be used for funding purposes. If it is used in funding, KVA should be analyzed together with FVA.
(2) KVA can be theoretically hedged. However if KVA is hedged, its hedge position might require additional capital.

7.2. Tax Valuation Adjustment (TVA)

Just as KVA has caught the attention of practitioners, a further adjustment — Tax Valuation Adjustment (TVA) is attracting some (albeit much lesser) interest. Green (2016) discusses this topic and mainly puts forth the context that much of CVA management is likely to involve a warehousing risk (i.e. keeping risk within the bank albeit with central oversight and mitigation) as opposed to actually offloading the risks externally. While net PV change is zero when a hedge offsets the moves in an underlying, if the hedge is warehoused[2]

[2] Another effect from warehousing is a potential increase in capital. This is because if a single-name CDS is used to hedge CVA, it may qualify for exclusion of CVA

(i.e. not done externally), it may not be possible to recognize (for tax purposes) P&L from this hedge even if P&L from the underlying has to be recognized. This mismatch can lead to tax incurred, since there is an asymmetry in taxes payable on profits whereas losses do not lead to a tax refund (although they could be offset against future taxes — or even past taxes). This asymmetry could rightly warrant an adjustment for taxes from warehousing CVA, hence TVA.

7.2.1. *Practicalities of TVA and putting things in context*

First, we observe that the tax asymmetry is not necessarily as extreme because losses can be offset against future profit (if there is no possibility to claim back past taxes). So this may be more of an issue of funding the taxes paid assuming they will eventually balance out. There will be a permanent cost if say risk warehousing leads to profits in one region that cannot be offset against losses in the underlying in another region — but this is likely a situation where better internal arrangements can at least mitigate. Alternatively, if some of the mismatch is structural, i.e. repayment is not expected within the life of the firm, then TVA is likely to be material — but then the question arises as to whether such CVA hedging is appropriate. Thus, the amount of TVA is likely to be less significant than one might originally assume. This may still be substantial if there is (as is likely) significant risk warehousing over a large number of counterparties.

A further consideration is whether TVA is really so different from the general treatment of tax in a business. After all, if a business makes a profit, it gets taxed and if it makes a loss, it might not be possible to claim except against future taxes.[3] So this asymmetry

capital charges. But this does not happen with warehousing. So even KVA will be different between the two approaches.

[3]It has been argued that derivatives pricing was predicated on a replication strategy being employed, hence no P&L impact in theory apart from profit margins charged for the trade. In practice, various model parameters have tended to be unhedgeable, e.g. mean reversion in a short-rate model that affects the price of a Bermudan swaption in excess of the maximum European or copula

exists already. Further, with different legal entities and multiple jurisdictions in which a firm operates, it is quite possible for some subsidiaries to be making profits while others are making losses and it is unlikely that the institution can offset profits and losses globally before considering tax. Despite the above, it does not appear that there was a valuation adjustment for taxes in derivatives or indeed other businesses prior to the 2008 financial crisis.

We thus must be clear on whether we are addressing a new situation (e.g. risk warehousing) with significant tax implications or whether TVA is just another adjustment that has been thought up by inspired professionals, anxious to compensate for the failure to fully account for the cost of maintaining their positions prior to 2008.

Naturally, given the complexities of taxation, we can at best work with a much simplified estimate of TVA. For a reader who is still interested in this, we refer to the work of Green (2016).

7.3. Fixed Costs

While on the topic of taking account of all costs in maintaining a position, we wish to mention some other costs in running a derivative business.

(a) Middle Office staffing costs in marking positions daily;
(b) Operations costs in settling cash flows of trades and posting collateral;
(c) Costs of risk management professionals to oversee risks of desks and globally;
(d) Costs of quants to develop and model validators to assess the pricing and risk models;
(e) Costs of compliance personnel to ensure regulatory requirements are adhered to;
(f) Costs of IT personnel and IT systems;

---

correlation between 2 rates in a CMS spread option. Even deep out-of-the-money swaptions tend not to be directly hedgeable but are risk-managed with positions in swaptions with strikes closer to the money. Thus, in reality, derivatives trading leads to P&L events over time, with a dispersion of profits around the expected amount due to the profit margins of trades.

(g) Costs of premises for staff and equipment;
(h) Costs of staffing the trading and sales desks.

While it might seem that we are going overboard with taking account of costs in valuation, there is a valid concern in that derivatives positions tend to have long lives (e.g. some instruments have 40-year maturities) and require a lot of active management (e.g. daily marking of positions and settlement of collateral). The relevant question here is whether certain costs are quasi-fixed (e.g. premises) or whether increased volume of trades will lead to higher cost (e.g. more hardware requirements or support staff).

If we are to fully account for costs, it is arguably sensible to make adjustments for (non-fixed) costs that grow with the amount of business done. This might be as simple as adding a fixed charge for the whole business, or a fixed charge per set quantity of trade or a different charge depending on trade complexity. We do not however feel there is a need to come up with any more complex model than that.

7.4. Brief Summary of Rules on Regulatory Capital

We discuss the situation from the onset of Basel 2.5 and beyond (including Basel III). Very briefly, Basel 2.5 requires RWA to be calculated as follows:

$$\text{Market Risk RWA} = \text{Multiplier} \times (\text{VAR} + \text{SVAR} + \text{IRC} + \text{CRM})$$

Basel III in addition requires a charge for the CVA market risk.

FRTB replaces VAR and SVAR with ES and liquidity horizons for calculations are no longer fixed at 10 days but vary with the asset class and more specific features of the underlying instrument. Further, FRTB replaces IRC with DRC (that applies to equities in addition to debt but only default and not credit migration is accounted for) and CRM is to be replaced by the new securitization framework and computed only by a standard formula.

Further, there are components of Credit Risk RWA and Operational Risk RWA.

7.4.1. *Market risk capital*

Currently (i.e. under Basel 2.5), this is based on calculations prescribed under the standardized method or VAR and SVAR under the internal model method. Under Basel III, there is additionally a need to take account of a market risk charge for variability of CVA.

7.4.1.1. *Internal model method*

Banks with approval from supervisory authorities may use the internal Model for the measurement of market risk capital. In Basel 2, in the internal model approach, market risk should be measured by 99% VAR at a 10-day horizon.

7.4.1.2. *Standardized method*

Banks which do not have approval to use the internal model for the measurement of market risk use the standard model. In the standard model, the capital depends on only trade properties and not on market conditions.

7.4.1.3. *Fundamental review of the trading book*

In Basel Committee on Banking Supervision (2013), BCBS proposed to replace 99% VAR in risk measurement to 97.5% ES which captures the tail risk better. They also proposed to use the model calibrated to market data of the stressed period. Under FRTB, there is also no longer a standardized 10-day liquidity horizon. Rather, liquidity horizon will vary across asset classes and even across different type of assets within the same asset class (e.g. longer liquidity horizon for High Yield corporate credit spreads than Index Grade Sovereign credit spreads).

7.4.2. *CVA risk capital (market risk)*

In Basel III (Basel Committee on Banking Supervision, 2017), there is also a requirement for capital for CVA variability. The charge can be computed by the standard method (Basic Approach) or advanced method (Standardized Approach).

Standard Method (Basic Approach) for CVA Risk: Banks which do not have approval to use an internal method must use the Basic Approach. In the Basic Approach, capital charge is based on standard features of the trade, such as maturity.

Advanced Method (Standardized Approach) for CVA Risk: Banks which have approval to use an internal method may use the confusingly named Standardized Approach, which (like the new Standardized Approach for Market Risk in the Trading Book under FRTB) is based on sensitivities. Here, CVA risk charge is based on a sensitivities-based VAR where risk factors are counterparty credit spreads, as well as risk factors that drive regulatory CVA (e.g. interest rates, FX, equity values). Regulatory CVA is similar to accounting CVA (as discussed in Chapter 2), but must not recognize own default (i.e. DVA).

7.4.3. *CCR capital*

Capital requirement for CCR is given by $c\text{RWA}_{\text{CCR}}$ where c is a capital multiplier which is currently 8% (and at the discretion of national supervisors, a capital buffer could be added), RWA_{CCR} is a risk-weighted asset of CCR.

$$\text{RWA}_{\text{CCR}}(t) = 12.5 \times w \times \text{EAD}(t)$$

where w is the risk weight and $\text{EAD}(t)$ is the exposure at default.

In short, the CCR part of market risk capital is computed by EAD.

The methodology to calculate EAD will be described afterward.

Regarding risk weight, under Basel II (Basel Committee on Banking Supervision, 2008), there are two methodologies: standardized method (Part 2 II) and Internal Ratings-Based Approach (Part 2 III). The calculation of risk weight in Internal Rating-Based Approach is given in Section B.6.1 of Appendix B.

Under Basel III, for the calculation of $\text{EAD}(t)$, both CEM and SM are replaced by the Standardized Approach (SA-CCR) (Basel Committee on Banking Supervision, 2014). Therefore, $\text{EAD}(t)$

is calculated by SA-CCR or the Internal model. It is given in Section B.6.1 of Appendix B.

In SA-CCR, EAD(t) is a function of values and features of the contract but reflected in a simplistic way. For example, an example is made to reflect moneyness of options by weighting by their Black–Scholes delta based on regulatory prescribed volatilities.

Internal Model Method: The calculation of EAD(t) in the Internal Model Method is given in Section B.6.1 of Appendix B.

Final Note: Given the complexities of the Basel III rules, we devote an Appendix at the end of the book to discuss it in more detail. This section only intended to give a flavor of some of the concepts involved.

Part III

Computing XVA in Practice

Chapter 8

Typical Balance Sheet and Trade Relations of Banks and Implications for XVA

A typical financial institution engages with a range of counterparties. Typically, there are collateral arrangements with fellow financial institutions and larger funds and some major corporates. Also, deals done across different assets tend to have different maturities (with interest rates including cross-currency swaps being long dated and equities being short dated in nature). The different types of business arrangements and maturity profile of deals across assets have significant implications on the importance of XVA and also the computational challenges that one will face in implementing this. We thus wish to explore this topic here.

For the efficient use of the resources of the bank, to reduce XVA and regulatory capital is one of the important aspects of the trading business. We will also discuss some methodologies to reduce XVA and the capital of the bank. Part of the contents in this chapter is based on the private communication with Tan.

8.1. Prevalence of Collateralization Agreements

As previously discussed, standard CSA agreements (based on high-quality collateral) will strongly mitigate counterparty risk and also reflect funding in the base curve, hence more or less removing a large amount of CVA, DVA and part of FVA.[1] (We do not however claim that these quantities do not need to be computed in an XVA system, since typical collateral arrangements provide for at least one business day to post collateral, and a conservative assumption might be for up to two weeks of Margin Period of Risk — until collateral is received.) It is true that we will still have KVA, since there is (market risk-related) capital incurred in entering even collateralized deals. However, as discussed earlier, KVA is really about economic value added rather than actual cost. Further, MVA will remain because regulators have insisted on exchange clearing of derivatives or alternatively for initial margin to be posted to an independent account under SIMM.

Thus, XVA (outside collateral arrangement varieties) primarily comes about from

(a) Uncollateralized deals (CVA, DVA, FVA)
(b) Collateral arrangements with a high Minimum Transfer Amount (MTA) or Threshold (CVA, DVA, FVA)
(c) Initial Margin requirements of exchange traded or exchange-cleared deals, or where required by regulators to be posted to an independent account as per SIMM (MVA)

All the above additionally can attract KVA.

To put things in perspective, the majority of deals with fellow financial institutions, funds and some large corporates will likely be collateralized. However, with regulators requiring exchange clearing of standardized deals, a lot of these deals will instead move to exchanges and be subject to initial margin requirements. This greatly increases the importance of modeling initial margin, i.e. MVA. Further, even for deals not cleared on exchanges, there is now a regulatory requirement for posting collateral to an independent account for uncleared margin, hence leading to MVA as well.

[1]If we had chosen a base curve to be based on OIS in the currency concerned, then there will still be FVA if we had other collateral arrangements (e.g. USD OIS or choice of collateral).

However, even among collateralized counterparties, operational convenience may lead to the choice of a high MTA, with associated FVA implications. We anticipate this to be for large corporates or other (primarily non-financial) institutions less used to coping with daily cash flows. Naturally, we anticipate a lower volume of deals between banks and these institutions than for the fully collateralized case or the exchange-cleared case.

Finally, with some exceptions,[2] uncollateralized deals are more likely to take place with smaller counterparties or industrial concerns who really do not wish to deal with the logistics or are not up to the financial sophistication of settling margin regularly. We expect even less frequent deals with some counterparties and some deals to be of smaller notionals, although there could be many such counterparties.

8.2. Maturity of Deals Across Assets

To understand XVA implications, next we consider the maturity of the deals.

By its nature, interest rates is a long-dated business, with institutions trying to borrow (via bonds or mortgages), lock in (e.g. via swaps) or protect from (e.g. via swaptions) the cost of borrowing over a long horizon (e.g. up to 30 years). Further, the international variations of these (i.e. cross-currency swaps to convert between domestic and foreign borrowing) also work similarly. Then there are Inflation and Longevity products which cater to the needs of pension funds and where the horizons are even more extreme (e.g. up to 50 years). Even yield-bearing products in Rates tend to be long-dated (e.g. 30 years for PRDC), being aimed at corporate clients and attempting to take account of interest rate differentials on forward FX rates which are not expected to be realized.

By contrast, Equities is a far shorter horizon business (under 5 years), with the aim to acquire yield by a more retail or fund management clientele. A similar situation exists for Credit, with lower grade borrowers having access to the market for shorter periods

[2]Notable examples are sovereigns who insist on one-way CSA.

(under 10 years). And Commodities tend to be less about long-term protection than near-term moves (e.g. next 2 years). There is also more FX hedging over short horizons by corporates with production and sales in multiple economies and currencies.

8.2.1. CVA cost and capital implications[3] of long maturities

Long maturities are substantial for CVA and have imposed significant capital costs because the potential variance of risk factors increases over time, thereby increasing uncertainty and potential losses. Typical models are based on Wiener processes where the variance grows linearly with time. In this type of model, variance in interest rates tends to grow cubically with time.

To illustrate cubic growth of variance, let us consider the simplest short-rate process, the Ho–Lee model $dr_t = \theta(t)dt + \sigma dW_t$.

A discount bond is given by

$$
\begin{aligned}
D(t,T) &= E_t^Q\left[\exp\left(-\int_t^T r_s ds\right)\right]\\
&= E_t^Q\left[\exp\left(-\int_t^T \left(r_t + \int_t^s \theta(u)du + \sigma\int_t^s dW_u\right) ds\right)\right]\\
&= \exp\left(-r_t(T-t) - \int_t^T \theta(u)\int_u^T dsdu\right)\\
&\quad E_t^Q\left[\exp\left(-\sigma\int_t^T\int_u^T dsdW_u\right)\right]\\
&= \exp\left(-r_t(T-t) - \int_t^T \theta(u)(T-u)du\right)\\
&\quad E_t^Q\left[\exp\left(-\sigma\int_t^T (T-u)dW_u\right)\right]
\end{aligned}
$$

[3]For the impact of skew to CVA calculation (Ji, 2017).

$$= \exp\left(-r_t(T-t) - \int_t^T \theta(u)(T-u)du + \frac{1}{2}\sigma^2 \int_t^T (T-u)^2 du\right)$$

$$= \exp\left(-r_t(T-t) - \int_t^T \theta(u)(T-u)du + \frac{1}{6}\sigma^2(T-t)^3\right)$$

Then if we are only interested in the random part of the SDE of the discount bond, we find

$$\begin{aligned} dD(t,T) &= -(T-t)D(t,T)dr_t + \cdots dt \\ &= -(T-t)\sigma D(t,T)dW_t + \cdots dt \end{aligned}$$

This means it has log-normal variance given by

$$\sigma^2 \int_t^T (T-s)^2 ds = \frac{1}{3}\sigma^2(T-t)^3$$

and we can see cubic growth of the variance of interest rate.

Notice in contrast that if a stock has SDE $dS_t = \mu S_t dt + \Sigma S_t dW_t$, then the variance is $\Sigma^2(T-t)$.

Whereas typical deals are done based on a PV close to zero at inception, the potential change in value is clearly more widely distributed over time (Fig. 8.1). Given CVA takes account of how much a counterparty could potentially owe you, it is calculated as an option, whose value grows over time. Note further that a swap done at par today can become in-the-money (i.e. counterparty owes

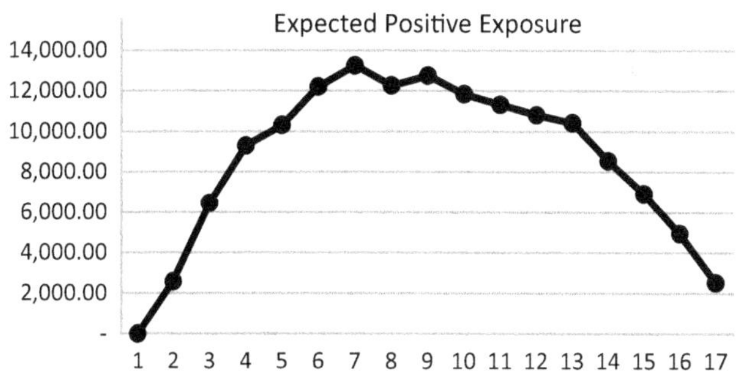

Fig. 8.1: EPE of swap over time.

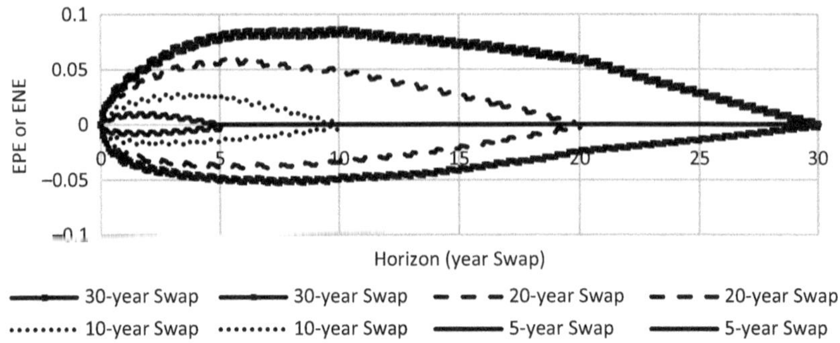

Fig. 8.2: Exposure profiles of swaps of different maturities.

the bank money) over time due to market moves, with a significant resulting increase in CVA.

In short, XVA is likely to be a lot bigger for long-maturity instruments than shorter maturity instruments. This suggests high XVA for interest rates and inflation, notwithstanding their lower vols than equities.

Figure 8.2 illustrates the exposure profiles for various standard market instruments in interest rates, foreign exchange and inflation where maturities are the longest. It clearly demonstrates how much wider exposure profiles are for long-maturity swaps (e.g. 30 years) vs short-maturity swaps (e.g. 5 years). Given CVA is effectively the integral of EPE multiplied by probability of default, the area under the graph shows that long-maturity swaps have far bigger (much greater than linear growth) CVAs than short maturity swaps.

(ENE in the above graph is relevant for DVA in the sense that the above graphs are based on swaps receiving the floating leg, and the ENE is thus equivalent to the EPE of swaps paying the floating leg.)

Figure 8.3 illustrates the EPE and ENE profiles for various forward-starting swaps. It again highlights the dominance of long-maturity deals. This is a precursor to understanding swaptions whose underlying start in forward.

Figure 8.4 compares EPE profiles of physical-settled swaptions of different moneyness vs an ATM forward swap. It can be observed that after the exercise date of 10 years, an ATM swaption has the same profile as the underlying ATM forward swap. Further, it can

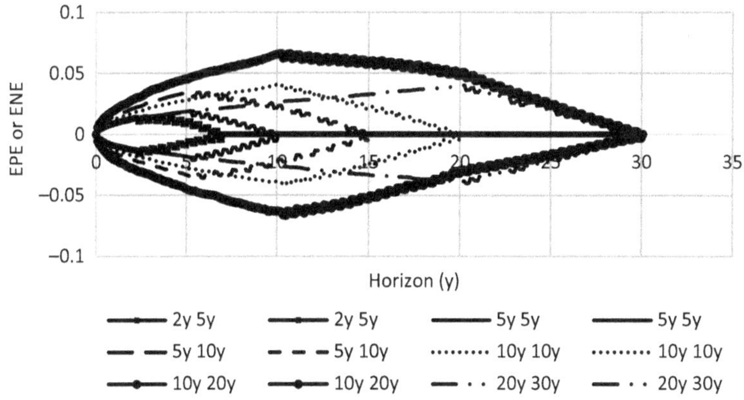

Fig. 8.3: Exposure profiles of forward starting swaps.

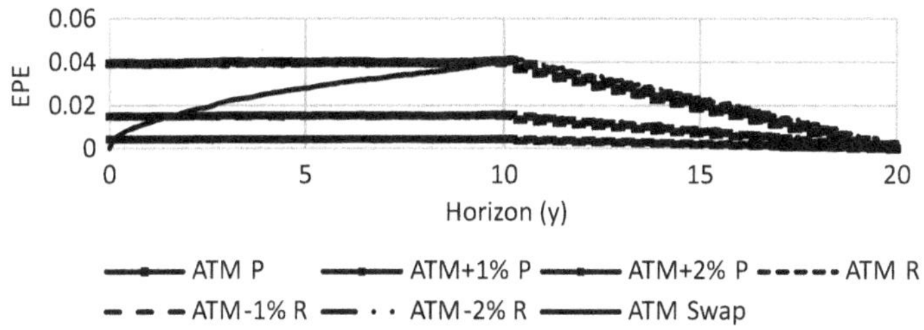

Fig. 8.4: Exposure profiles of 10-year physical swaptions of different moneyness vs ATM swap.

be seen that EPE is far bigger for the ATM swap than OTM swaps (i.e. strike 1% or 2% away from ATM), and this gives a perspective that impact of smile (which affect the value of OTM swaptions) is much less in CVA than in pricing, since swaptions contribute most to CVA when they become ITM and intrinsic value dominates.

For a cross-currency swap, at each coupon date, one party pays Libor in currency A, while the other pays Libor plus a spread in currency B; at maturity, the party paying Libor in currency A has to pay the notional of currency A while the party paying Libor in currency B has to pay the notional of currency B.

Figure 8.5 shows how exposures for cross-currency swaps are far bigger than those for standard swaps. (Here we are receiving domestic currency, so ENE reflects how much the foreign leg might cost in

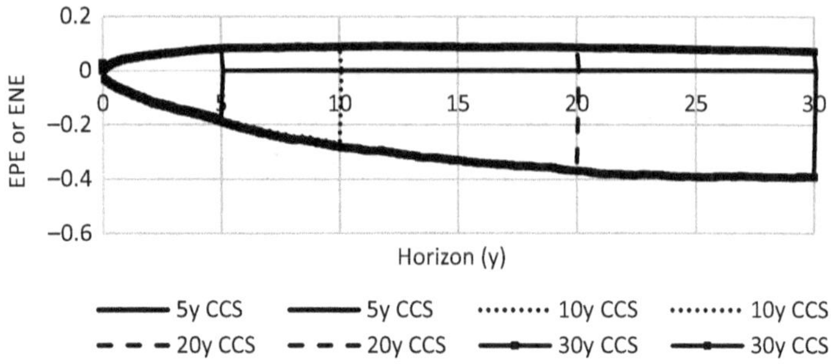

Fig. 8.5: Exposure profiles of cross-currency swaps of different maturities.

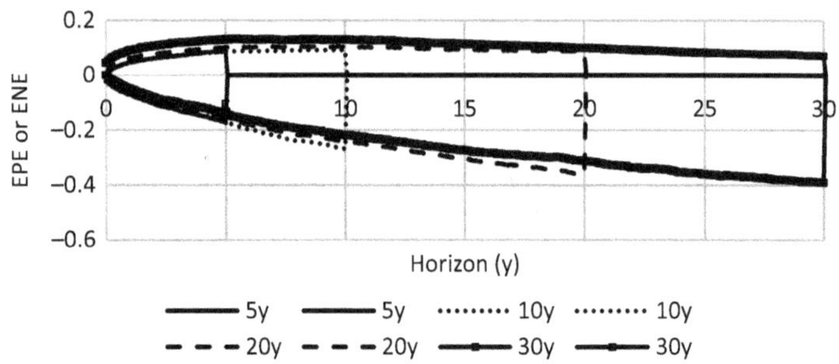

Fig. 8.6: Exposure profiles of inflation asset swaps of different maturities.

domestic currency terms.) Contrast the EPE/ENE of swaps to be under 0.1 for 30 years vs up to 0.4 for cross-currency swaps. The reason for the far larger exposure is because for a cross-currency swap, the notional of each leg must be repaid at maturity, and this notional leads to a very large FX exposure, which dominates typical interest rate exposures.

Now considering inflation asset swaps, we encounter a similar situation (Tan, private communication) (Fig. 8.6). In this case, we receive Libor plus a spread and pay a coupon indexed by inflation at coupon date, and at maturity, we pay the notional adjusted by inflation while receiving a non-adjusted notional. PV at time 0 is close to 0, but cash flows are not balanced, we receive more coupons early in the life of the swap and pay more toward the end of the swap. Similar to the case of cross-currency swaps, it is the notional

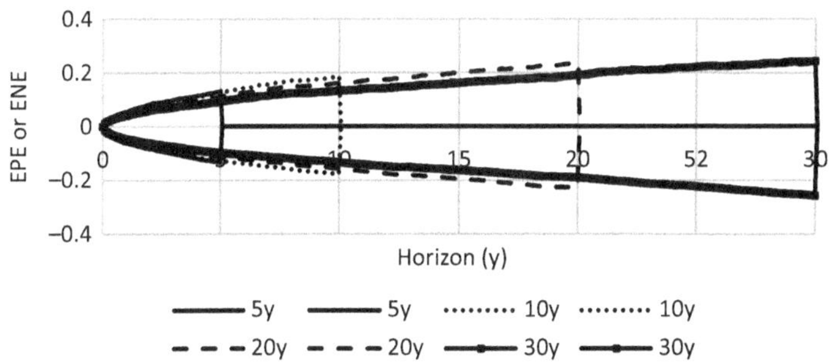

Fig. 8.7: Exposure profiles of inflation zero swaps of different maturities.

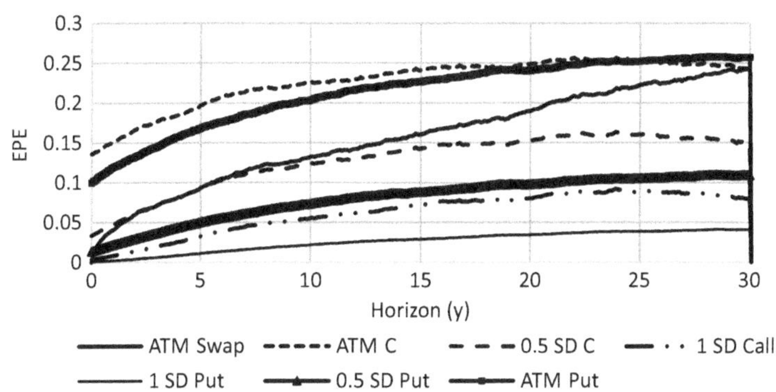

Fig. 8.8: Exposure profiles of 30-year options on inflation zero swap vs ATM inflation zero swap.

exchange at maturity that leads to a far bigger exposure. In fact, exposure profiles look similar to the cross-currency swap.

To better understand the inflation asset swap, we can simply consider the inflation zero swap, where the only cash flows are at maturity: one party pays fixed and the other pays the ratio of inflation index at maturity vs start date, i.e. I_T/I_0 (Fig. 8.7). You can immediately see that one side of the exposure of the inflation swap is comparable to the exposure for this product.

Another purpose of understanding this product is that it is analogous to the exposure of an FX forward corresponding to one unit of the domestic currency today.

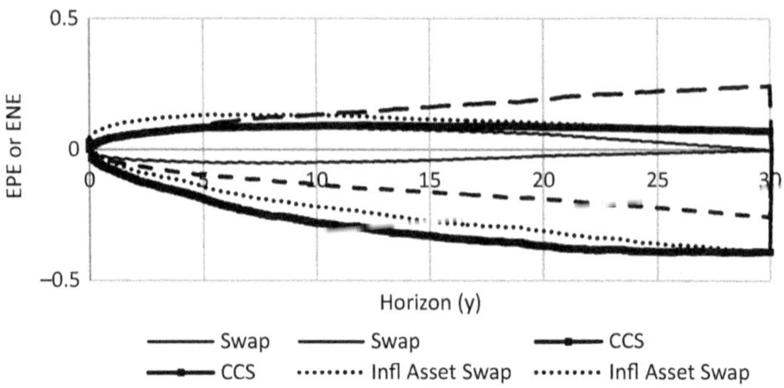

Fig. 8.9: Exposure profiles for the 30-year swap, cross-currency swap, inflation asset swap & inflation zero swap.

Having looked at inflation zero swaps (and hence FX forwards) earlier, we can now consider options on the inflation zero swaps (similarly FX options) in Fig. 8.8. We see that the exposure at expiry for an ATM inflation swap is comparable to that of an ATM inflation option. We see further that OTM inflation options have far smaller exposures than ATM options.

Thus, again as in the case of swaptions, we recognize that smile is not that important for CVA because the bigger contributors to CVA are ITM options, where intrinsic value dominates.

Finally, to put things in perspective, we show exposure profiles of a 30-year swap, cross-currency swap, inflation asset swap and inflation zero swap (or FX forward) together in Fig. 8.9. We can see that the exposure profile for the standard swap is by far the tightest, showing how the notional exchange of the other products really leads to high exposures and hence CVA and capital.

Figure 8.9 gives some insights into considerations that are worthwhile in product design to reduce CVA and capital, which we discuss later in this chapter.

Table 8.1 gives a rough indication of the contribution to Counterparty Credit Risk (CCR) capital of various instruments and asset classes. We had to give a fairly large range for our estimates because the exact composition of the balance sheet will vary between banks. But it should be obvious that swaps, cross-currency swaps and FX forwards by far dominate CCR capital contribution at 50–70%.

Table 8.1: Indication of the contributions to the CCR.

Category	Instrument	Low	High
Linear IR & FX	Swaps, CCS and FX Forwards	50%	70%
IR	Non-Standard Swaps (incl Basis but not CMS)	5%	10%
IR	IR Options (Swaptions, Caps, Bermudans)	2%	7%
IR	IR Exotics (CMS, Spread, Ranges)	0%	3%
Inflation	Inflation ZC and YoY Swaps	1%	5%
Inflation	Inflation Options	0%	2%
Inflation	Inflation Exotics (incl LPI)	0%	2%
FX	FX Options	1%	3%
FX	FX Exotics (Barriers, Multi-FX, PRDC)	0%	2%
Credit	Credit Deriv (CDS, CDS Index, Tranches, Opt)	5%	15%
Equities	Equities Linear (incl TRS)	2%	7%
Equities	Equities Options	1%	5%
Equities	Equities Exotics	0%	3%
Commodities	Commodities (Swaps, Forwards, Options)	0%	5%

In contrast, exotics across all asset classes all likely to account for CCR capital between 0% and 10%. (The 10% is likely a significant overestimate.) This suggests that the role of accurately capturing exotics is not that essential for XVA modeling, but instead earlier on we have shown what really matters is to appropriately deal with long-maturity IR and FX linear instruments.

8.2.2. *Modeling implications of long maturities*

A further consideration of long maturities is the increased complications in models. Interest rates drive FX and equity forward, and whereas the effect is rather muted over short maturities due to far smaller interest rate vols, modeling stochastic interest rates becomes necessary over long maturities. This adds additional factors to the FX model over long horizons (Rebonato, 2004 and Clark, 2011). What is worse is that extreme paths of interest rates can affect FX rates significantly and lead to potentially unrealistic FX forwards. Note that the issues discussed in this section are common to the ones in Long-Dated FX (PRDC) modeling.

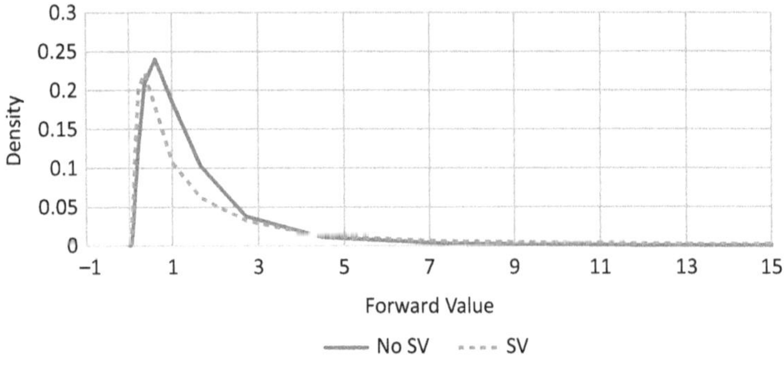

Fig. 8.10: Density of 30-year forward.

Here we point out that a long horizon allows for model weaknesses and the unrealistic features that result to become accentuated. For example, a stochastic volatility model on spot FX or equity that is used to capture better smile for short maturities can explode over time, leading to unfathomably high scenarios of FX or equity (Fig. 8.10).

For example, if there is an upward sloping skew (which is captured by positive correlation between spot and stochastic vol), then using some strong but still plausible Heston parameters (vol of vol 0.46, mean reversion speed 0.75, correlation 0.7) with initial vol of 0.15 leads to the 99.9^{th} percentile of 30-year forward being about 41.2 times the T0 value vs 9.8 times in the absence of stoch vol. In contrast, the 99.9^{th} percentile of a 5-year forward is about 7.5 times the T0 value vs 2.8 times in the absence of stoch vol. While the 99.9^{th} percentile is an extreme tail, such scenarios actually feed into CVA. In fact, this is compensated for by having lower values of forward in the majority of the distribution (e.g. median of 30-year forward is 0.5 times of T0 value with stoch vol vs 0.7 without stoch vol). Given that CVA considers scenarios where the netting set has a positive PV, we see that the distortion is definitely not limited to the tail.

Similarly, when calibrating a local vol model to match smile over various expiries, the shape of local vols necessary to match short expiry smile may extremely constrain our free parameters such that we may end up with zero local vol (if variance over maturity is

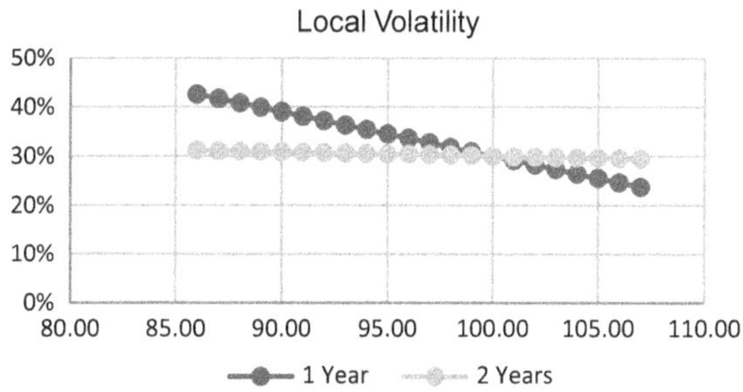

Fig. 8.11: FX skew local volatility.

decreasing, for example) at longer maturities or it may not even be possible (due to negative forward variance).

For example, in the FX (USD/JPY) market, skew is steep for short expiry (shorter than 1 year). In this situation, if implied volatility for low strike (for example, 10 delta of put option) is too large at 1 year and that at 2 year is relatively smaller, too large local volatility at 1 year can make even zero local volatility too large to explain the implied volatility at 2 year.

It is illustrated in Figs. 8.11 and 8.12. Here we assumed local volatility of the form $\sigma(t, x(t)) = a + bx(t)\exp(-ct^2)$ and tried to calibrate it to the linear skew surface. In our calibration, averaging of local volatility is adopted as an implied volatility representation following (Derman *et al.* 2016).[4]

In this example, local volatility is steep for 1 year and almost flat for 2 years. However in this local volatility model, implied volatility for 2 years has almost the same steepness as 1 year. That is, the model cannot fit to the above volatility surface which has steep implied volatility in 1 year and relatively flatter one for 2 years.

The simplest way to illustrate this is to consider a case of vol which is just time dependent. Suppose the vol up to 25 years is 20%, then accumulated variance is $0.2 \times 0.2 \times 25 = 1$. Now, if vol up to 30 years is 18%, accumulated variance is $0.18 \times 0.18 \times 30 = 0.972$, which means variance between 25 years and 30 years is negative (-0.028)

[4]Actually, implied volatility should be a square root of the average of square of the local volatility, but the difference should be negligible in this discussion.

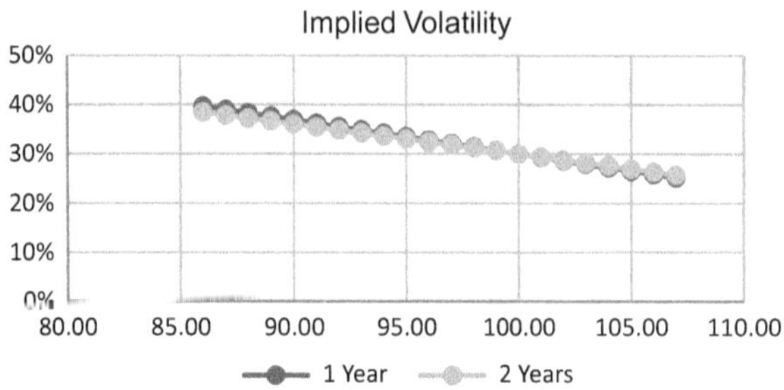

Fig. 8.12: FX skew implied volatility.

which is not permissible. We see how fitting a time-dependent vol up to 25 years constraints our degrees of freedom in that we only have the time-dependent vol between 25 years and 30 years to fit the 30-year vol.

To reason in the same way, instead we had used a local vol model and fitted the smile up to 25 years, quite likely we would have enforced a minimum variance for the set of options of 30-year maturity with different strikes. And we may not be able to fit the given market values well.

Notice how this is just a 2% vol difference and yet the model is unable to accommodate. Such differences can well be due to market inefficiencies from lack of liquidity at the long end. Alternatively, perhaps the market is telling us that the true model dynamics are not as prescribed by the model (e.g. time-dependent vol) but something else (e.g. if you want to have higher short-term vols but lower long-term vols, jumps might be a possible candidate). But the main point is that for long horizons (given we never truly know market dynamics and have to work with imperfect data), fitting vol targets over a bunch of previous (shorter) maturities severely constrains a model's ability to continue fitting the remaining vol targets.

Whereas skew can be captured via the Cheyette model in interest rates, the convexity term can lead to rather unrealistic rate scenarios over time. This, if added to a long-dated FX model for spot FX, can lead to explosive FX forwards.

For example, if you have a log-normalish skew driving domestic rates, then over a 30-year horizon, extreme tail percentiles of realized

Table 8.2: Percentiles of FX spot for flat and skew cases.

Percentile	Flat	Skew
0.01	0.18	0.16
0.03	0.24	0.23
0.05	0.30	0.29
0.10	0.41	0.39
0.30	0.84	0.75
0.50	1.34	1.22
0.70	2.13	2.01
0.90	4.11	4.22
0.95	5.60	5.79
0.98	6.98	8.63
0.99	10.05	16.75
1.00	26.00	83.58

FX spot (starting from a spot of 1) can be much larger than when flat normal rate vols are used, as illustrated in Table 8.2.

Cheyette model is represented by Markov state variables

$$dx(t) = (\kappa(t)y(t) - x(t))dt + \eta(t, x(t), y(t))dW(t)$$
$$dy(t) = (\eta^2(t, x(t), y(t)) - 2\kappa(t)y(t))dt$$

Discount factor is given by

$$D(t,T) = \frac{D(0,T)}{D(0,t)} \exp\left(-G(t,T)x(t) - \frac{1}{2}G^2(t,T)y(t)\right)$$

where

$$G(t,T) = \int_t^T \exp\left(-\int_t^u \kappa(s)ds\right) du$$

with $x(t)$ and $y(t)$ being the state variables, $\kappa(t)$ being the mean reversion speed, $\eta(t, x(t), y(t))$ being volatility (which importantly can depend on state variables and so can capture smile) and $D(0,T)$ being the discount factor up to maturity T as seen at time 0.

Given the above, we advise to be careful of model weaknesses and limitations when coming up with models over long horizons. Often, simplicity is preferable if robustness is desired. We note that for XVA modeling, we definitely need stochastic interest rates as part of the general framework (since there will be many counterparties largely doing rates products), and horizons needed are likely to be long (at least 50 years).

8.3. Capital Reduction Measures

Following the financial crisis of 2008, regulators have responded by mandating a massive increase in capital charges to ensure financial institutions are well capitalized to weather future crises.

For example, Basel 2.5 has introduced Incremental Risk Charge (IRC) (i.e. loss at 99.9% level over a one-year horizon for credit positions over and above VAR[5]) and Comprehensive Risk Measure (i.e. similar to IRC but for Correlation Trading). Additionally, to have guard against aggressive internal models by having a non-risk-based backstop, banks have been required to maintain capital as a percentage of leverage ratio reaching 10.5% after taking account of the countercyclical buffer. Further, CVA VAR is introduced, and in any case a more realistic capture of CVA (generally larger) by industry and recognition of FVA as a cost by market participants have led to an overall picture of far higher costs of doing business. This is even before the onset of the Fundamental Review of the Trading Book (FRTB) under Basel III in 2022 with even more punitive capital charges. The details about the regulatory capital was discussed in Section 7.1.

The response of industry has been to attempt to reduce capital charges where possible in light of a very challenging operating environment. This included modifying the way some business is done and introducing changes to typical products in our businesses.

8.3.1. *Mandatory termination agreement*

The Mandatory Termination Agreement is an attempt by banks to reduce the capital charges from CCR by limiting the horizon

[5]VAR is loss at 99% level over a 10-day horizon. The further the tail (i.e. 99.9% vs 99%) and the longer the horizon, the larger the potential loss will be.

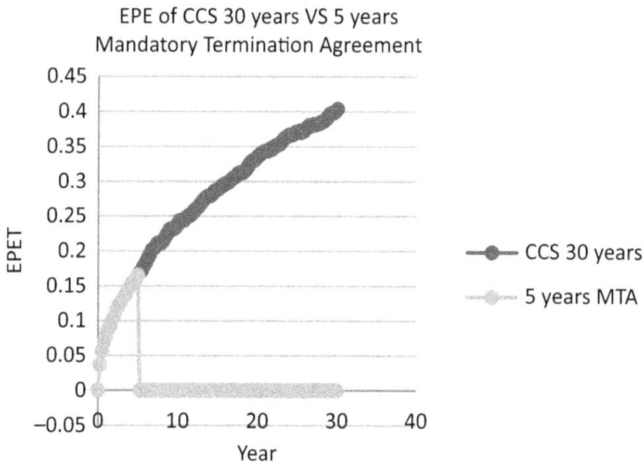

Fig. 8.13: EPE for cross-currency swap for first 5 years vs 30 years.

of the exposure. Specifically, the agreement is that the deal will terminate at a fixed horizon (with 5 years being typical), at which point the deal with be marked-to-market and the PV will be settled in cash.[6]

One can see then that this horizon becomes the last date for which CVA, DVA and FVA are relevant. Imagine now that you have a 30-year cross-currency swap but the Mandatory Termination Agreement specifies a horizon of 5 years, then your exposure to the counterparty is over 5 years and you only need to fund over 5 years. Given variance of risk drivers and hence exposures grow with time (and even more than linearly for rates), this can lead to a massive difference in exposure.

CVA of 30-year cross-currency swap in Fig. 8.13 is USD 286,069 and that with 5 years Mandatory Termination Agreement is USD 27,196.

[6]Naturally, if the bank and counterparty are still in good terms (and still desirous of doing business with each other in light of their strategy and circumstances like credit rating), then they will simply continue the deal, after having settled the mark-to-market in cash. Or the bank can loan the counterparty the cash if both so desire.

8.3.2. *Mark-to-market (MtM) cross-currency swaps*

Adoption of different standard products for some assets is also a response to the desire to reduce capital. We had discussed the MtM cross-currency swap in Section 5.3.

Here, we see again the benefit of exposure reduction of the MtM cross-currency swap vs the traditional cross currency swap (with fixed notionals).

CVA of MtM cross-currency swap in Fig. 8.14 is given by USD 46,799, which is a significant reduction from USD 286,069 for the original cross-currency swap.

The reason for the huge reduction in exposure is because any changes in the FX rate over time triggers a (potentially quarterly) rebalancing of the notional of one leg (the USD leg), so that the swap is not going to be too in-the-money to either party.

Note that similar capital reduction occurs for the Notional Reset Inflation Swap.

8.3.3. *Capital implications and securitization*

Finally, we should note that Basel III which will come into effect in January 2022 does not make any provision for the use of internal risk

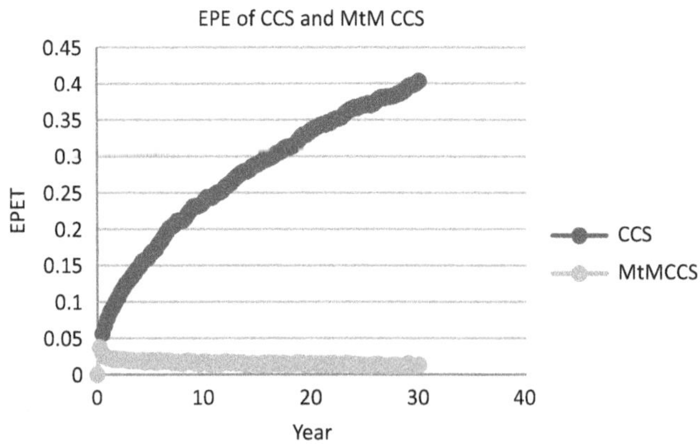

Fig. 8.14: Diagram of EPE of MtM cross-currency swap vs traditional cross-currency swap.

models for Correlation Trading (i.e. tranches of securitized assets — CDOs, MBS, etc.). This is likely to lead to a far higher cost of capital in doing some of that business, which has led many institutions to exit that space. The winding down of those portfolios will potentially mean that most institutions will no longer need to worry about XVA for Correlation Trading in securitized products.

Chapter 9

Framework for Computing XVA

In this chapter, we shall sketch a framework for computing XVA in practice. Whereas traditional derivatives pricing is analyzed from the perspective of individual deals, XVA needs to be understood at the portfolio level. This naturally suggests a different perspective and presents challenges in terms of computational constraints and data availability and consistency.

As is explained in Section 2.3, the main component in the calculation of CVA and FVA is the calculation of Expected Positive Exposure (EPE) (when credit spread is independent of market factors). In the calculation of EPE, we need to compute derivative values on each Monte Carlo path. Here the derivative valuation is the calculation of the conditional expectation value. Thus, we need to calculate the conditional expectation value on each simulation path (Fig. 9.1).

9.1. CVA and the Netting Set

At the heart of CVA is the legal framework for resolving a company in the event of bankruptcy. The existence of CVA after all is due to the asymmetric treatment of positions from a defaulted counterparty — i.e. if the counterparty owes you money, you will join the queue

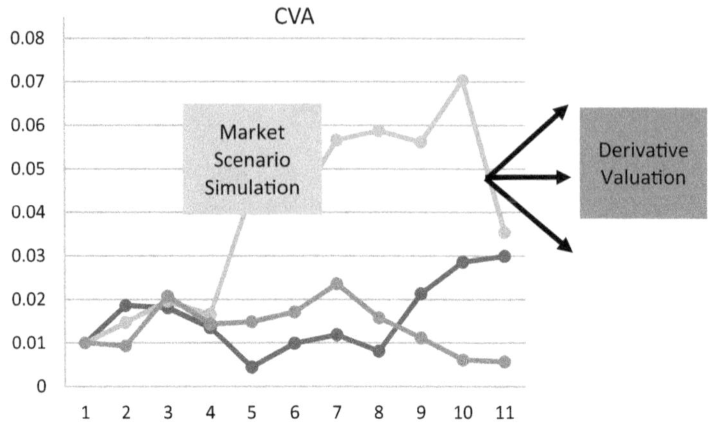

Fig. 9.1: EPE calculation.

of creditors claiming whatever can be recovered; if you owe the counterparty money, you still have to pay.

Here, we should be aware that large corporations tend to have many subsidiaries operating in multiple jurisdictions. In general, it may not be possible to net assets and liabilities of these different subsidiaries across jurisdictions. For example, suppose you deal with a corporation with a US subsidiary and a UK subsidiary. You owe the US subsidiary \$100 million and the UK subsidiary owes you \$150 million. If it goes bankrupt, then you still have to pay its US subsidiary the full amount of \$100 million, even though really as a whole the company owes you \$50 million across its subsidiaries.

To mitigate the risk in this situation, in most of the derivatives contract, the exposures between counterparties are netted. It is called netting.

This brings us to the concept of a netting set — i.e. the portfolio of all trades which we may legally net against each other for a given counterparty in the event of its bankruptcy. It should be clear from the above that CVA must be computed at a netting set level.

We cannot stress enough that CVA should be considered at a netting set level, rather than individual trade level. To take a stylized example, suppose you do a USD swap with a counterparty where you receive fixed 2% semi-annually and pay Libor quarterly over 10 years.

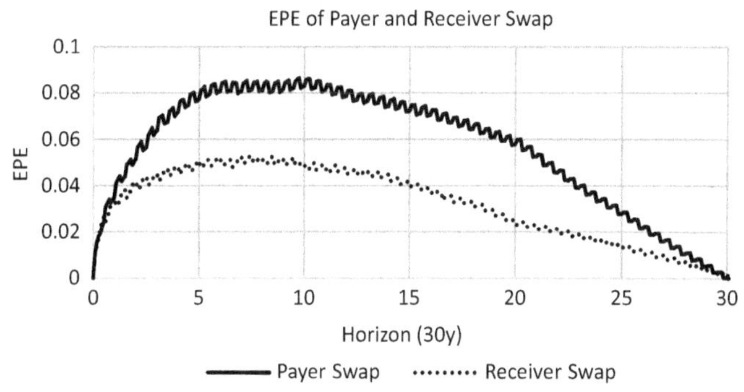

Fig. 9.2: CVA of payer swap and CVA of receiver swap. Net is 0.

Suppose you do another swap with the same counterparty where you pay fixed 2% semi-annually and receive Libor quarterly over 10 years, then clearly you will have a positive CVA for both trades, whereas they cancel and so the combination should have 0 CVA. While in practice you would not have two exactly offsetting trades with the same counterparty, it is likely that many trades offset to a large degree. For example, if you are dealing with a hedge fund over time, you are likely to do some swaps where you pay fixed, then at a future date, you might do a swap where you receive fixed, and the net effect will be a far smaller interest rate exposure than the sum of your absolute exposures (Fig. 9.2).

Whereas it is quite possible to come up with analytic formulae for CVA at the instrument level (e.g. after all, CVA on a (forward starting) swap is just a swaption), at the portfolio level, analytical formulae are far less likely to exist. Given the large number of trades in a netting set, most likely CVA has to be computed by Monte Carlo simulation. The efficient method to calculate sensitivities of XVA for the netting set level is discussed in (Kenyon and Green (2014)).

Naturally, DVA can use the same netting set.

Funding Set

For FVA however, it should be observed that strictly funding constraints might not correspond to counterparty level. More specifically, where collateral is posted, there is the question of whether the collateral can be rehypothecated (i.e. posted onward to a further counterparty). If so, this allows for funding to take place across counterparties. This gives rise to the concept of a funding set — i.e. portfolio of trades for which the net value needs to be funded (in light of collateral and other arrangements).

This is a complex topic. For computational and logistic constraints, many institutions however compute FVA based on the same netting set level as used for CVA.

9.1.1. *XVA model is a hybrid model*

In the netting sets, there can be derivatives of several (over 10) currencies and in the calculation of exposure, and we need to simulate interest rates and FX of these currencies simultaneously. (The simulation of other assets such as inflation, equity and commodity are generated on the top of interest rates.) This multicurrency interest rates and FX hybrid model (cross-currency model) has been developed for the derivatives pricing area, especially for the pricing of Powered Reverse Dual Currency (PRDC). Most of the global banks are well experienced with FX hybrid models, and so it is natural to use them for XVA calculation.

Note that typically the FX hybrid model has a feature for controlling FX volatility skew and other sophisticated features. However, in calculation of XVA, calculation burden is huge and we need to compromise to use a simpler model. For example, quite likely the XVA model does not control the FX skew.

Issues about correlations between rates and FXAs were stated earlier and the XVA model is constructed by multiple uses of cross-currency models. We need to fix a base currency in which exposure is calculated. Calibration of the cross-currency model is done between the base currency and other currencies. Let the number of currencies in the portfolio be N_{cr}, the base currency be C_0 and other currencies be C_i $(i = 1, \ldots, N_{\mathrm{cr}} - 1)$. The calibration of the single-currency model is done for each currency independently. The calibration of FX volatility with respect to the base currency is then carried out, taking account of stochastic interest rates.

Let us illustrate by considering Hull–White rates for all currencies, and a log-normal spot process for FX (vs the base currency). The calibration is done in the following steps:

(1) Base Currency Rates: $dr_t = \kappa(t)(\theta(t) - r_t)dt + \sigma(t)dW_t$ where $\sigma(t)$ is calibrated to interest rate swaption markets or historical rates for the base currency.
(2) Rates in Currency i: $dr_t^i = \kappa^i(t)(\theta^i(t) - r_t^i)dt + \sigma^i(t)dW_t^i$ where $\sigma^i(t)$ is calibrated to interest rate swaption markets or historical rates for currency i.
(3) FX for Currency i vs Base Currency: $dS_t^i = (r_t - r_t^i)S_t^i dt + \lambda^i(t)S_t^i dV_t^i$

where $\lambda^i(t)$ is calibrated to FX options markets or historical FX spot for currency i, but taking account of $\sigma(t)$, $\sigma^i(t)$ and the correlations $\rho_{\text{IR,IR}}^i(t) = dW_t dW_t^i$, $\rho_{\text{IR,FX}}^i(t) = dW_t dV_t^i$, $\rho_{\text{IR,FX}}^{i,i}(t) = dW_t^i dV_t^i$.

However, it is quite likely that the result of this calibration will not recover (implied or historical) vols for FX crosses (i.e. between currency i and j). It is indeed possible to recover implied vols for FX crosses by calibrating the correlations $\rho_{\text{IR,IR}}^i(t)$, $\rho_{\text{IR,FX}}^i(t)$, $\rho_{\text{IR,FX}}^{i,i}(t)$.

However, this may not be desirable. A lot of FX exposure for CVA is about conversion of linear non-FX products (e.g. interest rate swaps) into a base currency. Clearly, there is more liquidity in these linear products in their own markets than for options on FX crosses, especially for long expiries. Thus, even considering that risk neutrality is the result of hedge considerations, it is unlikely that exposures to vols on FX crosses can be hedged. Thus, at the portfolio level, given the dominance of linear products in their own currency, it might be more appropriate to consider historical correlations and accept the discrepancy in CVA for options on FX crosses.

9.2. Cash Flow Aggregation

A typical netting set will involve thousands of trades. Pricing via Monte Carlo typically involves simulating risk factors for each of the cash flow dates.

However, OTC trades are not standardized: for example, swaps typically are done with cash flow dates based on the date of inception.[1] Thus, in practice, a portfolio with thousands of trades

[1]For example, USD and EUR swaps tend to have the start date 2 days after inception.

Table 9.1: Portfolio of interest rate derivatives.

Instrument	Cash flow dates
1: USD swap	10 years, quarterly float, semi-annual fixed, start 15 Jan 2018
2: EUR swap	10 years, semi-annual float, annual fixed, start 12 Mar 2018
3: USD swap	20 years, quarterly float, semi-annual fixed, start 5 Mar 2018
4: EURCHF option	Expiry 6 Jul 2018
5: USDJPY cross-curr swap	20 years, quarterly, start 13 Feb 2018
6: USD swaption	Expiry 12 Feb 2020 into 10-year swap
7: EUR swaption	Expiry 17 Jul 2028
8: USD swap	5 years, quarterly float, semi-annual fixed, start 12 Apr 2018

will have cash flow dates spanning most days in the year. This will significantly increase computational time in the Monte Carlo, as computational time is generally proportional to the number of timesteps.[2]

Suppose our portfolio has instruments as described in Table 9.1.

Then any grid that intends to exactly capture all cash flow dates will have to at least have 288 points, starting 15 Jan 2018, 13 Feb 2018, 5 Mar 2018, 12 Apr 2018, ... and ending 5 Sep 2037, 13 Nov 2037, 5 Dec 2037, 13 Feb 2038, 5 Mar 2038.

Thus, an approach is to come up with a standardized grid (e.g. with dates every 3 months) and then aggregate cash flows in a mapping onto the grid. A simple approach is to linearly assign a cash flow between the two nearest grid points. For example, say if you have a cash flow of €300 payable at time 7 months, and the nearest grid points are 6 months and 9 months, then the mapping could assign €200 payable at 6 months and €100 payable at 9 months.

[2]This is not always true in that some models like local vol require a small timestep (e.g. no more than 1 month) to generate risk factors that depend on realized values of other risk factors. However, in any case, Monte Carlo on a grid with daily timesteps will generally be prohibitively slow.

A more refined approach is based on a (globally) arbitrage-free interpolation of discount factors of different maturities

$$D(t,T) = \gamma \frac{D(0,T)}{D(0,T_j)} D(t,T_j) + (1-\gamma) \frac{D(0,T)}{D(0,T_{j+1})} D(tT_{j+1})$$

where T_j and T_{j+1} are on the standard grid, $T_j < T \leq T_{j+1}$ and $\gamma = (T_{j+1} - T)/(T_{j+1} - T_j)$. It is used in some of the banks (Andreasen, 2014; Antonov and Brecher, 2012). In this refined algorithm, in the above example, the assigned values at 6 months is €300 $\times$ $(7-6) \times D(0,7)/D(0,6)$ and that at 9 months is €300 $\times$ $(9-7) \times D(0,7)/D(0,9)$, respectively. This method preserves the PV of the portfolio to be the same as the original PV.

A more sophisticated approach may have to be considered to take account of options with exercise dates. One way might be to map to two options with standardized exercise dates, but strikes may have to be adjusted to take account of the change in exercise date as well.

For example, say if you have an option (European payers swaption) with strike 1%, notional of €300 and expiry at time 7 months, and the nearest grid points are 6 months and 9 months as above, then the mapping could assign €200 payable at 6 months and €100 payable at 9 months. However, if both the mapped options have a strike of 1%, the original option and the portfolio of the mapped options generally have different PVs. That is

$$300 \times \mathrm{PV}_{7\,\mathrm{month}}(1\%) \neq 200 \times \mathrm{PV}_{6\,\mathrm{month}}(1\%) + 100 \times \mathrm{PV}_{9\,\mathrm{month}}(1\%)$$

To resolve this problem, strike adjustment is well used for the practitioners of derivatives valuation (Andersen and Piterbarg, 2010; Hunt and Kennedy, 2005). That is, in this example, the strike of the options with expiry 6 months and 9 months K_{adj} is adjusted such that the sum of their PVs match the original option with expiry 7 months as follows:

$$300 \times \mathrm{PV}_{7\,\mathrm{month}}(1\%) = 200 \times \mathrm{PV}_{6\,\mathrm{month}}(K_{\mathrm{adj}}) + 100 \times \mathrm{PV}_{9\,\mathrm{month}}(K_{\mathrm{adj}})$$

When we use this adjusted strike K_{adj}, as a strike of options on the standard grid, the model reproduces the original PV of the option.

9.3. Number of Factors in the Interest Rate Model

As is stated in Section 9.1, CVA is calculated at the netting set level, as opposed to on individual trades. Therefore, even when the netting set consists of linear instruments such as interest rate swaps only, CVA depends on the correlation structure of the yield curve.

To illustrate the importance of the number of factors, we will show the relationship of CVA calculation and spread option valuation here. Let the netting set consist of a payer swap of 20 years with strike K_1 (swap1 hereafter) and a receiver swap of 10 years with strike K_2 (swap2 hereafter), both quarterly. The exchange of cash flows occur at times $[T_1, \ldots, T_{80} = 20]$ and $[T_1, \ldots, T_{40} = 10]$, respectively. Let us analyze their EPE observed at time grid T_j.

The positive exposure is given by $(A_1(T_j)(S_1(T_j) - K_1) - A_2(T_j)(S_2(T_j) - K_2))^+$ where $S_1(T_j)$ $(A_1(T_j))$ and $S_2(T_j)$ $(A_2(T_j))$ are swap rates (present value of basis point) of swap1 and swap2, respectively. The EPE of time T_j is given by

$$E(T_j) = E[(A_1(T_j)(S_1(T_j) - K_1) - A_2(T_j)(S_2(T_j) - K_2))^+|F_0]$$

where the numeraire is expected to be normalized in the expectation. Here because PVBP fluctuates less, it is a reasonable assumption to freeze it to its time 0 value and we can approximate it as

$$E(T_j) \sim E[(A_1(0)S_1(T_j) - A_2(0)S_2(T_j) - A_1(0)K_1 + A_2(0)K_2)^+|F_0]$$

This can be recognized as the value of a spread option (with a different gearing applied to each rate).

To illustrate the importance of correlation in CVA calculation more, we will analyze a more significant example. Let the netting set consist of a payer forward swap of 5–10 years and a receiver forward swap of 10–15 years with the same notional and strike. If we use a one factor model, the yield curve moves are almost exclusively parallel and exposure from the first swap and second swap cancel each other to a large extent, so that the net exposure observed before 5 years is close to 0. However, actually from the decorrelation between the shorter tenor rate and longer tenor rate, there can be significant exposure. To capture this correlation effect, we need at least two factors in the interest rate part of a CVA model.

9.4. Least-Squares Monte Carlo (LSM)

Pricing of derivatives tends to be either an analytic formula or one of a set of numerical techniques (i.e. numerical integration on a grid including copulas, PDE, Monte Carlo) (Piterbarg, 2003).

There is typically a trade-off between accuracy and speed. While a derivatives desk quoting on a product to a client will need extremely high accuracy to ensure it profits from the said transaction, even when risk managing the risk in the desk's portfolio at the end of the day, there is already a lower requirement on accuracy and the practical constraint that risks (e.g. delta, vega, and other sensitivities) on a large number of trades need to be computed within a finite time (at most a day). For a CVA or XVA desk, looking at thousands of trades across all counterparties dealing with the bank, the overriding requirement is certainly computational efficiency as opposed to accuracy.

Numerical techniques tend to be used to price exotic products: e.g. replication in CMS pricing often involves numerical integration, Bermudan swaptions and callable rate products tend to require a PDE[3] (Grid calculation) as does FX exotics under the Local Stochastic Vol model and path-dependent products tend to require Monte Carlo simulation. Typically, Monte Carlo simulation is the slowest of the above and a single pricing may take over a second. This can be prohibitively expensive for a portfolio of thousands of trades, and especially where sensitivities are required.

On the other hand, Monte Carlo simulation has a benefit of that computational cost increases linearly as the number of factors increases, where in the Grid calculation it increases exponentially. In

[3]A PDE can only be used if a model that is Markovian in a small number of state variables (e.g. Hull–White or Cheyette in interest rates) is used in pricing. Specifically, this rules out using PDEs together with the Libor Market Model, for which we need a state variable against each Libor rate. The alternative is to use LSM described.

the XVA calculation, because it is calculated on the netting set level, the number of factors can be large. Therefore, Grid calculation is not an option and Monte Carlo simulation is necessary.

As has been stated in Fig. 9.1 already, the calculation of CVA boils down to the calculation of conditional expectation values at future times. In the practice of derivatives valuation, future conditional expectation value is necessary in the valuation of a callable derivative (Bermudan Swaption). Therefore, we can borrow the techniques to calculate future conditional values from derivatives valuation. In the Monte Carlo simulation, we typically use LSM for the calculation of future conditional expectation values.

9.4.1. *LSM for Bermudan swaption (callable swap)*

In the valuation of Bermudan Swaption, the value at exercise time T_i is given by $V(T_i) = \max(\text{Cont}(T_i), Ex(T_i))$, where $\text{Ex}(T_i)$ is an exercise value and $\text{Cont}(T_i)$ is a continuation value at time T_i. Exercise value is an analytical function of a state variable but continuation value is not. Calculation of continuation value at future time T_i is necessary for the valuation of Bermudan.

The LSM approach effectively approximates continuation (conditional expectation) value by regressing the prices at a future point in time against state variables as seen at an earlier point in time, i.e. the pricing function becomes a linear regression based on some chosen basis function of the state variables.

The basic idea is you first generate a set of paths and evaluate the exercise values along this path. You now have the state variables $\theta(T_j)$ and the exercise values. By regressing the values of the derivatives by state variables, you will have a predictor function for the continuation value $\text{Cont}(T_i) = \hat{f}(\theta(T_i))$. Next, you generate an independent set of paths and apply this predictor function to get the value $V(T_i)$ of payoff for each of these paths conditional on the realized value $\theta(T_i)$ of your state variable at an earlier time t.

We illustrate this below with the payoff from a payers swaption. Let S_t be a swap rate started at time t. The calculation is done backward. So let the value at time T_{n+1}, $V(T_{n+1})$ already be calculated. For the valuation at time T_n, we need continuation value

$\text{Cont}(T_n)$ and exercise value $\text{Ex}(T_n)$. Exercise value is given by $\text{Ex}(T_n) = \text{PVBP}_{T_n} \max(S(T_n) - K, 0)$, where PVBP_{T_n} is the present value of basis point at T_n, and K is the strike and is an analytical function of the state variables. On the other hand, continuation value is not given by the analytic function. It is represented by the conditional expectation value

$$\text{Cont}(T_n) = E[V(T_{n+1})|F_{T_n}]$$

In LSM, the conditional expectation value is evaluated by regression. That is, on each Monte Carlo path, there is a value of Swap Rate $S(T_n)_p$ and the value at T_{n+1}, $V(T_{n+1})_p$ $(p = 1, \ldots, N_{\text{path}})$. Here, we adopt the Swap Rate as the explanation variable and the conditional expectation value is assumed to be approximated as $f(S(T_n)) = \beta_0 + \beta_1 S(T_n) + \beta_2 S(T_n)^2 + \beta_3 S(T_n)^3$. The regression is done between $S(T_n)_p$ and $V(T_{n+1})_p$ and the regression coefficients $\beta^T = (\beta_0, \beta_1, \beta_2, \beta_3)$ are estimated as

$$\beta = C^{-1} E[X^T Y]$$

where X refers to the explanatories $(S(T_n), S(T_n)^2, S(T_n)^3)$ in the equation above, Y is the dependent variable $V(T_{n+1})$, X^T is the transpose of X and $C = E[X^T X]$. Expectation values are evaluated by the Monte Carlo simulation (Fig. 9.3).

(Details about the plausibility of LSM in the calculation of conditional expectation value will be discussed in Section 9.7.) The

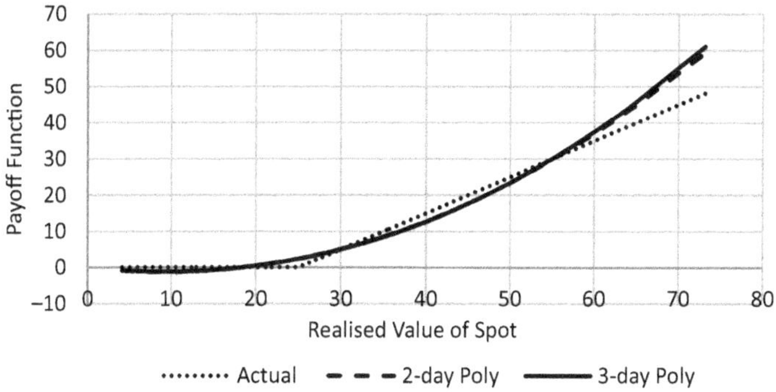

Fig. 9.3: Illustration of LSM.

multiple application of regression for the Bermudan Swaption is a reminiscent of Deep Learning.

9.4.2. *LSM for CVA calculation*

Note that this approach is particularly suited for CVA, since we generally need to generate the paths for our risk factors relevant to all our positions across our various counterparties.

On each path, we need to calculate exposures of the counterparty (which is a sum over the derivatives portfolio), which is represented as a conditional expectation value.

Therefore, LSM is naturally applied to the calculation of CVA and improves the efficiency of the calculation significantly.

LSM is used for the valuation of callable derivatives, however it is also useful for the calculation of CVA of the non-callable derivatives.

For example, when we calculate CVA of swaps and European swaptions portfolio, we need to calculate the value of swaps and swaptions on each Monte Carlo path. In most of the interest rate models used in the CVA calculation, there is an exact formula for a swap and a European swaption but evaluating their PVs thousands of times can still take significant computational time. This is particularly relevant because there can be a huge number of swaps (and swaptions) in the netting set and we can benefit from a technique to evaluate it efficiently.

If we start by using the standard numerical algorithm to price each instrument for a reduced set (e.g. 500) of paths, then we can use the least-squares regression to obtain a predictor function for each instrument. Now, along each path of the risk factor we have generated (generally this is a far larger set of paths), we simply apply this predictor function to get the PV. The predictor function is typically a polynomial of state variables and calculation is very fast. In this way, the number of computations is greatly reduced.

In the above example of CVA of swaps and European swaptions (or other non-callable derivatives), LSM is a method of interpolation rather than statistical inference as that in the valuation of the Bermudan Swaption and convergence of LSM is faster than that of the Bermudan Swaption. This methodology of LSM is similar to the machine learning. Here estimation of predictor function corresponds training in the supervised learning.

On the other hand, when we calculate CVA of a Bermudan Swaption (or callable exotic derivative), LSM is naturally used as follows. Before the calculation of CVA, the PV is calculated beforehand. In the calculation of PV, the future values of the derivative are calculated as a (predictor) function of the state variable in LSM on the exercise date. We can use this function for the calculation of CVA.

One thing we need to be careful about for the CVA of a Bermudan Swaption (callable derivative) is that the value of a Bermudan at time T depends on not only the state variables at that time but also their trajectories. In a trajectory, if the Bermudan Swaption is exercised before time T, the value of the Bermudan is the value of the Swap which is exercised (for the physical-settled swaption). Therefore, for the CVA calculation, the trajectories of state variables are stored to calculate exposure.

Note that we can use grid interpolation instead of LSM with a similar logic Green (2016). That is, for each CVA time, generate equidistant grid in state variable space. Calculate the value of derivatives at the grid point. For the calculation of CVA, generate Monte Carlo paths and calculate the value of the derivatives portfolio using polynomial interpolation as is stated by Pelsser (2000). However, the combination of grid and Monte Carlo simulation makes the logic more complicated and we explain only the LSM technique hereafter.

LSM can be applied to VAR calculations on Monte Carlo simulation, which is the core part of the MVA and KVA calculations. It will be discussed in detail in Chapters 10 and 12.

9.4.3. *Limitations of LSM*

LSM is based on regression and the quality of the predictor functions is naturally dependent on the choice of basis functions. Typically, for simplicity, basis functions tend to be chosen to be a low-order polynomial (e.g. X, X^2, X^3, XY, $X^2Y, \ldots$) in some combinations key risk factors (e.g. S&P 500 level or 10-year USD swap rate)

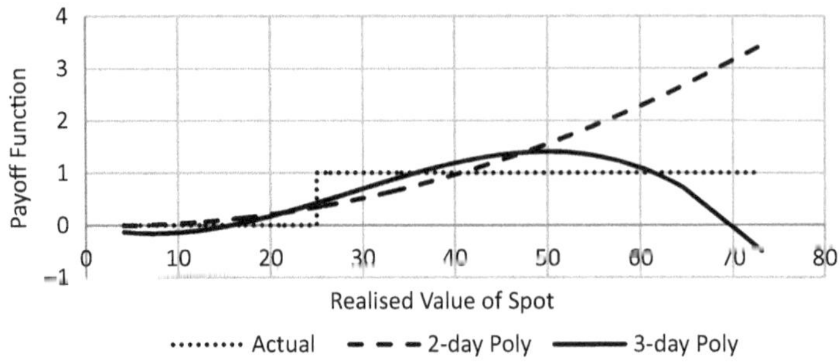

Fig. 9.4: Illustration of tail behavior on digital call option.

relevant to the derivative. While polynomials tend to behave well locally, tail behavior can be extreme. Thus, their original use in estimating optimal exercise is appropriate, but for generating all PVs for purposes of computing CVA, they can be less suitable.

The best way to see it is by considering a digital call option. Here the true payoff is 0 below strike 25, and 1 above that. But whereas close to the strike, a polynomial can try and approximate it, any polynomial will struggle very badly as the tail would either go to ∞ or $-\infty$ (Fig. 9.4).

A solution could be to split the state space into regions and have different regressions in each region (e.g. we could split the state space into two regions here — one below 25 and one above) and the payoff is actually linear in each region. An inspired choice of region boundaries requires knowing the payoff intimately. However, it may be effective to more generally split any payoff into a few regions, based on the assumption (usually suitable) that most derivatives behave linearly (in terms of the underlying) at both tails — e.g. when deep in-the-money, a call option behaves like the underlying.

However, recognizing that tail behavior is not accurately captured by the linear regression. Andersen has proposed a modification whereby the regression is used to determine certain key features such as whether an option is exercised, but otherwise the payoff evaluation is not dependent on a blind application of the predictor function (Andersen and Piterbarg, 2010).

A further problem of regression is that the entire explanatory power has to lie in the state variables. This can be a problem for short horizons, since we typically work with diffusion processes for risk factors and time is needed for diffusion processes to accumulate quadratic variation.

Figures 9.5 and 9.6 show plots of the payoff of the earlier 4-year expiry call option, but with use of explanatory being the stock price as of 3 years, or as of 3 months. The explanatory power of the stock price at 3 months is very low, as can be seen from the almost no discernible trend in the scatter plot.

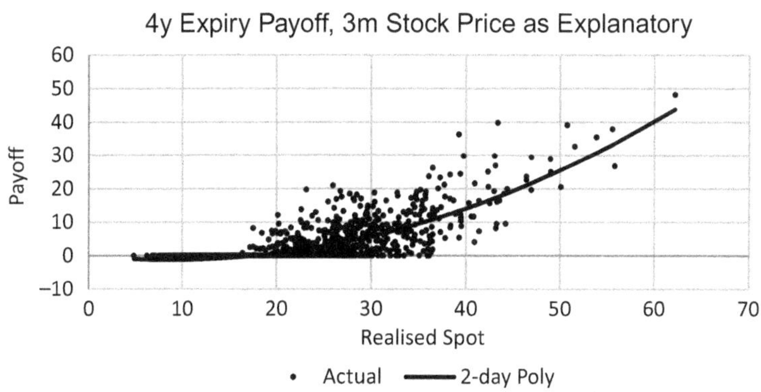

Fig. 9.5: 4-year expiry payoff, 3-year stock price as explanatory.

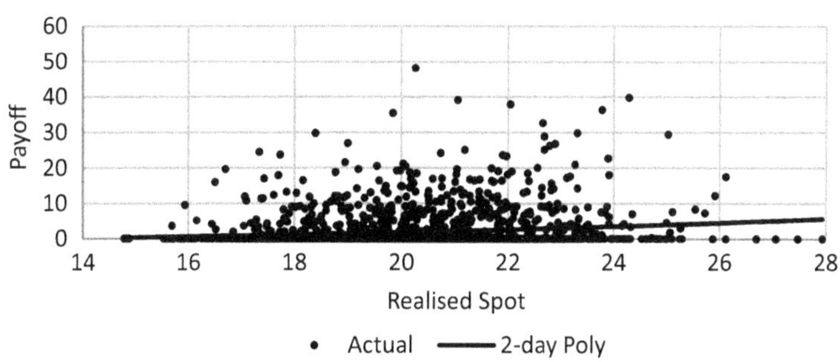

Fig. 9.6: Four-year expiry payoff, 3-month stock price as explanatory.

The background (as to why we seek to use stock price at a date before exercise as explanatory) is that suppose a product has early exercise at annual intervals, we can be in a situation where comparing the continuation value (i.e. exercise at time 4 years) is necessary vs immediate exercise say at 3 years. While it is unusual to have to compare against exercise at 3 months, this stylized example demonstrates the limit of explanatory power in LSM.

A further problem is that sometimes risk factors generated for purposes of CVA[4] are done in the physical measure, which is not necessarily the same as the risk-neutral measure used for pricing. This means that it is possible that the scenarios for risk factors generated may not be consistent with the market data used for pricing. In short horizons, due to the slow growth of variance of a diffusion over time, there is a possibility that there is a large region where the risk factors do not overlap, so that predictive power of the regression is poor. For more details of this, see discussion in Chapter 11, in the context of the discussion of limits to hedging and the mix of physical measure for simulation and risk-neutral measure for pricing.

One solution is to artificially increase the vol of predictor variables. While this may distort any PVs obtained from the predictor function, this may be a necessary price to pay to have meaningful results. Note however if the predictor function is used to determine option exercise as opposed to full payoff, the impact may be more limited. This is very much akin to the idea of the Green–Kenyon Shocked-States Augmentation, which is discussed in Chapter 10, regarding computation of KVA and MVA.

[4]Note here that there is regulatory CVA used to hold capital against counterparty credit risk, which should theoretically be based on the physical measure, as opposed to accounting CVA which is charged based on expected losses from counterparty defaults and should be computed under the risk-neutral measure if it is hedgeable via CDS. Even so, regulatory CVA requires the use of market CDS spreads implied probabilities of default where available, breaking the "purity" of using the physical measure, advocated by some authors.

9.5. The Need for Simplicity of Models

In Section 8.2, we explained how model performance can be problematic if we are interested in long horizons. For example, stochastic vols needed to match short-term skew can explode after a few years (e.g. 5 years); matching interest rate skew over short horizons can lead to zero or negative forward variance as implied by longer dated instruments; complex interest rate models (e.g. Cheyette) can lead to unrealistic paths of FX forwards in long horizons (e.g. 20 years). This topic was already discussed in Chapter 8.

This brings us to the general consideration that in XVA, having to deal with a large number of counterparties and the entire spectrum of deals (hence involving potentially all assets and over long horizons), we cannot overemphasize the importance of having a robust model. This usually means a simpler model, which is also less accurate (Tan, 2014).

Interest rates tend to be the foundation for other risk factors, since FX and equity forward processes are driven by interest rates, e.g. $X(t,T) = X_t \frac{D^f(t,T)}{D(t,T)}$, where X_t is spot FX at time t while $D(t,T)$ and $D^f(t,T)$ are domestic and foreign discount factors, respectively until maturity T. This means a complex interest rate model will affect FX and equity forwards, and strongly suggests keeping interest rate models simple if possible.

Potentially, perhaps sticking to the Hull–White or Cheyette (if skew is deemed necessary) is preferable than the Libor Market Model.

For equity and FX, again the consideration is that the exposure model needs to work over long horizons. While stochastic vol may be useful in realistically captured skew dynamics in some markets (e.g. equities), the explosive behavior can instead suggest it might be better to stick with the log-normal spot (or local vol if deemed necessary).

For credit intensity or spread processes, we should recognize that with a Hull–White model, negative values are possible. And a negative credit intensity or spread implies a negative probability of default — a logical impossibility. Further, if we wish to take a pragmatic approach and just ignore a small set of paths with negative intensities, it turns out that credit vols tend to be rather high, so this set is uncomfortably large.

For example, if credit spread is 0.02 and Hull–White mean reversion is 0.05 while vol is 0.025, probability of term credit spread being negative over 5 years is greater than 20%.

Ideally a model which could avoid negative credit spreads is preferable, including CIR or log-normal. Both these suffer from numerical issues. For CIR, the issue is correlating default times with other processes; for log-normal, even to get the value of a survival probability requires evaluation of a conditional expectation (perhaps by LSM). Potentially other possibilities exist, e.g. Cheyette with some suitable parametrization of local vol. However, a consensus does not seem to have been reached.

9.6. Implied Calibration or Historical Calibration

One of the most important parts in the practice of derivatives valuation is calibration. There are two types of calibrations: (1) implied calibration and (2) historical calibration. In the practice of derivatives valuation, implied calibration is preferred. Historical data represents risk factors in the past but implied data is the present estimation of risk factors from the price of traded instruments. For hedgeable quantities, the latter reflects the cost of hedging.

Basically the parameters needed in the XVA calculation are divided into two categories: (1) parameters for credit risk of counterparty and (2) parameters that drive market risk of exposure. Credit risk parameters include Probability of Default (PD) and Loss Given Default (LGD). LGD is difficult to estimate and to use a fixed number for different categories (e.g. by regions, sectors and ratings — say 40% for high-rated large corporates, 0% for firms with minimal tangible assets) is the market standard. Therefore PD, which is equivalent to the hazard rate, is the more important credit risk parameter to be estimated.

Regarding estimation of PD, in traditional counterparty risk management methodologies, historical calibration is frequently used.

Regarding market risk parameters, in any market (interest rate, FX, equities, commodities or traded credit products) and in any model, the parameters necessary are drifts μ_i, volatilities σ_i and correlations $\rho_{i,j}$ of stochastic processes illustrated by

$$dS_i(t) = \mu_i(S_i(t), t)dt + \sigma_i(S_i(t), t)dW_i(t)$$
$$\rho_{i,j}(t)dt = dW_i(t)dW_j(t)$$

For both credit risk factors and market risk factors, in traditional counterparty credit risk management (for regulatory capital), historical calibration is sometimes used. Banks use Potential Future Exposure (PFE) to set the credit limit. For the calculation of capital of counterparty risk, the calculation of exposure is necessary. When considering the use of historical calibration, one must balance the likelihood of passing backtesting (a requirement that model suitability is validated by testing on past history) vs a need to recover market prices of traded instruments. If the drift is not matched, it is very unlikely that exposure for capital purposes would be consistent with traded prices. If vols are not matched, then only options would not match traded prices, whereas these vols are also used for exposures of linear products (with far greater volumes) and there is no reason why matching traded prices of options should be a criteria of quality. Further, quantities like correlation are not necessarily hedgeable and thus there is little clear rationale to object the use of historical data to estimate correlations.

However, for the XVA calculation in front office, implied calibration is often preferred in most of situations. In fact, Basel III rules even require CVA capital to be based on risk-neutral processes. The rationales for using the risk-neutral calibration are:

(1) XVA is the net adjustment to the price of a derivative and it is calculated in the framework of arbitrage-free valuation. For the value to be arbitrage-free, the drift and vol of the stochastic process and the PD should be the one from arbitrage-free theory. That is, PD should be from the CDS market and drift should be

from the cost of funding rate and the vol should be from prices of traded options.

(2) The XVA desk will hedge XVA (especially CVA) using single-name CDS or CDS indices. To hedge effectively, the model should be calibrated to hedge instruments.

(3) Market risk of XVA should also be hedged. Regarding volatilities of market risk factors, implied volatilities reflect the cost of vega hedging in the option market.

However, as will be discussed in Chapter 11, there is a limit to CVA hedging due to constraints on the availability of single-name CDS and also a pragmatic consideration on the liquidity of option markets vs that of linear products. Thus, even for XVA, the use of historical calibration for quantities like correlation (and occasionally vol) can sometimes be justified.

9.7. The Estimation of Conditional Expectation Value by Regression (LSM)

In this section, how LSM is useful to calculate conditional expectation value is explained. Let one-dimensional state variables for the model $X(t)$ be Markovian. The conditional expectation value at time t, $E[V(T)|F_t]$ is a function of $X(t)$, i.e. $f(X(t)) = E[V(T)|X(t)]$. Let the function $f(x)$ be well approximated by a simple function, for example the polynomial function $\tilde{f}(x) = a_0 + a_1 x + a_2 x^2 + a_3 x^3$.

Let us consider the expectation value

$$E[(V(T)-\tilde{f}(X(t)))^2] = E[V(T)^2]-2E[V(T)\tilde{f}(X(t))]+E[\tilde{f}(X(t))^2].$$

Here using the tower rule, we have

$$\begin{aligned} E[V(T)\tilde{f}(X(t))] &= E[E[V(T)\tilde{f}(X(t))|X(t)]] \\ &= E[E[V(T)|X(t)]\tilde{f}(X(t))] = E[f(X(t))\tilde{f}(X(t))] \end{aligned}$$

Then we have a relationship

$$\begin{aligned}
&E[(V(T) - \tilde{f}(X(t)))^2] \\
&\quad = E[V(T)^2] - 2E[f(X(t))\tilde{f}(X(t))] + E[\tilde{f}(X(t))^2] \\
&\quad = E[V(T)^2] - E[f(X(t))^2] \\
&\qquad + E\left[(f(X(t)) - \tilde{f}(X(t))^2\right]
\end{aligned}$$

Therefore, the function $\tilde{f}(x)$ which minimizes $[(V(T) - \tilde{f}(X(t)))^2]$ also minimizes $E[(f(X(t)) - \tilde{f}(X(t))^2]$.

That is, the function $\tilde{f}(x)$ which minimizes

$$\sum_{j=1}^{N_{\text{path}}} \{V(T)_j - \tilde{f}(x(t)_j)\}^2$$

in the Monte Carlo simulation best approximates the conditional expectation value $f(x) = E[V(T)|x]$.

Chapter 10

Calculation of KVA and MVA

As has already been stated in previous chapters, calculation of KVA (and MVA) is computationally intense when the internal model (or even the Standardized Approach under Basel III) is used. In this section, we will discuss the computational burden. KVA is given by

$$\text{KVA} = \int_0^T \lambda_{\text{capital}}(u)\phi(u)E[K(u)]du$$

where $K(u)$ is capital observed at time u, $\phi(u)$ is the bank's survival probability and $\lambda_{\text{capital}}(u)$ is cost of capital. Therefore, we need to calculate the expectation value of capital observed at a future time. Since we need to calculate capital on the scenarios generated by the Monte Carlo simulation, it can be a huge computation burden.

Given the earlier formula on capital, we wish to separately consider the counterparty (including CCR and CVA risk charge) and the traditional market risk aspects.

IRC currently (i.e. pre-FRTB) pertains mostly to debt securities where bonds tend to dominate, so capital computations relating to these should not be too complex. Its successor DRC extends this further to equities, but here single names tend to be underlyings for vanilla payoffs while indices tend to have at least 30 underlyings so that the impact of a single default is more limited. CRM by contrast involves the most complex of Credit Correlation Trading, which is in wind-down mode in many institutions. Further, the 99.9% 1-year tail (required for these measures) does not lend itself easily to modeling efficiencies, and Basel III rules will replace CRM with a new securitization framework with a standardized formula by January 2022. Thus, we shall not discuss any of these metrics further.

Hereafter, we separate KVA as

$$\mathrm{KVA} = \mathrm{KVA}_{\mathrm{CCR}} + \mathrm{KVA}_{\mathrm{CVA}} + \mathrm{KVA}_{\mathrm{Mkt}}.$$

From the discussion of Basel III capital requirements in Sections B.6 and B.7 of Appendix B, we further summarize the computation requirements of KVA calculation as follows:

- Standardized method requires sensitivities calculation for Market Risk RWA (excluding CVA RWA), but otherwise no calculation more complex than PV is required.
- Banks will always have to compute capital charge under the standardized method, due to leverage ratio and output floor if using the internal method.
- Banks using the internal method need an Expected Shortfall (ES) (tail) calculation for market risk RWA, EEPE (a CVA-like calculation of Exposure at Default) for CCR RWA, a sensitivities calculation for CVA RWA and an extreme tail calculation for DRC, with no other charges being subject to internal calculations.

10.1. Calculation of KVA for Counterparty Risk (CCR and CVA Part of VAR/SVAR)

CCR and CVA capital are calculated at the netting set level.

In Basel III, CCR capital at time t is given by

$$\mathrm{RWA}_{\mathrm{CCR}}(t) = 12.5 \times w \times \mathrm{EAD}(t)$$

where w is a risk weight dependent on probability of default (PD), loss given default (LGD) and effective maturity (M), while

$$\text{EAD}(t) = \alpha \times \text{Effective EPE}(t)$$

$$\text{Effective EPE}(t) = \sum_{k=1}^{\min(1\,\text{year},\text{maturity})} \text{Effective EE}_{t_k}(t)\Delta t_k$$

$$\text{Effective EE}_{t_k}(t) = \max(\text{Effective EE}_{t_k}(t), \text{EE}_{t_k}(t))$$

where expected exposure $\text{EE}_{t_k}(t) = E[V^+(t_k)|F_t]$ is calculated in the bank's internal model and $\alpha = 1.4$ is a regulatory multiplier. Note that since CCR capital is floored at 0, EE can be considered to be floored at zero, so not too dissimilar in concept from EPE as defined for accounting CVA.

CVA capital is given by sensitivity-based VAR of regulatory CVA, where shocks are applied to counterparty credit spread, as well as market risk factors (such as interest rates, equity values, FX and credit spreads for credit derivatives). Here, regulatory CVA is closely related to accounting CVA (per Chapter 2) but where DVA cannot be recognized, i.e.

$$E\left[\int_0^T \max(V(t), 0)D(0, t)(R-1)\lambda(t)dt\right]$$
$$= \text{LGD}\int_0^T E[\max(V(t), 0)]D(0, t)d\,\text{PD}(t)$$

where loss given default is $LGD = R - 1$, R is the counterparty's recovery rate, probability of default is PD which satisfies $d\text{PD}(t) = \lambda(t)dt$, $\lambda(t)$ is the counterparty's default intensity at time t, $V(t)$ is portfolio value at time t and $D(0, t)$ is value of a discount bond with maturity t, with the equality obtained by assuming independence between credit spreads and market factors.

Therefore, in KVA_{CCR} and KVA_{CVA}, we need to calculate a quantity similar to expected exposure in a scenario generated by Monte Carlo simulation. We will describe the calculation methodology. Here the valuation model is typically based on a low-dimensional Markov process $x(t)$. (Typically, it is a Gaussian process $dx(t) = \sigma(t)dW(t)$). Prior to KVA calculation, CVA should have already been calculated for the netting set. In the CVA calculation, the netting set value $V(t_k)$ at future time t_k is already evaluated as a function of the Markov process $V(t_k, x(t_k))$ (Fig. 10.1). This value is represented as an analytic function if LSM is used in CVA calculation (Fig. 10.2). It is a grid function if a grid is used in the calculation of CVA. In the driftless Markov process, the conditional probability distribution function from time t to t_k, $P(t, x(t); t_k, x(t_k))$, where $t \leq t_k$ is given in a simple closed form and the conditional expectation value $E[\max(V(t_k), 0)|F_t]$ is calculated by a numerically efficient method which is used in the calculation in a Markov Functional model.

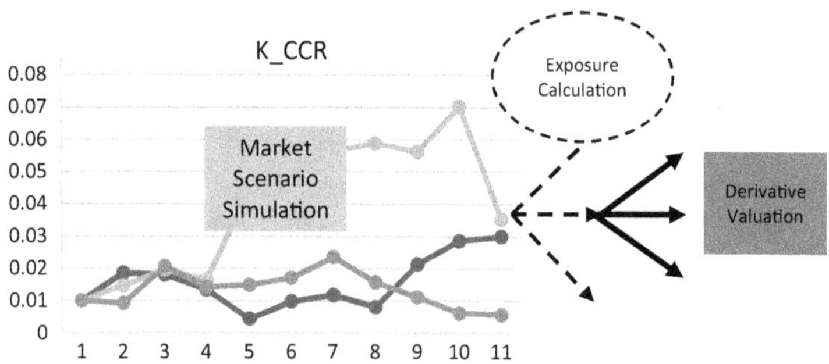

Fig. 10.1: CCR KVA calculation.

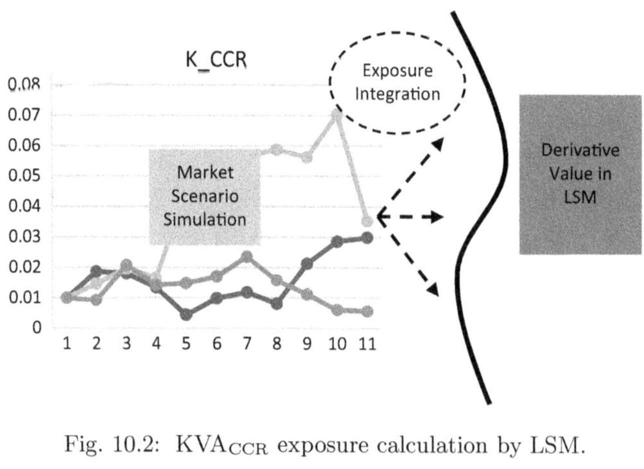

Fig. 10.2: KVA_{CCR} exposure calculation by LSM.

(For details about the efficient numerical calculation of conditional expectation values, see Pelsser (2000)).

In conclusion, calculation of exposure in KVA_{CCR} and KVA_{CVA} is done with extra numerical computations after calculation of CVA. In the finalized Basel III (or SA-CVA), CVA capital depends on market risk sensitivities of CVA and extra simulation is necessary but the calculation is done with the technique discussed in Section 10.2.

10.2. Calculation of KVA for Market Risk (Non-CVA Part of VAR/SVAR) and MVA

In this section, KVA_{Mkt} will be discussed. Typically in the trading book of an investment bank, market risk is hedged and market risk capital should be much smaller than notionals of the underlyings but is still significant due to leverage.

Market risk capital is given by VAR and Stressed VAR (currently) or ES (once Basel III comes into effect in January 2022) of the portfolio. Simply put, to calculate KVA_{Mkt} we need to perform simulations (generate scenarios) three times: for the expectation value of capital, the VAR or ES of capital and the valuation of each derivative in the portfolio (Fig. 10.3). Here, the dimension of VAR or ES (e.g. 10 buckets for yield curve sensitivities) is much larger than that of the underlying model (one or two factors). For the efficient calculation of VAR or ES in Monte Carlo simulation,

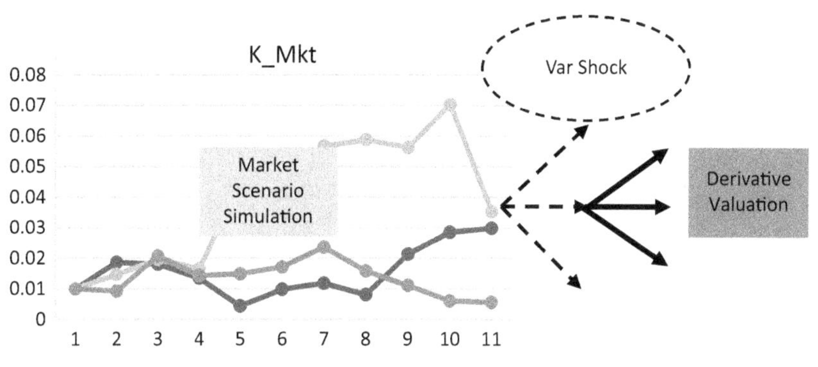

Fig. 10.3: Three times simulation for Mkt risk KVA.

Green and Kenyon (2015) introduced the Green–Kenyon Shocked State Augmentation (GKSSA) method and tested its application on an Interest Rate Swap portfolio.

For the calculation of $\mathrm{KVA}_{\mathrm{Mkt}}$, the portfolio can contain any kind of derivatives including Linear Products (like Interest Rate Swaps, FX Forwards, Cross-Currency Swaps), Plain Vanilla Options (like European Swaptions, CMS Caps, CMS Spread Options, FX Options) and MultiCallable Products (like Bermudan Swaptions, Callable CMS Spread Swaps, etc.). Here the calculation of $\mathrm{KVA}_{\mathrm{Mkt}}$ of Linear Products and Plain Vanilla Options will be discussed. Note that GKSSA can be applied to callable exotic derivatives also, but the convergence can be much worse.

Note that GKSSA is so named because the state space is augmented using historical shocks to risk factors. Here in our presentation for sensitivity-based VAR, augmentation of state space is not used. However, for convenience, we call it GKSSA.

Note that our illustration below is based on VAR, but almost all of the discussion will apply to ES as well.

The calculation of VAR inside of the Monte Carlo is common in MVA. In CCP MVA, typically Historical VAR is used, but the portfolio consists of Swaps and Plain Vanilla Swaptions, while in SIMM[1] MVA, sensitivity-based VAR is adopted but the portfolio can contain Swaptions and callable exotic derivatives in addition.

10.2.1. *GKSSA for sensitivity-based VAR*

GKSSA is a combination of the following ideas:

(a) Apply extra random shocks. Some of them can be orthogonal to state variable movements and the dimensionality of the model is increased.
(b) Apply LSM to evaluate VAR (or ES).

---

[1]The SIMM formula for independent initial margin takes sensitivities to risk factors as inputs and applies a fixed set of parameters (i.e. prescribed correlations and volatilities) to produce this amount. It can be interpreted as VAR based on sensitivities and certain assumed parameters for normal/log-normal risk factor distributions.

(c) Compress portfolio to a single set of regression function.
(d) Augment space of regression by using Historical shock as an extra random shock.

There are typically two types of VARs: one is sensitivity-based VAR and the other is Historical VAR.[2] In Historical VAR, VAR is calculated based on historical returns of market risk factors. Historical returns (movements) include large market shocks (especially in Stressed VAR), and large movements of the market are taken into account properly. On the other hand, in sensitivity-based VAR, we estimate VAR based on sensitivities (greeks) applied to risk factors generated from typically parametric distributions. Because sensitivities are based on infinitesimal movement of market risk factors, this approach can be inaccurate for a large market movement.

Here the discussion will be divided into two parts. First, we consider a sensitivity-based VAR. In this case, we do not need large VAR shock and (a)–(c) of GKSSAs above are used. The idea of augmentation which is relevant to Historical VAR will be discussed in Section 10.2.2.

We assume that a one-dimensional Markov interest rate model is used and valuation of the Plain Vanilla Swap and other European Swaptions on the Monte Carlo paths is done by analytical calculation. The arguments should be the same if we use other models including (low-dimensional) multifactor models.

In sensitivity-based VAR, VAR is explained by a large number of variables, namely around 10 buckets of deltas and vegas are used. That is, VAR is based on a multidimensional (10×2) problem. On the other hand, typical models used for interest rate dynamics of

[2]Strictly, there are two concepts: (1) distributional assumptions (i.e. parametric or historical) and (2) computation of VAR (i.e. sensitivities-based via Taylor expansion or full revaluation including the use of a grid). Usually, parametric distributions require a sensitivities-based approach because we need around 10,000 paths of risk factors; in contrast, historical distribution generally uses 260 business days of past shocks for VAR, so full revaluation (or enhanced by pre-computed grid) is possible. In the rest of the chapter, we avoid distinguishing these details further and assume that historical VAR is based on the full revaluation while sensitivities-based VAR has parametric distributions.

XVA are low-dimensional models. This discrepancy of difference in dimension makes application of LSM to VAR calculation difficult. In GKSSA, this discrepancy is resolved as follows.

In the KVA (SIMM MVA) calculation, we need to generate scenario paths of state variables. On each generated path, we will calculate sensitivities (Deltas and Vegas).

We assume to use the bump and revalue approach: that is, we bump yield curve points and volatilities in each bucket and revalue the portfolio. *Here, a one-dimensional model process represents the parallel movement of the yield curve and bumping of volatilities should be orthogonal to it.*

Orthogonality of Delta shock to state variable movements in the one-dimensional Markov model is illustrated in the following example. Let there be a portfolio which consists of a Payer Swap of length 5 years and a Forward Receiver Swap which starts in 5 years and ends in 10 years. The parallel Delta of this portfolio is close to 0 and state variable movements cannot capture any meaningful sensitivity of the portfolio to true market shocks. However, in Historical VAR if there is a large shock for the yield curve between the 5-year and 10-year portion, the portfolio can suffer a large loss in this shock and contribute to VAR significantly. To take into account these situations, we need to enhance the dimension of Delta movements also.

The issue about dimensionality is common for both Vega and Delta, but to illustrate the point more clearly we explain only the calculation of Vega.

At a given time grid t_j, the calculation of Vegas is schematically described as follows. Let Markov state variable (parallel movement of the yield curve) be represented by x and movement of volatility be represented by y. (Here 1 bucket is assumed for volatility.)

In the bump and revalue technique, the state variable and volatility for valuation are represented by Fig. 10.4. Here, filled circles represent Monte Carlo paths in the original valuation and white circles represent those corresponding to bumps.

Now we increase the number of buckets in volatility to 2 by introducing variable z which represents the volatility bump of

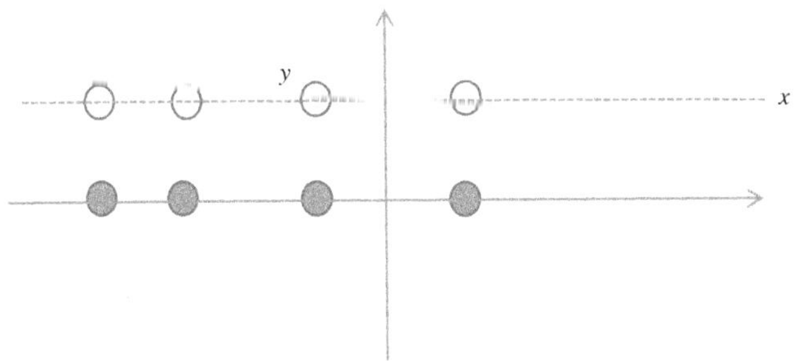

Fig. 10.4: Bump and revaluation on the Monte Carlo path.

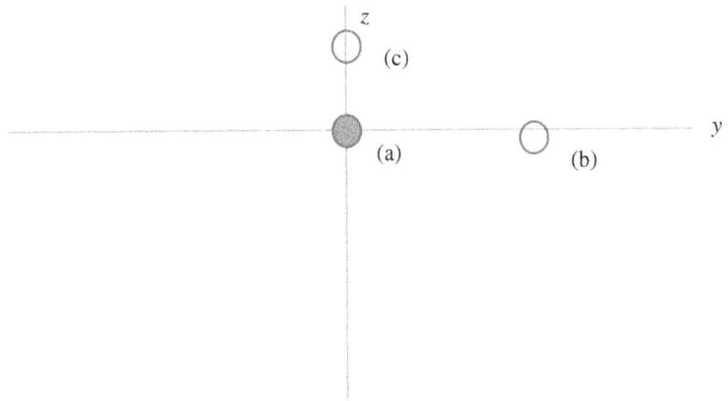

Fig. 10.5: Bump and revaluation with two buckets.

another bucket. Then when we see (x, y, z) space from the x direction, the (y, z) plane is given by Fig. 10.5.

As seen in Fig. 10.5, in the calculation of Vegas of two buckets, we need to calculate PV on three scenarios of volatilities. (Here one-sided bumping is assumed.) For example, to calculate Vega of y in direction $v(y + \delta, z) - v(y, z)$, we use points (a) and (b). As the number of buckets increases, the number of points to simulate increases. If there are n buckets of Vegas and the number of paths in the Monte Carlo simulation is N_{Path}, then the total number of paths needed is $N_{\text{Path}} \times (n + 1)$.

Here, in $(n + 1)$ scenarios, only two of them are used for each individual Vega calculation. *If we can use all of the $(n + 1)$ scenarios in all of the calculations of Vegas, the calculation can be more* *efficient.* This efficiency is realized as follows for the two Vegas bucket cases:

(1) For each Monte Carlo path, the random shock is applied to two variables of volatilities (y, z) on top of the random Markov state variable x. This random shock other than the state variable process is called *extra random shock* henceforth. That is, 3D random variables are generated as (x_i, y_i, z_i) $(i = 1, \ldots, N_{\text{Path}})$. Here, both random variables y and z are generated from arbitrary distributions like the normal or uniform distribution. Because we are interested in sensitivity, both y and z should be close to 0.
(2) On each of the generated path (x_i, y_i, z_i), we calculate the portfolio value $v(x_i, y_i, z_i)$. Here, the function $v(x, y, z)$ is evaluated analytically or by a simple numerical calculation.
(3) Conduct a 3D regression with explanatory variables (x_i, y_i, z_i) and dependent variable being the portfolio value $v(x_i, y_i, z_i)$. The regressed function $\bar{v}(x, y, z)$ is used as a functional form of the portfolio value as a function of three variables. Vegas on the path are given from the partial derivative of the regressed function. That is, Vega of bucket y is given by $\partial \bar{v}(x, y, z)/\partial y$. Note that even for typical nonlinear Plain Vanilla products such as the European Swaption, Vega should depend on whether it is ITM, ATM or OTM strongly. To take into effect the dependence of Vega on forward level (x), we need cross terms in the regression such as xy, x^2y, x^3y, x^4y. Note that the cross term should include higher degree polynomials in the state variable x but should be linear in the extra shock y because we are interested in a minimal bump of volatility.
(4) From the sensitivity, calculated in (3), we compute VAR and capital $K(t_j)$ for the given Markov state x at time t_j.
(5) Compute expectation value of the capital $E[K(t_j)]$ by averaging $K(t_j)$ for all of the Monte Carlo paths.

In the actual calculation of capital, the number of buckets in Vega and Delta is of the order $O(10)$. We can generalize the above methodology to the higher-dimensional case.

In the above algorithm, model volatility (not market volatility) will be bumped. However, for most of the simple models such as the Hull–White model, model volatility has, at least approximately, a simple relationship to normal or log-normal market volatility (For example, with respect to the Hull–White model, see Tan (2012)). Therefore, we can map model Vega to Market Vega.

Note that for the Delta calculation, bumping of the yield curve needs to be done independent of the Markov process x. This is illustrated in the Hull–White model as follows:

> In the Hull–White model, the discount factor observed at t for maturity T when the Markov state variable is x is given by
>
> $$D(t,T,x) = \frac{D(0,t)}{D(0,T)} \exp\left(-\frac{\Xi(t)}{2}(B^2(t,S) - B^2(T,S)) + B(t,T)x\right)$$
>
> in the S forward measure. An extra shock for Delta is given to the factor $D(0,T)$ and the Delta shock can be independent of the state variable movement.

The above argument about sensitivity-based VAR is intended to illustrate the necessity of increasing dimension for the calculation of VAR or ES on the Monte Carlo simulation. In practice, sometimes we can use an analytic formula to calculate the sensitivity of Plain Vanilla products. In this situation, we do not need the above algorithm. However, in most of the cases, Historical VAR or ES is used in the calculation of capital in the Internal Model Approach to market risk. The logic is naturally extendible to Historical VAR or ES calculation, as will be discussed in Section 10.2.2.

In Green and Kenyon (2015), the authors apply GKSSA to a swap portfolio. The Swap is a linear derivative and they use a first-degree polynomial in the regression (they use both the Swap Rate and Annuity as explanatory variables to capture nonlinearity of the Swap portfolio), but for nonlinear derivatives like the European Swaption, we need to adopt a higher degree polynomial. As noted in Green and Kenyon (2015), GKSSA is not suitable for callable derivatives because it distorts the volatility.

10.2.2. *GKSSA for Historical VAR (or ES)*

When sensitivity-based VAR is used, the random shock of volatility is small but when Historical VAR is adopted, we need a significant movement to have an accurate result. Especially when ES is adopted as in FRTB under Basel III, capturing large movement is essential. Green and Kenyon introduced large shocks to LSM and developed GKSSA. In GKSSA, they use Historical shocks as an extra random shock instead of small perturbation in sensitivity-based VAR. This ensures that the regression is carried out in a large enough space to capture tail effect in VAR (and ES).

In their methodology, for each Monte Carlo path given by a state variable x_i ($i = 1, \ldots, N$), they apply one of the Historical shocks and generate scenarios of yield curve and volatility. On the generated scenario, the portfolio value v_i is calculated. Regression is done between explanatory variables which represent the scenario and value v_i. Note that in this case, to capture the nonlinear movement of the portfolio value, the regression function should be a nonlinear function of not only the state variable but also the extra shocks.

Historical VAR (or ES) on each path is calculated by applying Historical shocks. Here because the portfolio is compressed and valuation is reduced to regressed functions which is typically a polynomial, the calculation burden is reduced significantly.

The application of LSAC to historical VAR is tested in Sections 10.4.4 and 10.4.5.

10.3. KVA of FRTB CVA (Standardized Approach)

In FRTB, banks which meet some criteria can calculate their CVA capital with FRTB CVA. Here the Standardized Approach (SA-CVA) is necessary for any bank which adopts FRTB CVA. In SA-CVA, capital requirement is based on sensitivity-based VAR and we need to calculate sensitivities on the paths of Monte Carlo simulation. Here, sensitivity (Delta, Vega) to market risk factors are necessary. Therefore, we need to calculate sensitivity of regulatory CVA (exposure) on Monte Carlo paths.

We can calculate sensitivities of exposures for non-callable derivatives by combining GKSSA in Section 10.2 and exposure calculation as explained earlier in the chapter. Let $E(t,T) = E[\max(V(T),0)|F_t]$ be an exposure of time T observed at t. To calculate sensitivities, we need to calculate the exposure when a (bucket of) market risk factor y_j is bumped, i.e. $E^{y_j}(t,T)$. Here the market factor y_j can affect both the portfolio value $V(T)$ and the distribution of the state variable from time t to T. In the typical model, when the market factor is after T, it affects only $V(T)$ and if it is from t to T, it affects only distribution of the state variables. Therefore, $E^{y_j}(t,T)$ can be calculated as follows:

Apply GKSSA to portfolio value at T and generate the value with market factor y_j bumped as a function of state variable $V^{y_j}(T, x(T))$.

Calculate conditional expectation value when market risk factor y_j is bumped, i.e. $E^{y_j}(t,T) = E[\max(V^{y_j}(T),0)|F_t]$.

10.4. Numerical Example of Calculation of Market Risk KVA

Our methodology to calculate sensitivity-based VAR of a portfolio by Monte Carlos simulation (GKSSA) is tested for an interest rate derivatives portfolio. We use a one factor Hull–White model for the test.

10.4.1. *Test 1*

Here we tested application of GKSSA for the calculation of Vegas on Monte Carlo paths. In Test 1, we analyze basic effectiveness of GKSSA for multiple buckets of Vegas. The assumption for the test is listed in Table 10.1 and the portfolio is given in Table 10.2. Strikes of the swaps are generated randomly.

Here, Monte Carlo paths are segregated into three groups depending on the value of the Markov variable at observation time, namely lowest 10%, medium 80% and highest 10%. Regression is done in this group independently with the constraints that the regression function matches at the boundaries of the groups. This grouping makes LSM very stable.

Table 10.1: The settings of Test 1.

Vega observation date	2 years
Vega buckets	[2,3], [3,4], [4,5], [5,6], [6,7] years
Spot rate	1.0%
Base volatility	0.5%
Number of paths	10,000
State variable	x
Extra shock for volatility bucket j ($j = 1, \ldots, 5$)	$y[j]$
Regression function	$a_0 + a_1x + a_2x^2 + a_3x^3 + a_4x^4 + \sum_{j=1}^{5} y[j]\{b_{j0} + b_{j1}x + b_{j2}x^2 + b_{j3}x^3 + b_{j4}x^4\}$
jth Vega	$b_{j0} + b_{j1}x + b_{j2}x^2 + b_{j3}x^3 + b_{j4}x^4$

Table 10.2: The portfolio consists of the following coterminal swaptions.

	Start	End	Strike	Pay/Receive	Long/Short	Notional
Swaption 1	3 Years	10 Years	0.017915	Payer	Long	1
Swaption 2	4 Years	10 Years	0.008067	Payer	Short	1
Swaption 3	5 Years	10 Years	0.006644	Payer	Long	1
Swaption 4	6 Years	10 Years	0.014432	Payer	Short	1
Swaption 5	7 Years	10 Years	0.018467	Payer	Long	1

Here, the state variable follows a drift-less Markov process $x(t)$, where $dx(t) = \tilde{\sigma}(t)dW(t)$. The volatility $\tilde{\sigma}(t)$ is bumped in the Vega calculation. Note that $\tilde{\sigma}(t)$ is approximately proportional to the normal volatility of the swaption.

The Vega for each bucket is given in Figs. 10.6–10.10. Here, the large dots represent Vegas from GKSSA and the small dots are Vegas from the bump and revalue approach.

The results indicate that the GKSSA technique is basically suitable for calculation of multibuckets of Vegas on Monte Carlo paths. We can see that Vegas from GKSSA fit to those of the bump and revalue approach on most of the domain.

10.4.2. *Test 2*

In Test 1, for each Vega bucket, there is one swaption whose expiry falls into it. In the actual portfolio, there are many swaptions for

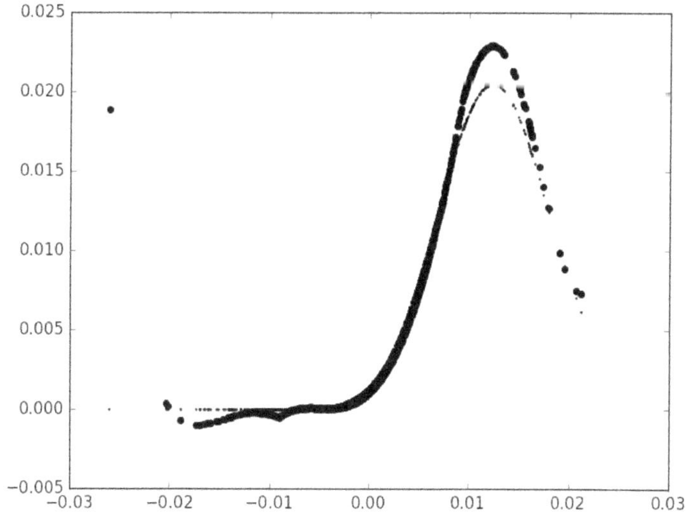

Fig. 10.6: Bucket 1.

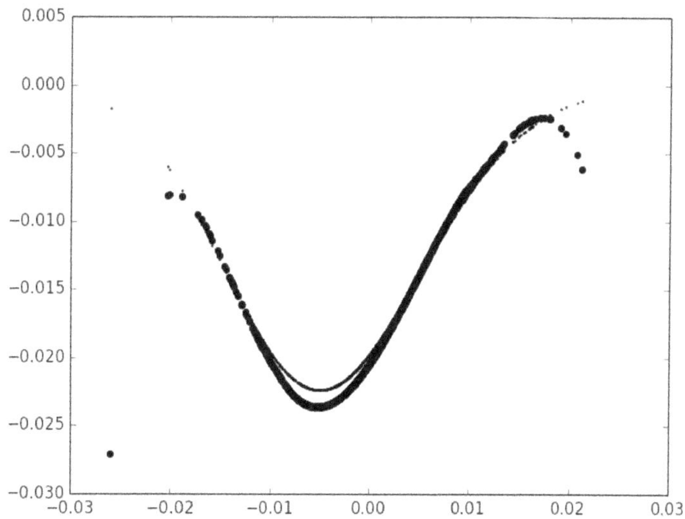

Fig. 10.7: Bucket 2.

each Vega bucket. In Test 2, we analyze the effect of many swaptions on the stability of GKSSA. Here, there are 10 swaptions for the Vega bucket of 3 years (1 year from observation date). In actual portfolios, the number of swaptions for the bucket is likely to be much larger,

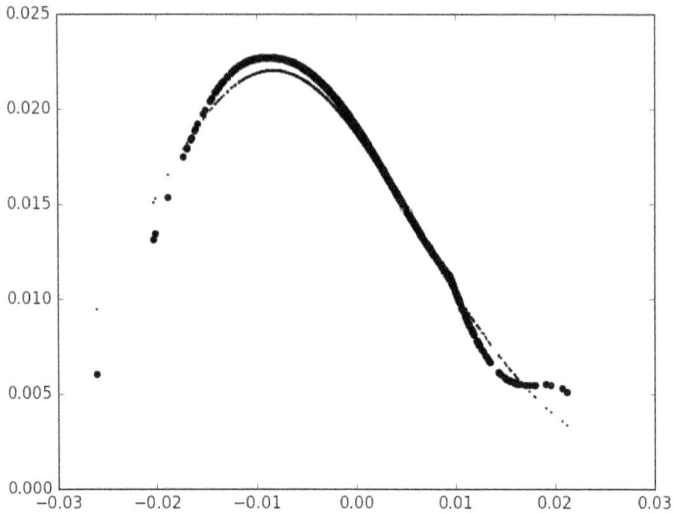

Fig. 10.8: Bucket 3.

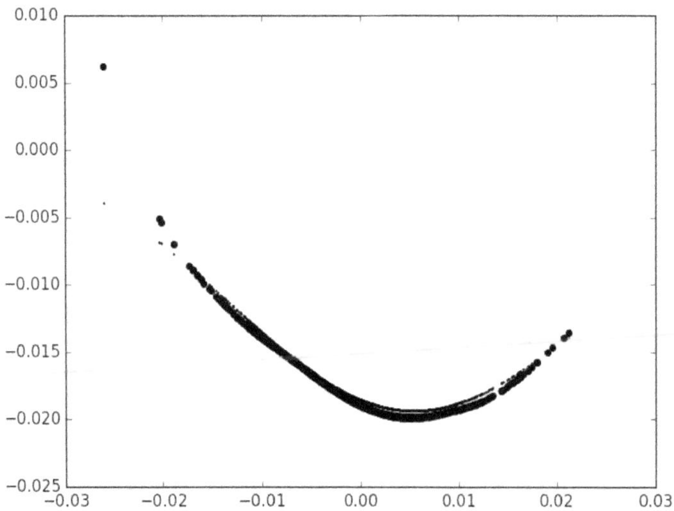

Fig. 10.9: Bucket 4.

but with the assumption that 10 swaptions approximate the behavior well. Here we analyze only one Vega bucket. In this portfolio, half of them are long positions and the other half are short positions.

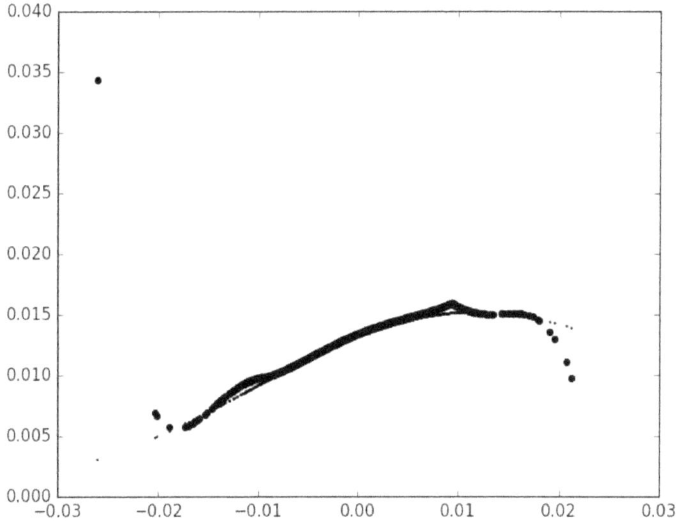

Fig. 10.10: Bucket 5.

Table 10.3: The setting of Test 2.

Vega observation date	2 years
Vega bucket	[2,3] years
Regression function	$a_0 + a_1x + a_2x^2 + a_3x^3 + a_4x^4$ $+\sum_{j=1}^{1} y[j]\{b_{j0} + b_{j1}x + b_{j2}x^2$ $+ b_{j3}x^3 + b_{j4}x^4\}$

Notional and strike is generated by uniform random numbers to simulate an actual portfolio (Table 10.4).

The results are as in Fig. 10.11.

The results indicate that increasing the number of swaptions in the same bucket will not deteriorate the convergence of LSM.

10.4.3. *Test 3*

In Test 3, GKSSA is applied to Deltas of a swaption portfolio. Here the portfolio consists of swaptions with expiries 3, 4 and 5 years. The setting of the regression is given in Table 10.5.

Figures 10.12–10.16 are comparisons of Deltas between GKSSA and the bump and revalue approach. Small dots correspond to the

Table 10.4: Portfolio for Test 2.

	Start	End	Strike	Pay/Receive	Long/Short	Notional
Swaption 1	3 Years	10 Years	0.023511	Payer	Long	0.797645
Swaption 2	3 Years	10 Years	0.008793	Payer	Short	0.722771
Swaption 3	3 Years	10 Years	0.005614	Payer	Long	0.800891
Swaption 4	3 Years	10 Years	0.006109	Payer	Short	0.071083
Swaption 5	3 Years	10 Years	0.014825	Payer	Long	0.8775
Swaption 6	3 Years	10 Years	0.015493	Payer	Long	0.606841
Swaption 7	3 Years	10 Years	0.024348	Payer	Short	0.274043
Swaption 8	3 Years	10 Years	0.016876	Payer	Long	0.518774
Swaption 9	3 Years	10 Years	0.019174	Payer	Short	0.568892
Swaption 10	3 Years	10 Years	0.016886	Payer	Long	0.951844

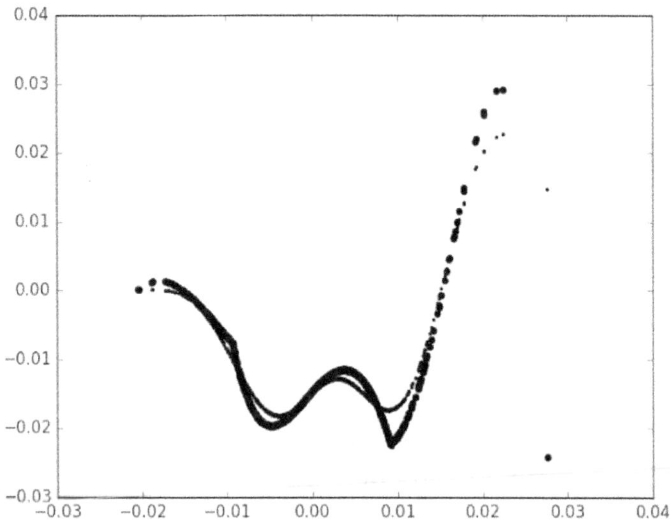

Fig. 10.11: Test 2.

bump and revalue results and large dots correspond to results from GKSSA. The graphs indicates that LSAC reproduce Deltas of the bump and revalue approach well.

Note that Fig. 10.15 gives unstable Deltas but this graph corresponds to a bucket of 5–6 years. This bucket should affect the value of the portfolio only through discounting and Deltas are small, so it will not affect KVA much.

Table 10.5: The setting of Test 3.

Delta observation date	2 years
Delta buckets	[2,3], [3,4], [4,5], [5,6], [6,7] years
Base spot rate	1.0%
Volatility	0.5%
Number of paths	10,000
State variable	x
Extra shock for rate bucket j ($j = 1, \ldots, 5$)	$y[j]$
Regression function	$a_0 + a_1x + a_2x^2 + a_3x^3 + a_4x^4 + \sum_{j=1}^{5} y[j]\{b_{j0} + b_{j1}x + b_{j2}x^2 + b_{j3}x^3 + b_{j4}x^4\}$
j^{th} Vega	$b_{j0} + b_{j1}x + b_{j2}x^2 + b_{j3}x^3 + b_{j4}x^4$

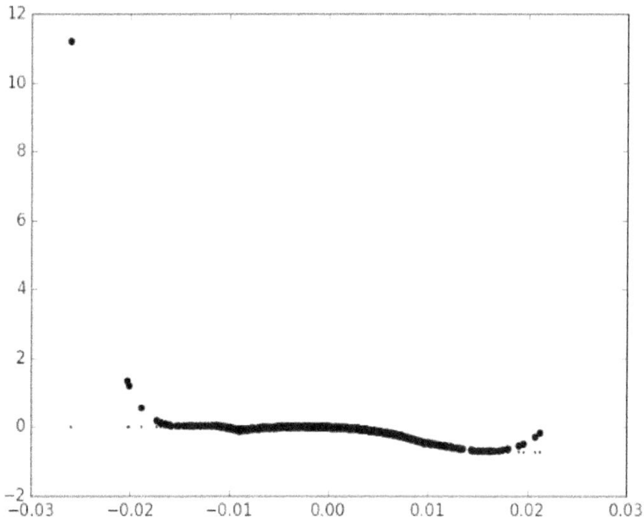

Fig. 10.12: First bucket.

10.4.4. *Test 4*

In the previous tests, sensitivities (Deltas and Vegas) are calculated by LSAC and the results are compared with the ones calculated by the bump and revalue approach. In the Internal Model Approach for market risk capital, Historical VAR is more commonly used than sensitivity VAR. To apply GKSSA to the Historical VAR approach,

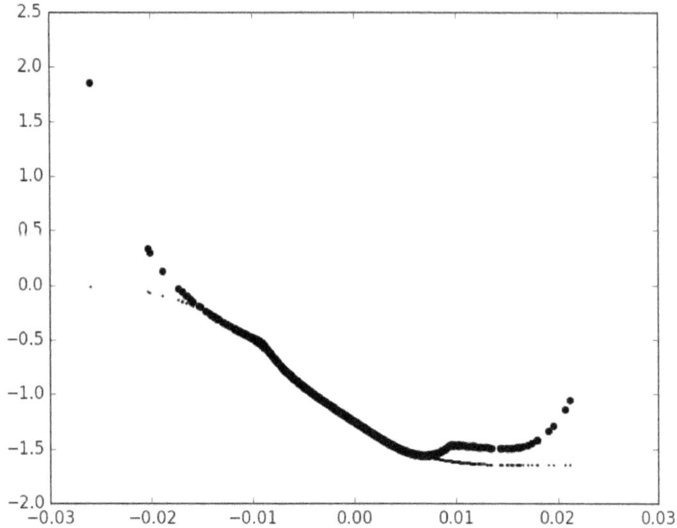

Fig. 10.13: Second bucket.

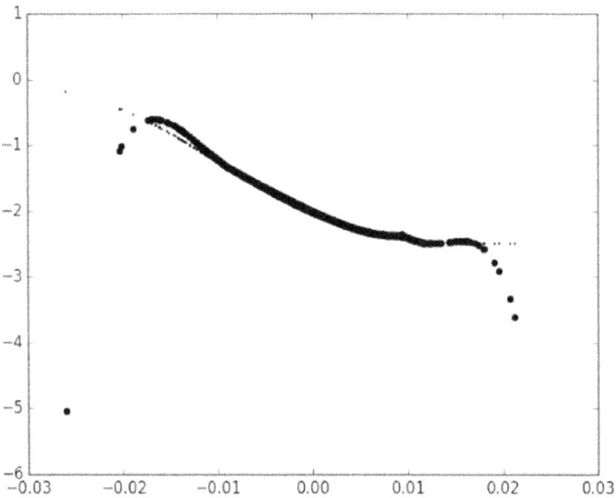

Fig. 10.14: Third bucket.

we need to check the applicability of GKSSA for large nonlinear market movements. To test this, we adopt a polynomial of degree 3 instead of degree 1 in the extra random shock to capture the

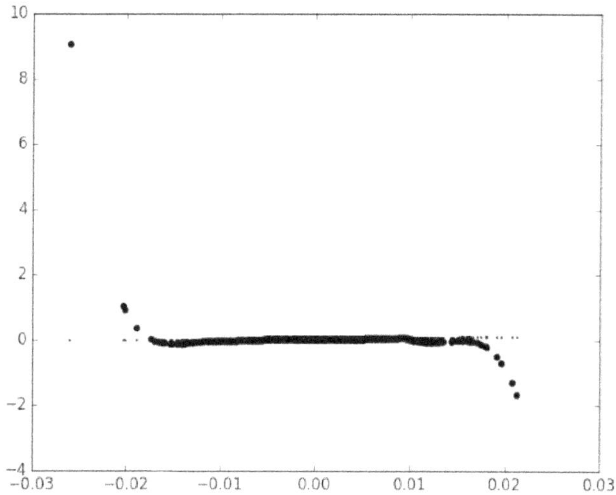

Fig. 10.15: Fourth bucket.

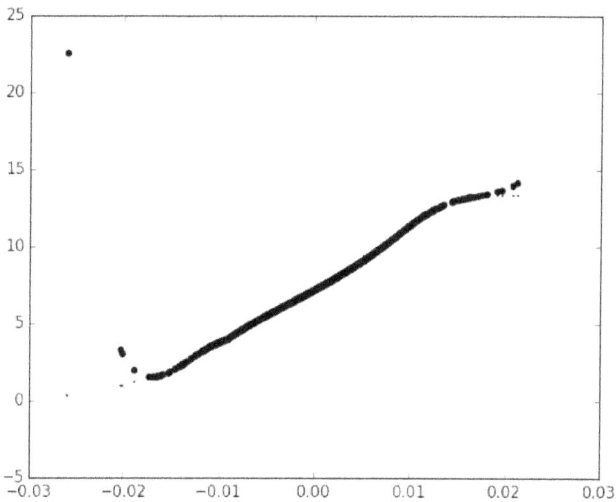

Fig. 10.16: Fifth bucket.

nonlinear nature of derivatives. In Test 4, there is one yield curve bucket.

LSM is conducted in the scenario given in Table 10.6.

Figure 10.17 is a scatter plot between the state variable x and the swap rate which starts in 3 years and ends in 7 years. You can

Table 10.6: The setting of Test 4.

Number of paths	1,000
Yield curve bucket	3 years
State variable	x
Regression function	$a_0 + a_1x + a_2x^2 + a_3x^3 + a_4x^4$ $+ \sum_{k=1}^{3} \sum_{j=1}^{2} y[j]^k \{b_{j0}^k$ $+ b_{j1}^k x + b_{j2}^k x^2 + b_{j3}^k x^3 + b_{j4}^k x^4\}$

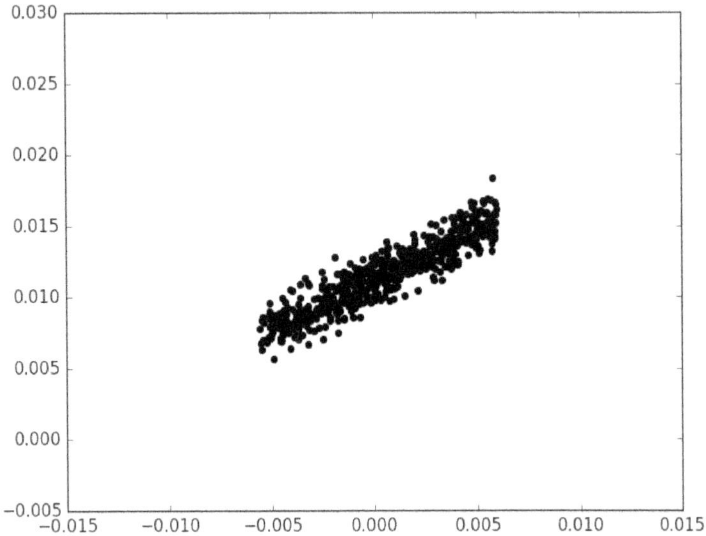

Fig. 10.17: Scatter plot between state variable and swap rate.

see that the extra random shock is sufficiently large to deviate from the swap rate.

Figure 10.18 is a 3D scatter plot with horizontal axes representing the state variable x and the extra random shock $y[1]$, while the vertical axis represents PV. Large dots give PV from the regression function and small dots represent the difference between the regression function and actual PV. The graph indicates that the regression function approximates actual PVs well in most of the area.

In Fig. 10.19, the data is represented in a 2D scatter plot where the horizontal axis represents the state variable and the vertical axis represents PV. (The extra random shock is degenerated.)

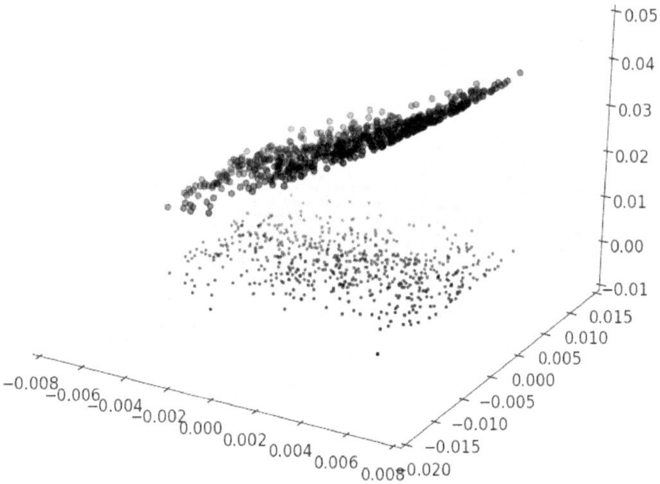

Fig. 10.18: 3D scatter plot of PVs and errors.

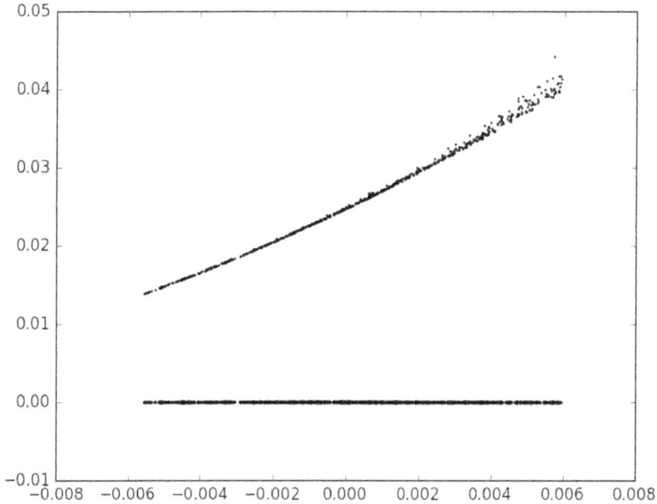

Fig. 10.19: 2D scatter plot of PVs and errors.

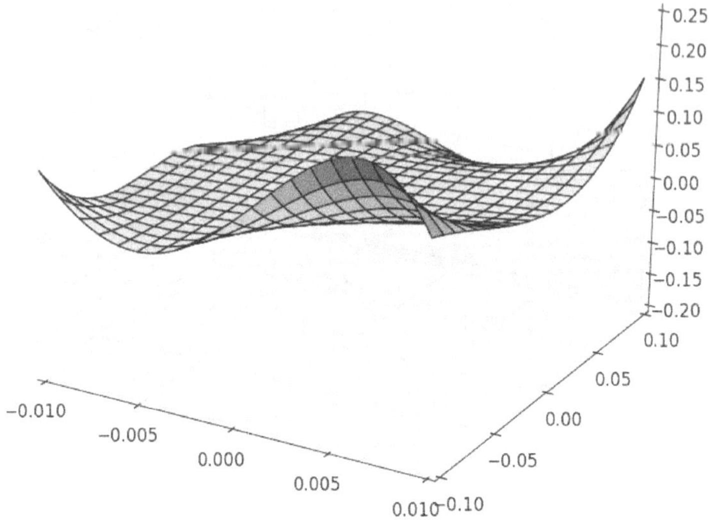

Fig. 10.20: 3D plots of the estimates surface.

Here large dots represent actual PV and small dots represents the quantity (actual PV − PV from the regression). You can see that the fitting error of the regression is almost negligible in most of the paths.

Figure 10.20 is 3D plots of the estimated surfaces of buckets 1 and 2, respectively. Here, the horizontal axes represent the state variable and the extra random shocks and the vertical axis represents estimated PV.

10.4.5. *Test 5*

In Test 5, to check the effectiveness of GKSSA in the multibucket case, the number of buckets is increased to two and the other conditions are the same as in Test 4.

In Fig. 10.21, as in Fig. 10.19, large dots represent actual PV and small dots represent the difference between actual PV and estimated PV. Because extra random shocks are applied to two buckets (3 years

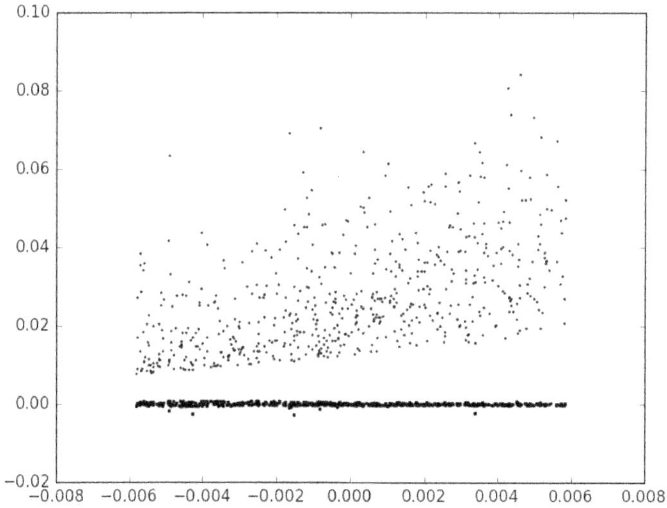

Fig. 10.21: 2D plot and error.

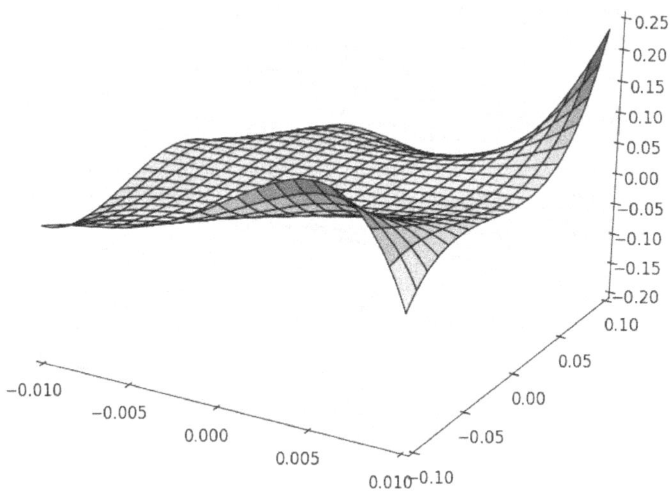

Fig. 10.22: Estimated surface for 3 years.

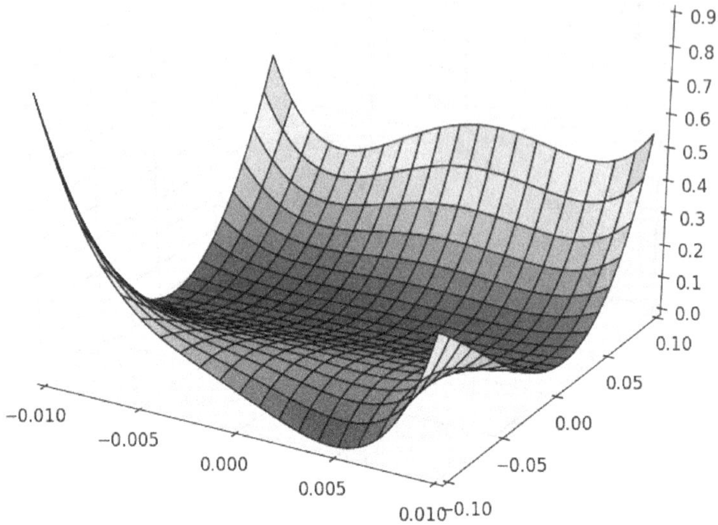

Fig. 10.23: Estimated surface for 4 years.

and 4 years), the deviation of PV as a function of state variable x is large but the fitting error (PV – estimated PV) is negligible.

Figures 10.22 and 10.23 give 3D plots of PV estimated by regression. In Fig. 10.22, the horizontal axes are the state variable and the extra shock $y[1]$, where in Fig. 10.23, the axes are the state variable and the extra shock $y[2]$.

10.5. Bucketing in LSM

In our test of GKSSA, Monte Carlo paths are bucketed into three buckets to have stable results. The methodology of bucketing for the case of Test 1 will be summarized here. Let paths be sorted in state variable x in ascending order and divided into three sets, namely higher 10%, mid 80% and lower 10%. LSM is done for the mid paths only. That is, for the mid bucket, we solve the following minimization problem:

$$\min_{\text{params}} \sum_{x_m \in \text{mid paths}} \left\{ a_0^C + a_1^C x_m + a_2^C x_m^2 + a_3^C x_m^3 + a_4^C x_m^4 \right.$$
$$\left. + \sum_{j=1}^{5} y[j]_m \{ b_{j0}^C + b_{j1}^C x_m + b_{j2}^C x_m^2 + b_{j3}^C x_m^3 + b_{j4}^C x_m^4 \} - v_m \right\}^2$$

where x_m recovers the mid bucket of the Monte Carlo simulation and v_m is the value of portfolio.

Now we have the regression function as follows:

$$a_0^C + a_1^C x + a_2^C x^2 + a_3^C x^3 + a_4^C x^4$$
$$+ \sum_{j=1}^{5} y[j] \{ b_{j0}^C + b_{j1}^C x + b_{j2}^C x^2 + b_{j3}^C x^3 + b_{j4}^C x^4 \}$$

Here, superscript C means center of the buckets.

Next, LSM for the higher bucket is done such that the regression function matches that of the center bucket at the boundary between these two buckets. That is, the regression function for the higher bucket is

$$a_0^H + a_1^H x + a_2^H x^2 + a_3^H x^3 + a_4^H x^4$$
$$+ \sum_{j=1}^{5} y[j] \{ b_{j0}^H + b_{j1}^H x + b_{j2}^H x^2 + b_{j3}^H x^3 + b_{j4}^H x^4 \}$$

Let state variable paths for the center bucket and the higher bucket be respectively, $(x_m, \ldots, x_n)$ and $(x_{n+1}, \ldots, x_N)$.

The following equations should hold:

$$a_0^C + a_1^C x_n + a_2^C x_n^2 + a_3^C x_n^3 + a_4^C x_n^4$$
$$= a_0^H + a_1^H x_n + a_2^H x_n^2 + a_3^H x_n^3 + a_4^H x_n^4$$
$$b_{j0}^C + b_{j1}^C x_n + b_{j2}^C x_n^2 + b_{j3}^C x_n^3 + b_{j4}^C x_n^4$$
$$= b_{j0}^H + b_{j1}^H x_n + b_{j2}^H x_n^2 + b_{j3}^H x_n^3 + b_{j4}^H x_n^4 \quad (j = 1, \ldots 5)$$

such that the regression function is continuous in state variable irrespective of the value $y[j]$. That is, the degree of freedom is reduced by 6 (the number of constraints). Here the left-hand sides of the above relationships are already given after the regression function of the center bucket is given. So let

$$\alpha = a_0^C + a_1^C x_n + a_2^C x_n^2 + a_3^C x_n^3 + a_4^C x_n^4$$
$$\beta_j = b_{j0}^C + b_{j1}^C x_n + b_{j2}^C x_n^2 + b_{j3}^C x_n^3 + b_{j4}^C x_n^4$$

By substituting the above relationship for a_0^H and b_{j0}^H $(j = 1, \ldots, 5)$, the minimization problem for the higher bucket is

$$\min_{\text{params}} \sum_{x_n \in \text{higher paths}} \Bigg\{ \alpha - [a_1^H x_n + a_2^H x_n^2 + a_3^H x_n^3 + a_4^H x_n^4] + a_1^H x_m + a_2^H x_m^2 + a_3^H x_m^3 + a_4^H x_m^4 + \sum_{j=1}^{5} y[j]_m \{\beta_j - [b_{j1}^H x_n + b_{j2}^H x_n^2 + b_{j3}^H x_n^3 + b_{j4}^H x_n^4] + b_{j1}^H x_m + b_{j2}^H x_m^2 + b_{j3}^H x_m^3 + b_{j4}^H x_m^4\} - v_m \Bigg\}^2$$

That is, the problem we need to solve is

$$\min_{\text{params}} \sum_{x_n \in \text{higher paths}} \Bigg\{ a_1^H (x_m - x_n) + a_2^H (x_m^2 - x_n^2) + a_3^H (x_m^3 - x_n^3) + a_4^H (x_m^4 - x_n^4) + \sum_{j=1}^{5} y[j]_m \{b_{j1}^H (x_m - x_n) + b_{j2}^H (x_m^2 - x_n^2) + b_{j3}^H (x_m^3 - x_n^3) + b_{j4}^H (x_m^4 - x_n^4)\} - v_m + \alpha + \sum\nolimits_{j=1}^{5} y[j]_m \beta_j \Bigg\}^2$$

where minimization is done for the parameters a_i^H and $b_{ji}^H (i = 1, \ldots, 4 \text{ and } j = 1, \ldots, 5)$.

Part IV

Managing XVA

Chapter 11

CVA Hedging, Default Arrangements and Implications for XVA Modeling

Derivatives pricing has been based on the idealized world where arbitrage can be eliminated by locking in a payoff via other instruments. Among other things, this assumes the existence of deep markets where actions of a participant will not move the market, the ability to borrow and lend at the same rate, and that market variables are continuous. Whereas in practice, none of the above strictly hold, derivatives pricing still works in general because the above "approximately" holds.

In the realm of CVA, we shall see that we are working in a far less efficient market. And this must be taken into account when considering implications for pricing.

11.1. Hedgeability of CVA

Theoretically, CVA can be hedged by buying protection via single-name CDS on the counterparty to which we are exposed. Practically, we need to consider that there is credit risk of the seller of the CDS, so we are still exposed to joint default (of counterparty and protection seller).

However, in practice, we run into the difficulty that the market for single-name CDS concentrates at the 5-year term with limited supply for longer maturities. And in any case, the reference names for CDS tends to be limited to the larger corporations (mainly located in North America, and some in Europe). Further, with the high capital charge of CDS trading and restrictive regulatory environment these days, many financial institutions have exited the business of single-name CDS (Green, 2016). This restricts the supply of single-name CDS, and in any case means pricing is less competitive. So hedging via single-name CDS is expensive if at all possible for various counterparties. The methodology to estimate the credit spread of the illiquid issuer by regression is introduced by Chourdakis *et al.* (2013).

An alternative is to seek to sell corporate bonds on the counterparty, but there are again restrictions in doing so: first, regulators are concerned about the effect on the health of corporates, and second, there is always the natural limitation that you can only sell as much notional of bonds as have been issued. And corporate bonds are not very liquid, so such hedging is costly. Overall, hedging CVA by selling corporate bonds is generally not a very viable solution either.

An approach taken is to hedge via CDS indices, for which a far more liquid market exists. However, there is a huge basis risk assumed, since a counterparty can default due to its own peculiarities even if the whole market is unaffected. Thus, hedging via CDS indices can at best be a proxy which protects an institution from heavy losses in a systemic market crash as opposed to an effective means of protecting the institution under normal conditions if it has exposure to a large counterparty. The details of quantitative analysis of hedging credit risk by index is discussed in Section 2.5.

We have remarked earlier in Chapter 6 that warehousing CVA risk attracts a different capital treatment to hedging via CDS. We will not discuss this any further here.

11.1.1. *Real-world pricing*

The lack of an effective means to hedge CVA brings us to the fundamental question of whether to price via the risk-neutral Q measure (as for derivatives) or the real-world P measure.

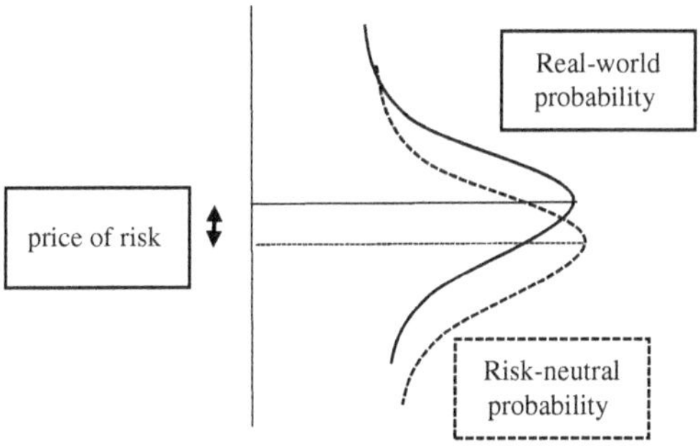

Fig. 11.1: Real-world measure and risk-neutral measure.

Practically, we can recall the example adapted from Baxter and Rennie (1996) about two horses A and B with probabilities of winning of 70% and 30%, respectively. If a bookmaker however finds 60% of customers wanting to bet on A winning and 40% wanting to bet on B winning, it should offer odds based on these percentages since effectively the customers betting on A winning will pay off those betting on B winning. The actual real-world probabilities do not matter. But the hedging cost is what becomes risk-neutral probabilities. This is the essence of much of derivatives pricing.

However, it only holds if you can hedge. Otherwise, realistically the real-world probabilities must apply. This appears to be the case for many counterparties when considering CVA calculations (Kenyon and Green, 2016).

Theoretically, going from the real-world measure to the risk-neutral measure involves a change in drift where the "price of risk" is eliminated, but there is no change in vol (Fig. 11.1). More practically, looking at the real-world however seems to involve using historical data[1] to estimate the vols and correlations of market risk factors (such as 1-year, 5-year, and 10-year USD swap rates, S&P closes, EURUSD spot). For example, say we have daily time series for market risk factors $\{X_i^j\}$, then we can compute their returns $\{R_i^j\} = \{X_{i+1}^j - X_i^j\}$ and subsequently take the empirical estimate of standard deviation $\{R_i^j\}$ and correlation of $\{R_i^j, R_i^k\}_{j \neq k}$.

[1]There can be an argument that the past does not need to repeat itself, so even claiming that the real-world measure should be based on historical returns is not necessarily valid.

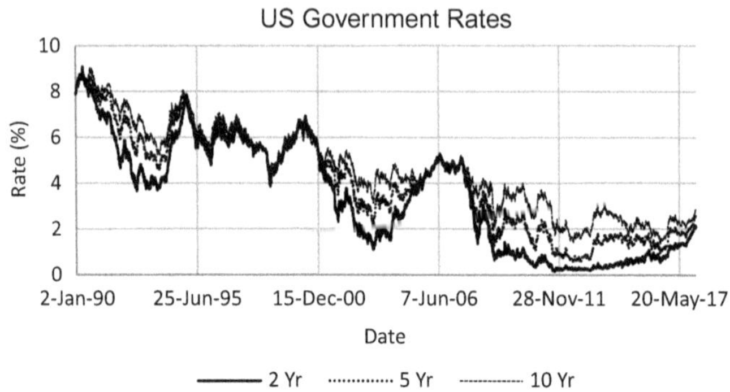

Fig. 11.2: US Government Bond rates.

Naturally, this leads to the question as to what period of history is relevant. Some have argued for using only recent history to consider only the current regime. For example, USD interest rates from 1979 to 1980 peaked close to 20% before going on a long decline thereafter. Throughout the 1990s, rates then dropped to below 5% and since 2001 have stayed far below that, briefly rising to about 5% from 2007 to 2008 before collapsing to near-zero levels today (Fig. 11.2). What part of history is relevant? The last year, the last 3 years, the last 5 years, or the last 10 years? Some have argued against using long history of the past because of changes in technology, geopolitics, the business environment, etc. But this argument is not just a philosophical matter. When ratings agencies considered credit ratings to give to subprime CDOs, they were partly encouraged that house prices had not dropped nationally in US for a 20-year period prior to 2005. Does it mean we need longer than 20 years of history?

11.1.2. *Practical and policy issues of using real-world measures*

From a practical perspective, using the real-world measure requires doing CVA by generating scenarios under a real-world measure, and then doing the valuation under the risk-neutral measure. This cannot be done in a single self-consistent valuation. There are some possibilities, such as using analytical formulae for valuation given the generated scenarios. Alternatively, the computation could be

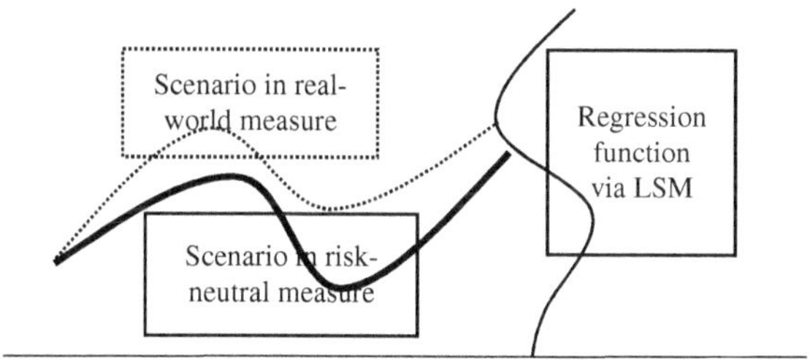

Fig. 11.3: Ideas of mixed real-world vs risk-neutral valuation.

done via pre-generating prices for different scenarios under the risk-neutral measure, and then using Least Squares Monte Carlo to obtain predictor functions, which we can then apply our real-world scenarios to (Fig. 11.3). In any case, care has to be taken that the valuation at the relevant point is under the correct measure.

Apart from the potential computational expense, a bigger implication on the use of the real-world measure for CVA is on the implications for fair value. The best way to illustrate this is by considering an example. Consider the Hull–White model $dr_t = \kappa\left(\theta\left(t\right) - r_t\right)dt + \sigma dW_t$, where our interest is in the long-run mean $\theta\left(t\right)$. Given our earlier discussion on pricing in the risk-neutral world, we should recognize that in a pricing model $\theta\left(t\right)$ is generally whatever is necessary to match the discount curve today. Specifically, note that in order to match the discount curve $D\left(0,t\right)$ today, we require

$$\theta\left(t\right) = -\frac{1}{D\left(0,t\right)}\frac{\partial D\left(0,t\right)}{\partial t} + \frac{1}{\kappa}\left[\left(\frac{1}{D\left(0,t\right)}\frac{\partial D\left(0,t\right)}{\partial t}\right)^2 - \frac{1}{D\left(0,t\right)}\frac{\partial^2 D\left(0,t\right)}{\partial t^2}\right] + \frac{\sigma^2}{2\kappa}\left(1 - \exp\left(-2\kappa t\right)\right) \quad \text{for all } t$$

Suppose instead we are interested in using the actual long-run mean for $\hat{\theta}(t)$ say based on history or long-term forecasts. Then it follows that we would not recover the prices of interest rate instruments today. Specifically, consider the current yield curve environment in 2016 with near-zero interest rates in EUR across all maturities and negative rates in the short end. Then we get the following rather ridiculous looking long-run mean $\theta(t)$ as in Fig. 11.4. Now suppose

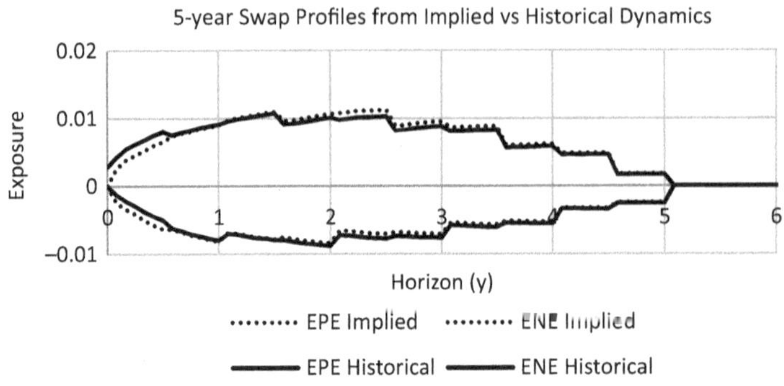

Fig. 11.4: Implied vs historical dynamics 5-year swap.

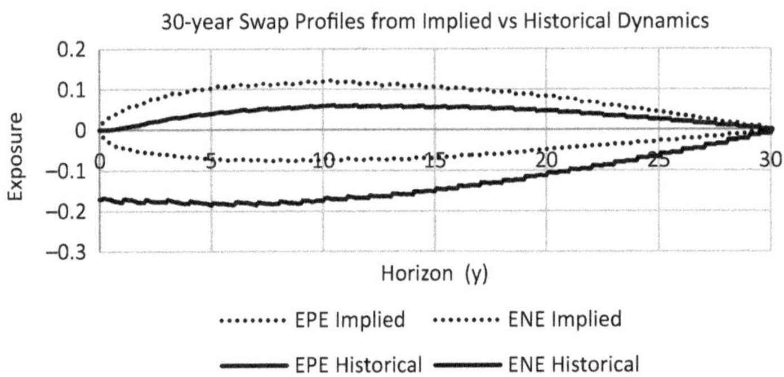

Fig. 11.5: Implied vs historical dynamics 30-year swap.

we believe the true long-run mean is 3%, based on history since 2001. Then it follows that using scenarios from the real-world measure to compute CVA will lead to much higher value for a swap that receives the floating rate than under the risk-neutral measure.

For Figs. 11.4 and 11.5, the historical calculations were based on a short rate of 0.3% and a flat long-run mean of 3%, which leads to a very asymmetric profile between the EPE and ENE, because market-implied long-term rates are very different from history.

From the diagrams, it is clear that the deviation between real-world CVA and risk-neutral grows substantially us as horizon increases, and this is troubling because interest rate instruments often have very long maturities, e.g. up to 30 years.

Further, if we consider the extreme case of zero vol, then it is clear that a swap that receives the floating leg will have value that increases over time, whereas a swap that pays the floating leg will have the opposite. What is substantial CVA might actually be 0 and vice versa for DVA, when we switch from risk-neutral to real-world probabilities. This leads to a very troubling policy implication: should we be in the business of rewarding traders for taking one side of the market (e.g. receiving the floating rate)? Is this effectively giving an incentive for a proprietary position (as far as allowable under regulations)[2] to bet on rates rising?

11.2. Valuation for Margin and Implications on MVA

MVA can arise due to initial margin demanded by exchanges. To properly take account of such MVA, one must take account of the approach by the exchange to determine the initial margin. Typically, products that are exchange traded or exchange cleared are vanilla in nature with straightforward valuation. Thus, there is little scope for major differences in valuation. Initial margin is then calculated by the exchange in light of expected volatility of the product. This is often based on historically observed volatility. If, however, the exchange were to change the margin calculation, then this needs to be factored into MVA computations. The consideration is particularly relevant to products where large margins could be demanded due to jumps in the underlying, e.g. CDS where the value will jump sharply if the reference name nears default.

A further consideration is that these days regulators have asked for margin to be posted by counterparties for uncleared products (typically more exotic or on less liquid underlyings than exchanges can cope with). The industry standard for this is ISDA SIMM, where the margin is based on sensitivities. The approach for calculation of this margin over time is also relevant to MVA and should be taken into account.

[2]Note that since hedging tends to be imperfect, the direction in which traders wish to leave themselves exposed if markets move unexpectedly is an implicit proprietary position.

We have already discussed the above topics in Chapters 6 and 10, and will not go into further detail here.

11.3. Uncertainty of Valuation at Default and Implications for Valuation

CVA is the amount an institution expects to lose due to default of its counterparty. Upon default, we would value all positions in a netting set, and if positive, the institution will have a claim as a creditor on the counterparty's assets. Naturally, the mechanics of default are relevant to determine the potential loss as a result of default.

First, it is far from clear what the recovery rate, i.e. percentage of amount owed that would be recovered upon default, is.[3] In fact, this varies widely across different counterparties, with industrial concerns that have productive capacity or retailers with stocks of goods generally having higher recovery rates, whereas firms in the service industry where the main assets are the staff may have near-zero recovery rates. The industry standard is to assume 40% for higher quality credit and lower where justified by the nature of the firm. Of course, the credit spreads implied from bond or CDS prices take account of both the actual probability of default and true recovery rate and not necessarily this assumed recovery rate.

But even the valuation that appears on default is not certain. Traditionally, the assumption is that upon default, the creditor is entitled to a claim on all cash flows immediately.[4] This suggests that on default, the valuation (on which claims are based) should be done using the risk-free rate, or in other words that CVA should not be taken into account.

[3]There is a further complication that recovery tends to take place a long time after default — potentially up to 10 years for financial institutions like Enron or Lehman. Of course, the recovery rate could be "adjusted" to take account of any loss of value from the time delay.

[4]There is potentially the issue of whether this accelerates the timing of cash flows due, e.g. if all coupons on a bond are payable immediately rather than over time. But that is a further complication that we shall not introduce here.

However, the wording of the ISDA master agreement says that valuation "may" take account of replacement cost of a derivative. Replacement cost would likely be the cost of finding an alternative counterparty, with comparable rating, to take the other side of the deal. This alternative suggests using that CVA of the counterparty (computed based on its credit prior to default) should be included in valuation post default. The problem here is the word "may", which does not assure market participants of the outcome. And different jurisdictions may well interpret this differently in the event of default.

These two approaches yield very different outcomes. In the case of risk-free valuation, there is an upward jump in value immediately upon default (since CVA is excluded whereas the counterparty is likely to have been weak credit just before default). In the second, this does not occur. Philosophically, one can argue that the upward jump in value in risk-free valuation can have the undesirable effect of giving a financial institution an incentive to push a counterparty into default in some circumstances. The use of replacement value however is more likely to lead to a contagion effect. Specifically, defaults are likely to be higher in the event of a systemic crisis, and so replacement value will be low and hit other institutions harder as a result.[5]

The two different treatments of valuation post default also have implications for FVA. After all, FVA is about funding costs for a position. What happens upon default clearly affects the cost of funding the position over its life (including if prematurely terminated by default).

The topic of FVA implications from risk-free vs risky closeout in default was discussed earlier in Chapter 4.

[5]Whereas a claim from a defaulted counterparty might take years to recover, valuation based on default assumptions enter a financial institution's balance sheet immediately, so contagion can be very swift.

Chapter 12

Managing XVA in Practice

By now, it should be clear that XVA is very much something to be considered at the level of large portfolios — all portfolios in a netting set for CVA and DVA, funding set for FVA, capital set for KVA and other segregated set (to which initial margin applies) for MVA. Ring fencing and integration of different regulatory environments are adding another layer of complexity. Clearly, there are operational considerations in light of this — namely data requirements and computational requirements. We shall start with a brief discussion of the setup of a financial institution to give further context to the subsequent discussion.

12.1. Operating Frameworks for Managing XVA

In most large banks, a fair amount of specialization occurs. Sales desks are responsible for facing off clients, structurers look at customizing payoffs to satisfy clients, while traders manage the risks associated with trades undertaken by looking at sensitivities to various risk factors and putting on hedges. There are then functions like Financial Engineering which are responsible for pricing models, support functions like IT and governance, and control functions like Model Validation, Risk Management and Finance.

Within the trading setup, typically, different desks deal with specific asset classes (e.g. Rates, FX, Equities, Credit) and specific products (e.g. exchange traded, linear, nonlinear, exotics). With CVA, FVA and MVA being essential components of the value of derivatives these days, the desks would also have to manage this risk. However, given the specialization of desks by asset class and products above, there is also likely to be the establishment of specialized desks dealing with managing counterparty exposure (CVA) and other valuation adjustments (FVA, MVA and KVA).

Managing CVA is not a new problem, with CVA having attracted attention since the early 2000s. By now, in many banks, there is a CVA desk which attempts to manage exposures to counterparties by hedging via single-name CDS or proxy hedging via CDS indices. (Actually, Basel III requires banks to have dedicated CVA desks if they wish to seek internal model approval for CVA capital.) If such hedging proves impossible, the CVA desk warehouses the risk, i.e. keep it in its own books. But in any case, by having a CVA desk, the traditional trading desks are typically relieved of having to worry about counterparty exposure, since they get charged for this by the CVA desk, which takes on the resultant risk. It is then up to the CVA desk to manage this CVA risk, while the traditional trading desks are free to focus on risk of their books to movements in market variables (rates, FX spot, etc.) (Fig. 12.1).

On the other hand, there is another design of hedging market risk and credit risk in combined derivatives and XVA desk (Fig. 12.2).

FVA and MVA (which is also funding related) are however newer, having attracted interest since perhaps 2010 or after. Traditionally,

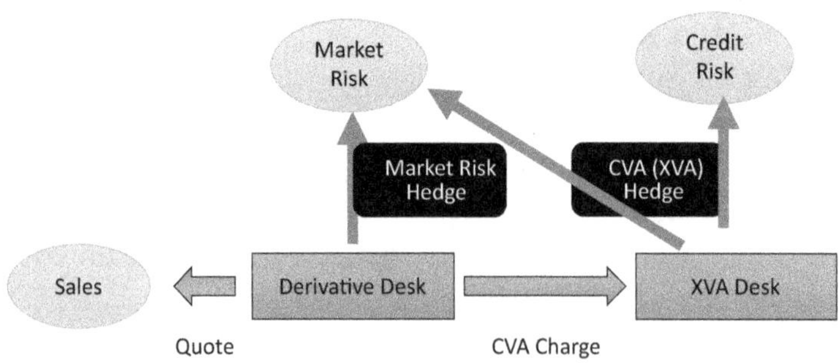

Fig. 12.1: CVA desk hedge CVA.

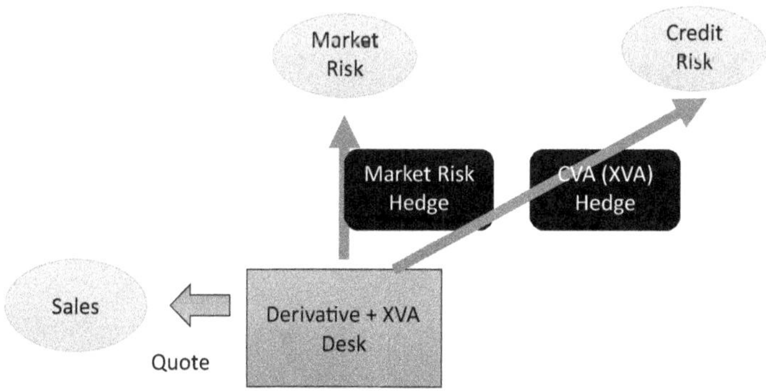

Fig. 12.2: CVA desk combined with derivatives desk hedge CVA.

funding is a function of Treasury. Individual trading desks will be charged for any borrowing to maintain their position by Treasury. And where positions require initial margin (per exchange clearing or SIMM), the amounts involved have to be funded. What is less clear however is what type of funding is provided by Treasury and hence whether the Treasury desk really manages FVA and MVA. Given that these days funding cost is extremely tightly linked to collateral, any desk that manages FVA and MVA would need to post and receive all sorts of collateral (in different currencies) from different desks and also provide uncollateralized funding (including under one-way CSA).

If Treasury just charges based on uncollateralized funding or standardized collateral, then it is really up to the desk to manage FVA itself. Of course, some internal functions in the bank different from Treasury can manage FVA and then face off with Treasury. Alternatively, the roles can be split. For example, cross-currency swaps are used to convert from funding under collateral in one currency to another, and clearly the cross-currency swaps desk can supplement an FVA desk in its function. Another consideration is the management of FVA and MVA together with CVA in a holistic XVA desk, which can then develop to deal with other non-internalized costs of maintaining a position (e.g. KVA) (Fig. 12.3).

Often, there is a danger of double charging: from treasury and from the XVA desk.

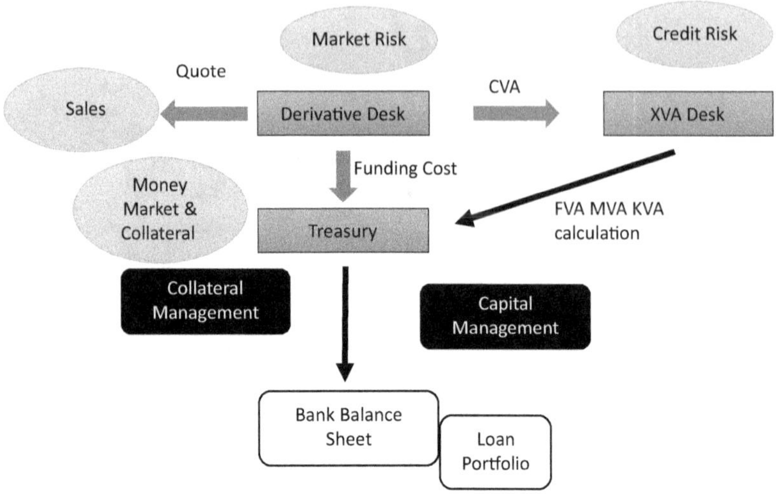

Fig. 12.3: Capital management and collateral management are assumed to be ran by treasury.

Whatever the setup of the bank, managing XVA still involves a significant computational exercise involving finding sensitivities of the bank's portfolios to different credit risk variables (e.g. Credit Default Spreads of different reference names), as well as different funding risk variables (e.g. OIS spreads under different currencies, bank's own funding spreads). This involves significant data and computational challenges that we address next.

12.2. Data Requirements of XVA

XVA involves valuing all trades in a given netting set, funding set or other aggregate set simultaneously. For all intents and purposes, it could be assumed that this would involve all market variables across all assets.

Traditionally, different desks in an investment bank operate autonomously. First, there is the natural consideration of using end-of-day market data for valuation, and clearly across different regions (e.g. Asia, Europe and North America) the closing times are very different. The use of closing data ensures better quality data for managing a desk's positions locally. However, it leads to inconsistencies when looking at the bank's positions globally. For

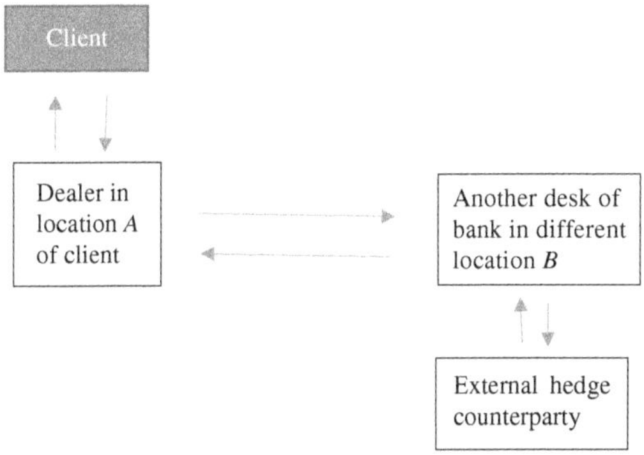

Fig. 12.4: Derivative desk is global in nature.

example, suppose a position (CVA position is global in nature) with USDJPY exposure was taken and at Tokyo close spot USDJPY was 102 and this was used to value the position in Tokyo. Suppose however that this position was offset by an equivalent position in New York, then net PV should be zero from the bank's perspective. If at New York close, USDJPY was 101, then net PV would not be zero if we valued the New York position separately. This suggests that from a macroperspective, and for XVA, we need to take closing values at a single point in time.[1] This could involve interpolating the marks of the market variables globally beyond market close or accessing alternative source of data. Most stocks and foreign exchange rates are trades 24 hours a day, 5 days a week.

Often a global snapshot is taken at the end of day in the most important trading areas: London, Hong Kong, Tokyo or New York.

In Fig. 12.4, the client does a deal with a desk of the bank in location A (same as client). This desk does an internal hedge with another desk in location B (different time zone). The desk in location B takes out an external hedge with a counterparty in its location. Now, if each desk values the hedge based on market close in its

[1]Strictly, for CVA of a netting set, we only need all positions in this netting set to be valued as of the same closing time. Similarly, for FVA of a funding set, all positions within need to be valued as of the same closing time, provided this is the same closing time as used for CVA. But splitting into separate closing times by netting set is probably logistically impractical, unless these netting sets are region specific.

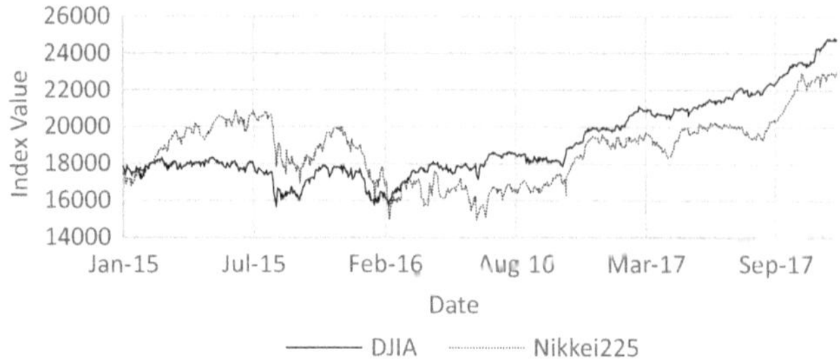

Fig. 12.5: Historical performance of DJIA and Nikkei 225.

location, then the overall PV may not be zero due to different market closing values.

A further reason to use a common closing time is that daily correlation of returns for different market variables can be very low if they are in different closing times. To analyze it, let us investigate the correlation of return of the Dow Jones Industrial Average and Nikkei 225 (Fig. 12.5). We can assume that the two indices are driven by and large by the same macroeconomic factor, because the Japanese economy is affected by the US economy and the correlation should be large. However, as shown in Fig. 12.6, the correlation of daily return is small (in an average 21%) and unstable, where that of two day return has a higher correlation (in an average 48%). We can assume the difference comes from the difference of observation periods. Indeed, when we analyze the correlation of adjacent days, the correlation is larger, as shown in Fig. 12.7. In this case, the observation period overlaps from the Nikkei close time to the DJIA close time. The US macroeconomic factor is assumed to move mostly in the US day time, which is included in the common observation period. Actually, the correlations are much more stable for weekly and monthly returns as seen in Fig. 12.8.

Second, different desks place different levels of importance on the marks for different types of market data — e.g. the money markets desk needs interest rates for very granular tenors at the short end of the curve, while much of the rates desk is more worried about the long end; the traditional FX options desk tends to be very concerned about short-term smile and skew over short maturities, whereas the long-dated FX desk is less worried about such accuracy but needs

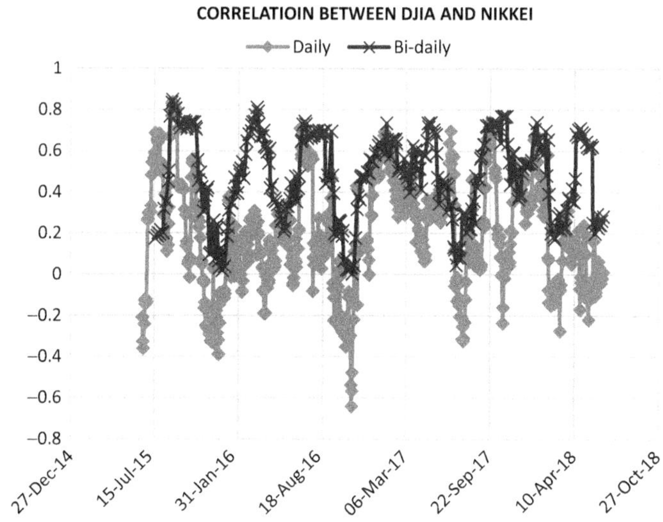

Fig. 12.6: Correlations of daily return and two days return. Average of daily return is 21%, where that of two days return is 48%.

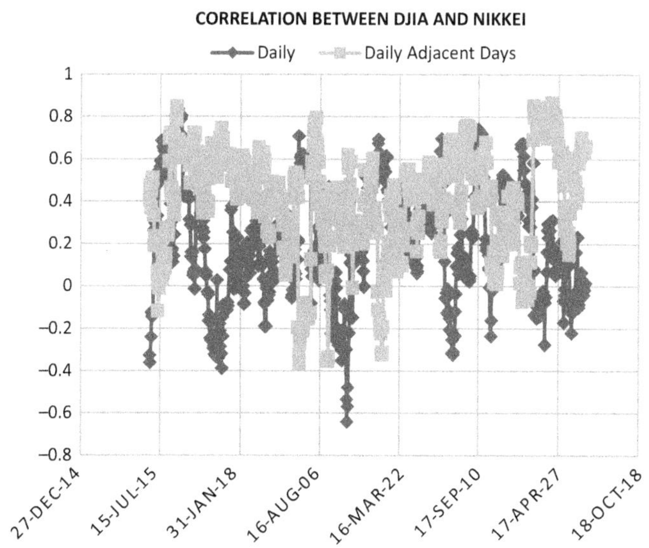

Fig. 12.7: Correlation between adjacent days.

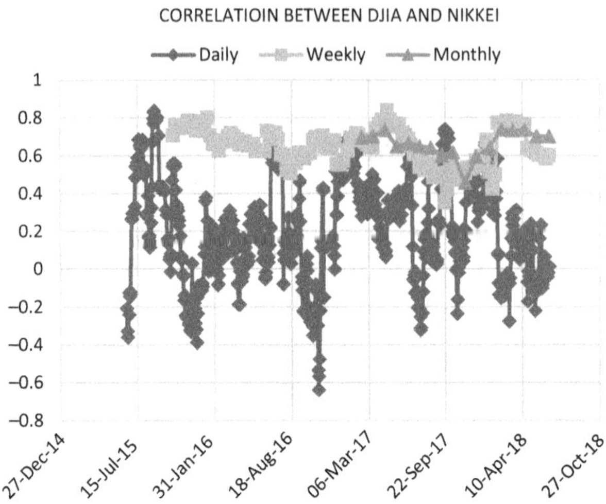

Fig. 12.8: Daily, weekly and monthly correlations.

good vol marks across maturities up to 30 years. Thus, whereas traders would mark market data conscientiously for the parts of the surface they need, these may be less reliable beyond — marks for FX vol from traditional FX options desk beyond 3 years may at times be suspect.[2] Thus, it is essential that we amalgamate the best components of the marks of different desks to come up with a single set of data for XVA.

Table 12.1 shows that long-maturity linear rates products (with no requirement for IR and FX vol for pricing) give rise to the need for curve and vol data for XVA. However, there is less supply of data for IR and especially FX vols as maturities increase. And part of the data may have to be amalgamated from various desks.

Finally, it is important to realize that XVA relies on good-quality data for all market variables arriving in a timely manner. Traditionally, data feeds in banking involve some degree of manual intervention, and a desk may be willing to roll over yesterday's market data if there is some failure to receive data deemed of lower importance in a timely manner — e.g. an Equities desk can perhaps

[2]Practically, what may happen is that a trader may update only the part of the vol surface he or she is interested in, leaving the other points stale (e.g. based on yesterday's values or worse).

Table 12.1: Sources of data for CVA.

Maturity	< 5 years	5–10 years	10–30 years	30–50 years
Source of CVA	Typically, longest instruments are linear rates products, so no need market for IR or FX vol to trade			
IR Curve	Money Markets Desk: Very rich curve with many nodes	Swaps Desk: Less granularity but still good liquidity		Data available for only a few Markets (USD, EUR, GBP)
IR Vol	Market Making Gamma Book: Very liquid	Vega Book: Partly market making but partly hedge till maturity, can be less liquid outside ATM		—
FX Vol	Short-Dated FX Desk: Good Smile Surface and Advanced Smile Modeling	Mid-Dated FX Desk: Less accuracy of vol surface and less sophisticated vol models due to need for stock rates	Long-Dated FX Desk (only available for some markets, e.g. USDJPY, AUDJPY, EURUSD)	—

afford to use yesterday's interest rate curve if something is wrong with today's. However, for XVA, generally it is not as acceptable to make a conscious decision to ignore bad data and use yesterday's, since we are now looking at all portfolios and it is not always clear when there is high dependence on the data that is being compromised. This often means that in an XVA desk, a high amount of coordination is necessary to ensure all relevant data is received before XVA can be processed, and substitution of data with fallbacks is only done as a last resort — this can nevertheless happen a lot more than ideal given the large amount of data from different sources involved.

Often internal market data are only controlled when they are related to live trades. Curves and surfaces are completed at the discretion of the traders but these interpolation or extrapolation are not benefiting from the same level of control and thus have an important impact on the XVA numbers.

Market practices can be consistent within each trading system but not taken together. It is therefore important to make the necessary transformation to get consistent market data.

12.3. Computational Requirements of XVA

XVA involves looking at the bank's entire portfolio of trades across counterparties, split into netting, funding or other aggregate sets. These are likely to involve thousands or tens of thousands of trades each. Further, to manage XVA, we need to compute sensitivities to different quantities, e.g. to credit spreads across different terms for XVA and to funding spreads of the bank for FVA. Traditionally, a sensitivity requires a bump and revalue operations $\frac{\partial V}{\partial \alpha} \approx \frac{V(\alpha+\delta\alpha)-V(\alpha)}{\delta\alpha}$, i.e. each sensitivity involves a separate call to the valuation function. This involves huge computational expense.

Moreover, the developments of the KVA and MVA make the computational burden much higher. As is given in Fig. 12.9, the calculation burden of CVA capital charge significantly increased for FRTB CVA. In the calculation of the KVA, we need to calculate the capital charge on the Monte Carlo path and the calculation burden can be huge.

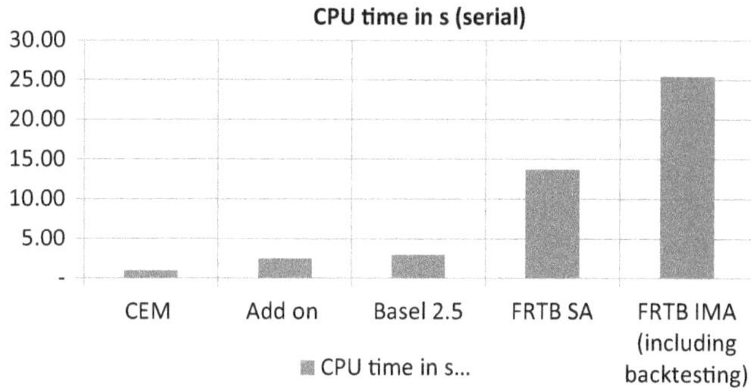

Portfolio
100 swaps
5 currencies
3 curves per currency
30-year maturity

Simulation
32k simulations
25 dates per year

Models	CPU time in s (serial)
CEM	0.55
Add on	1.56
Basel 2.5	2.89
FRTB SA	13.90
FRTB IMA (including backtesting)	25.73

Fig. 12.9: CPU time to calculate capital charge (Bouayoun, 2018).

12.3.1. *Faster and more robust models*

We have already discussed earlier in the book how the only way an institution can cope with the computational challenges of XVA is to have fast and robust models — i.e. rather than having some model (e.g. 3-factor PDE) that takes maybe half a minute for a single valuation, it is better to have simpler models that give rougher approximations to price and which happen to be less likely to fail under stressed market conditions. This further makes sense since a desk can cope more easily with a PV failure by manual intervention to analyze and remediate or apply a fallback on the price or risk of a given trade; however, this is much harder for an XVA desk with less expertise and a whole zoo of trades across all assets and where stressed conditions need to be applied at future horizons for CVA, etc. However, even so, generally Least-Squares Monte Carlo is needed so that really we can simulate a bunch of risk factors, then apply regression to obtain values of the portfolio based on realization of these risk factors.

12.3.2. *Faster computers*[3]

The computational expense of XVA really suggests that the problem would strongly benefit from an IT solution. A brute-force approach is to use more computing power, the very first step of which is to use multithreading. These days, computers are having more and more cores (e.g. 128 cores is now no longer unusual as of 2018), whereas the computing power of each core is no longer increasing as much. This suggests an approach that would better benefit from parallelization of the computations, which may well include a revisit of the code in derivatives pricing.

To increase the parallelism dramatically, the financial institution borrows the Graphics Processing Unit (GPU) from the gaming industry. Parallelization of GPU is really massive (up to 5,000 threads per machine). It fits well to the Monte Carlo simulation, which is used in XVA calculation. This does require substantial code rewrites as part of the functionality that is enhanced significantly is the processing power, but read–write of instructions is slow, and this can be a bottleneck based on the existing code.

The comparison of performance between GPU and CPU is given in Fig. 12.10.

Recently, Quantum Processing Unit (QPU) has been investigated to increase the speed of computation in finance dramatically. In a quantum computer, instead of binary digits (0 or 1), superposition of the states is used for the computation. It increases the number of states and speed of computation dramatically. The challenges for QPU is it needs a bespoke language and rewriting of the code is necessary.

Quantum computing relies on the quantic properties (superposition and entanglement) of a set of qubits. The two types of quantum computers currently in development are:

— Universal Gate quantum computer: It is the equivalent of a general purpose computer but with quantum circuits. Some versions with very few qubits exist.

[3]Part of the contents in this section are based on private communication with Dr. Assad Bouayoun.

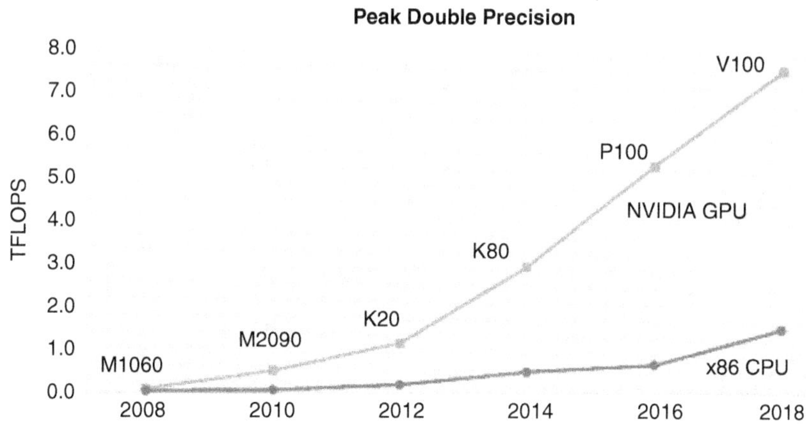

Fig. 12.10: The latest generation of GPUs from NVIDIA contain upwards of nearly 6,000 cores and deliever peak double-precision processing performance of 7.5 TFLOPS; note also the relatively minor performance improvement over time for multicore ×86 CPUs (Bouayoun, 2018).
Source: NVIDIA.

— Simplified version solving only ISING models can be tested (10^8 times faster than simulated annealing on a single core at most) developed by D-Wave®.[4]
  — These QPUs implement a quantum annealing algorithm, where qubits (quantum bits) can be prepared in a simple initial energy configuration where all qubits are both 0 and 1 (quantum superposition), and are then evolved to final configuration corresponding to a combinatorial optimization problem (QUBO).
  — This can be used for portfolio optimization or reverse stress testing.

Here we use QPU in the D-Wave sense only.

CPU and GPU have quite a long history in computational finance. There are some hardware of this kind available on the market, but QPU is still in the phase of development. Figure 12.11

[4]https://research.googleblog.com/2015/12/when-can-quantum-annealing-win.html.

Table 12.2: CPU, GPU vs QPU Bouayoun (2018).

	CPU	**GPU**	**QPU**
Access			
Local	Yes	Yes	no
Cloud	Yes	Yes	Yes
Language	all	most (CUDA)	bespoke
Debugability	easy	challenging	simulation
Quality	production	production	experimental
Hardware price	\$3k	\$6k	\$15M?
Development resources	yes	small expending community	niche
Types of algorithm			
SIMD (single instruction multiple data)	yes	**Yes but fast**	no
MIMD (multiple instruction multiple data)	**yes**	yes	no
MISD (multiple instruction single data)	**yes**	yes	no
QUBO (quadratic unconstrained binary optimisation)	yes but slow	yes but slow	**yes but fast**

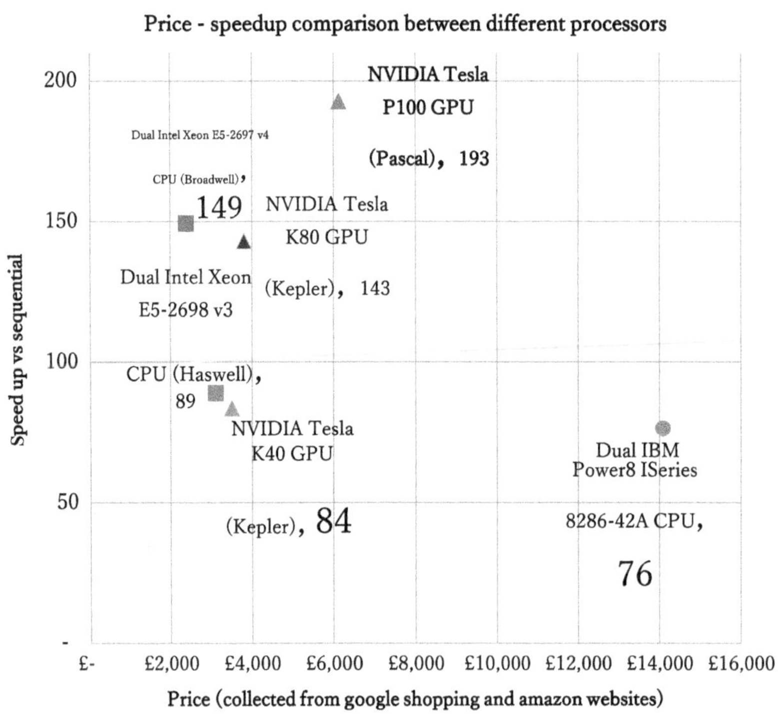

Fig. 12.11: Cost and performance of CPU and GPU (Bouayoun, 2018).

represents the costs and speeds of the computers available in the market.

12.4. Better Computational Algorithms

Furthermore, the computational challenges of computing multiple sensitivities for managing XVA risk can actually lend itself to the solution of Algorithm Differentiation (AD) techniques (Naumann, 2012; Luca and Giles, 2012). At its heart, the idea is that the pricing problem can be reformulated into a dual problem. In so doing, we can obtain all sensitivities together with a single call of the valuation function, rather than as a separate call per sensitivity. This comes at the expense of storing data for all sensitivities throughout the process — i.e. memory consumption will be far greater. A full description of Algorithmic Differentiation (AD) is beyond the scope of this book, but a brief description of the approach follows.

12.4.1. *Algorithmic differentiation (AD)*

Valuation algorithms can be rather complicated and typically Monte Carlo simulation is used in XVA calculation. However, valuation is given by the (very complicated) combination of binary and unary operations. That is, the valuation is represented as a composition of functions

$$\Theta \rightarrow U^1 \rightarrow \cdots \rightarrow U^j \rightarrow U^{j+1} \rightarrow \cdots \rightarrow U^n \rightarrow Y$$

where $\Theta \in R^N$ represents model parameters and $Y \in R$ is a value, intermediate states U^j can be a multidimensional vector $U^j = (U_1^j, \ldots, U_m^j)$ and the dependencies can branch into two. The dependencies between the variables are schematically given as solid arrows in the dependency graph in Fig. 12.13.

The model sensitivities of the derivative are given by $\partial Y / \partial \theta_i$ $(i = 1, \ldots, N)$.[5]

[5]Actually, we need sensitivity to market variables. However, as is discussed in Chapter 10, the model parameter sensitivity can be converted to market sensitivity by Jacobian and only model sensitivities are discussed here.

Here the number of model parameters N is usually large and the calculation cost of sensitivities is large.

From the chain rule, it is represented as

$$\frac{\partial Y}{\partial \theta_i} = \frac{\partial Y}{\partial U^n} \cdots \frac{\partial U^{j+1}}{\partial U^j} \cdots \frac{\partial U^1}{\partial \theta_i}$$

where summation of vector indices in the intermediate states are omitted.

The partial derivatives of each steps $\partial U_k^j / \partial U_l^{j+1}$ can be automatically assigned in the computer code. For example, if $V(U) = \exp(aU)$, $\frac{\partial V}{\partial(U)} = a \exp(U)$ and if $V(U_1, U_2) = U_1 + U_2$, $\frac{\partial V}{\partial(U_1)} = 1$, $\frac{\partial V}{\partial(U_2)} = 1$.

So if all the partial derivatives are stored when PV is calculated, the calculation of sensitivities is given by the multiplication of partial derivatives automatically in the computer. This is called algorithmic differentiation.

Here if we do the multiplication from the model parameters θ_i to PV Y, it is called forward propagation or tangent mode. The forward propagation corresponds to the dotted arrows in Fig. 12.12 and we need to iterate the propagations for all the model parameters to calculate all the sensitivities though most of the partial derivatives are common in all of the calculations. That is, the calculation cost for the sensitivities are about N times that of PV calculation and almost the same as that of bump and revalue method.

On the other hand, if we run the dependency graph backward from Y to Θ as in Fig. 12.13, we can calculate all of the sensitivities simultaneously with a small extra cost to PV calculation. This propagation is called adjoint mode. This calculation of algebraic derivative in the adjoint mode is called Adjoint Algorithmic Differentiation or AAD.

AAD makes calculation of sensitivities extremely fast (about four times the calculation time of PV), because calculation time of the partial derivative $\frac{\partial V}{\partial(U)}$ is of similar order as that of evaluating the function $V(U)$. However in AAD, all the partial derivatives on the dependency graph need to be stored in the calculation and memory consumption is huge.

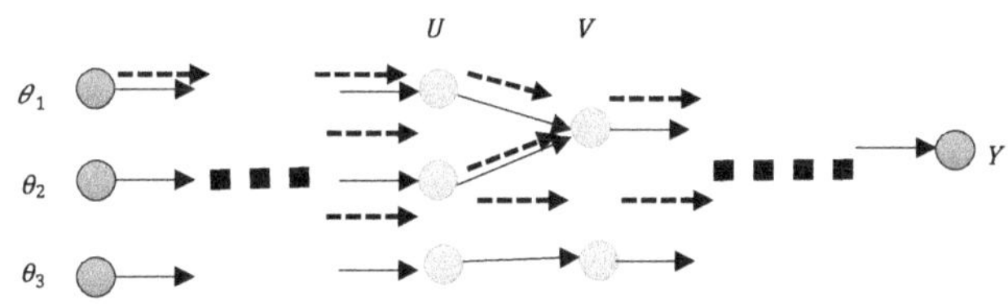

Fig. 12.12: Valuation and tangent mode.

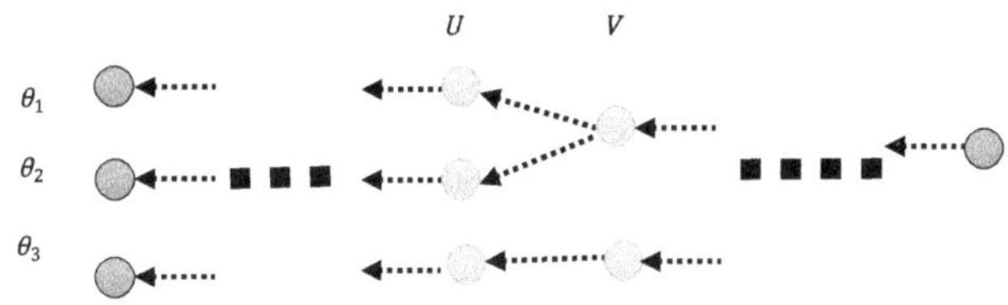

Fig. 12.13: Adjoint mode.

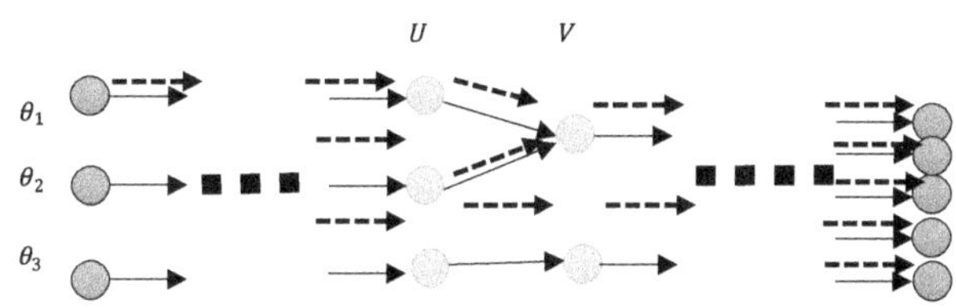

Fig. 12.14: KVA and MVA in AD.

For the calculation of greeks, we need derivative of one output (PV) by many input (parameters) and AAD is efficient. On the other hand, for the calculation of KVA and MVA, we need sensitivities on the Monte Carlo paths and the number of output (values on the Monte Carlo paths) are large (see Fig. 12.14). In this case, when we calculate the partial derivatives from the input parameters to the outputs (tangent mode), we can calculate the sensitivity for all the outputs simultaneously and adjoint mode is not necessary more efficient. Application of tangent mode calculation to SA-TB KVA will be discussed in Section 12.4.1.1.

12.4.1.1. *Implementation of AD for XVA calculation*

One of the most important areas of XVA where AD is useful is KVA and MVA, where Var calculation on Monte Carlo path is necessary.

In the calculation of the SA-TB KVA (and SIMM MVA), the sensitivity calculation of the exposure on the simulated market scenario is necessary. For the callable derivatives whose future value (exposure) $V(t, X(t))$ is typically calculated by LSM, we need to calculate $\partial V(t, X(t))/\partial\theta(t \rightarrow)$ on the simulated path. Here $\theta(t\rightarrow)$ means parameters for the time after t. So in this section, the issue about the application of AD of the exposure calculation for the Bermudan Swaption at a future time will be discussed.

Regarding KVA of SA-CVA, the technique in this section is also applied with extra calculation.

Typically XVA is calculated by the model which is based on a Markov process

$$dX(t) = \mu(t)dt + \sigma(t)dW(t)$$

For details of the interest rate (Hull–White) and FX process, see Sections A.2 and A.3 in Appendix A.

Note that in the SA-TB (and SA-CVA) KVA, we need sensitivities with respect to market parameters v_j. However, by calculating Jacobian

$$J_{ij} = \partial\theta_i/\partial u_j$$

we can convert model parameter sensitivities to market sensitivities.

To adopt AD, in the source code, partial derivatives should be assigned to all the relevant operations. To judge what are relevant operations and what are not, an approach to overload double variables using a template is commonly adopted (Antonov *et al.*, 2017b). When this approach is used, the quants of the bank need to rewrite all the relevant pricing library. So to introduce AAD is significant work when the existing library is large.

12.4.1.2. *Market risk KVA (standard approach) and SIMM-MVA for Bermudan swaption*

In this section, we analyze the application of AD to SA-TB-KVA for a Bermudan Swaption. All the issues about the application of AD to XVA will be discussed in this application.

Let the exercise dates of the Bermudan be $[T_1, \ldots, T_N]$. We assume the same XVA calculation dates as in the Bermudan exercise dates, but generalization to arbitrary dates is straightforward. We assume the use of the Hull–White model, but generalization to other Markov models is also straightforward. In this section, we omit the numeraire.

In the SA-TB, capital at time T_i is a function of the sensitivities $\partial v(T_i X(T_i))/\partial\theta(T_i \to)$, where $v(T_i X(T_i))$ is a future value at time T_i. We thus need to calculate it on the Monte Carlo path. Since we need to calculate sensitivities on all Monte Carlo paths, the calculation output is large. This is in contrast to the calculation of the sensitivities of PV, which has only one output.

In the Hull–White model (see Appendix A), the Markov process is

$$dX(t) = \sigma(t)dW(t)$$

and the discount factor is

$$D(t,T) = \frac{D(0,T)}{D(0,t)} \exp\left(\frac{\int_0^t \sigma^2(u)du}{2}(B^2(t,S) - B^2(T,S)) - B(t,T)X(t)\right). \tag{12.1}$$

To value the Bermudan swaption, we evaluate the exercise value $U(T_n, X(T_n))$ and the continuation value $V(T_n, X(T_n))$ in a backward manner. The value $v(T_i X(T_i))$ has the effect of an early exercise.

We conduct the backward evaluation of the Bermudan swaption as follows:

$$V(T_n, X(T_n)) = \max\left(\tilde{V}(T_n^+, X(T_n)), U(T_n, X(T_n))\right)$$
$$\tilde{V}(T_n^+, X(T_n)) = E\left[V(T_{n+1}, X(T_{n+1}) | F_{T_n}\right],$$

from time T_N to T_0.

We estimate the expectation value above using a regression with basis function $\psi(X) = (1, X, X^2, X^3)^T$[6] and coefficients of

[6] T means transpose of matrix.

$\beta_n^T = (\beta_n^0 \beta_n^1 \beta_n^2 \beta_n^3)$:

$$\tilde{V}\left(T_n^+, X\left(T_n\right)\right) = \beta_n^T \psi(X_n),$$

where we estimate β_n as

$$\beta_n^k = \sum_l C_{kl}^{-1} E\left[\psi_l\left(X_n\right) V(T_{n+1}, X_{n+1})\right] \qquad (12.2)$$

$$\text{and } C_{kl} = E\left[\psi_k\left(X_n\right) \psi_l\left(X_n\right)\right]$$

Note that we show the actual expectation value calculated by the Monte Carlo simulation in Chapter 9.

$$E[\psi_l(X_n)V(T_{n+1}, X_{n+1})] = \sum_p^{N_{\text{path}}} \psi_l(X_{n;p})V(T_{n+1}, X_{n+1;p})$$

$$C_{kl} = \sum_p^{N_{\text{path}}} \psi_k(X_{n;p})\psi(X_{n;p})$$

In the Hull–White model, if we do not calibrate the strength of mean reversion to the market, the parameters are the initial discount factor $D_j = D(0, T_j)$ and the volatility of Markov process $\sigma_j = \sigma(u)$ $(T_{j-1} < u < T_j)$.

As is apparent from (12.1), the exercise value is the analytic function of the state variable $X\left(T_n\right)$, volatilities σ_k $(k \leq n)$ and initial discount factors D_k $(k = n, \ldots)$.

The Markov process at time T_j depends on the volatility σ_k $(k \leq j)$.

$$X_j = X(T_j) = F(\{Z\}\{\sigma_0, \ldots, \sigma_j\}$$

where $\{Z\}$ represents the set of standard normal random numbers.

We next analyze the dependency of the Bermudan valuation on discount factor $D(0, T_n)$. For the Bermudan valuation, only the exercise values $U(T_m, X(T_m))$ $(m \leq n)$ depend on $D(0, T_n)$.

Hence, as Fig. 12.15 shows, the derivatives $\partial U(T_m, X(T_m))/\partial D(0, T_n)$ start the dependency graph and affect $V(T_m, X(T_m))$.

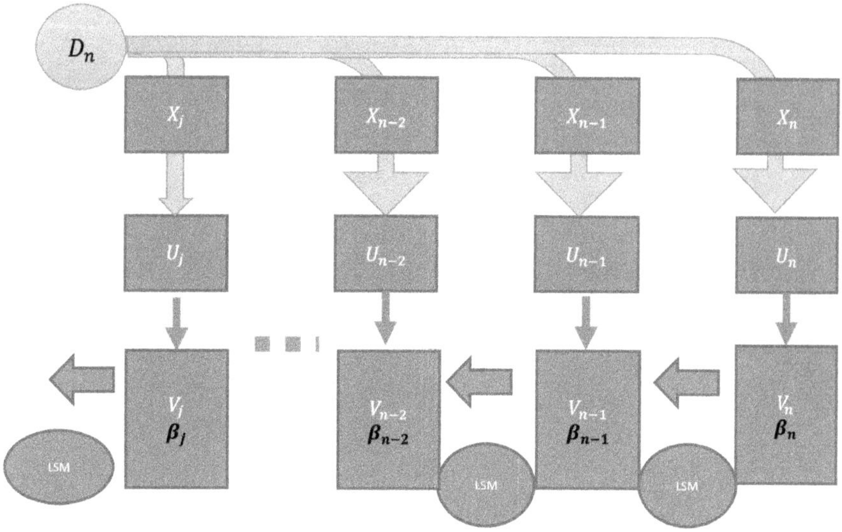

Fig. 12.15: Dependency graph for the initial discount factor.

In tangent mode, we can calculate the parameter derivative with the backward calculation of LSM. Here, in the calculation of β_{m} (12.2), only $V(T_{m+1}X_{m+1})$ depends on $D(0,T_n)$, and we can use

$$\partial\beta_m^k/\partial D(0,t_n) = \sum_l E\left[\psi_k\left(X_m\right)\psi_l\left(X_m\right)\right]^{-1} \times E\left[\frac{\psi_l\left(X_m\right)\partial V\left(T_{m+1},X_{m+1}\right)}{\partial D_n}\right].$$

Note that all $V(T_m, X_m)$ $(m \leq n)$ depend on $D(0,T_n)$ in the backward calculation. We illustrate the dependency of the Bermudan to the discount factor in Fig. 12.15.

Next, we investigate the dependency for model volatility. Volatility σ_j $(j < n)$ affects the state variable $X(T_n)$; thus, σ_j affects the valuation both directly and through its dependence on $X(T_n)$.

Thus, the dependency on volatility in the exercise value $U\left(T_n, X\left(T_n\right)\right)$ is

$$\frac{\mathrm{d}U(T_n,X(T_n))}{d\sigma_j} = \frac{\partial U(T_n,X(T_n))}{\partial\sigma_j} + \left(\frac{\partial U(T_n,X(T_n))}{\partial X(T_n)}\right)\frac{\partial X(T_n)}{\partial\sigma_j}.$$

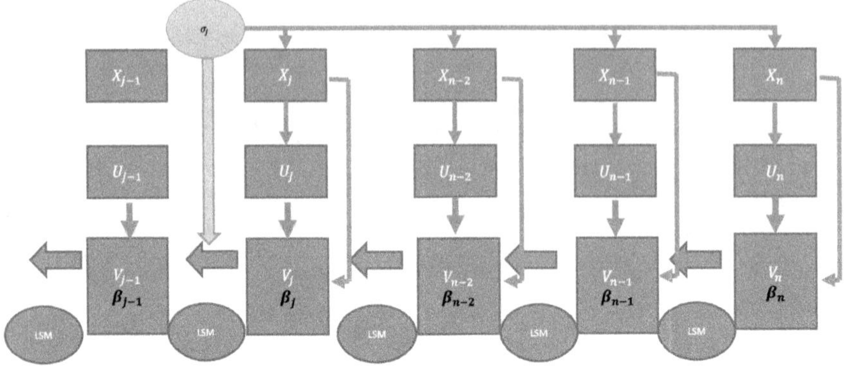

Fig. 12.16: Dependency graph for the volatility.

The continuation value also depends on X_n.

The continuation value at T_n^+ is

$$\tilde{V}\left(T_n^+, X_n\right) = \beta^T \psi(X_n)$$

where (12.2) gives β and it depends on X_n and $V(T_{n+1}X_{n+1})$. Hence, β depends on X_n, but the estimation of β is a statistical inference between X_n and $V(T_{n+1}X_{n+1})$, which depend on the evolution from X_n to X_{n+1}. Thus, in the ideal situation, σ_j and X_j $(j \leq n)$ do not affect the inference. Therefore, we can assume that β_n depends on σ_j only through $V(T_{n+1}, X_{n+1})$ (Antonov *et al.*, 2017a, 2017b).

Thus $\frac{\partial \beta}{\partial X_n} = 0$ and $\frac{\partial V(T_n^+, X_n)}{\partial X_n} = \beta^T \frac{\partial \psi(X_n)}{\partial X_n}$.

Figure 12.16 provides the dependency graph of volatility.

Note that the volatility σ_j affects all state variables thereafter and the derivative $\frac{\partial V(T_n, X_n)}{\partial X_n}$ is common to all sensitivities for $\sigma_j (j \leq n)$. By keeping these derivatives, we can improve the calculation speed significantly.

As we have shown above, when we calculate the derivatives using the chain rule following the dependency graph, we can calculate the sensitivities (delta and vega) for all paths simultaneously.

As the algorithm above shows, a significant part of the calculation is common for all sensitivities. We can make the calculation highly efficient by keeping these data.

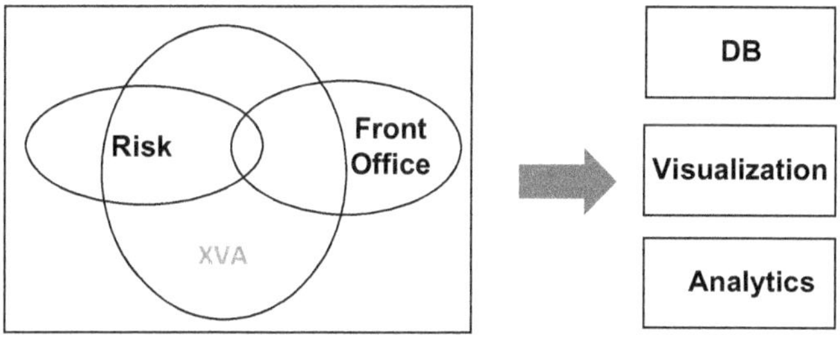

Fig. 12.17: Shareholders of XVA library (Bouayoun, 2018).

12.4.2. *The IT requirements for XVA*

From the observation in this section, the requirements for the derivatives valuation library after the financial crisis is given as in this section.

XVA library should consist of three main functions that is (1) database management, which is explained in Section 12.2. (2) analytics, which includes both valuation algorithms in Chapters 9 and 10 and AAD in Section 12.3.4; and (3) visualization as with the traditional derivatives pricing library Fig. 12.17. The XVA library is used in various parts in the bank, which include, but are not limited to the front office (trader), risk management function, treasury and finance.

In the library, the most important part is analytics, as with the traditional derivatives library (Fig. 12.18).

In the management of the library, the following functionalities should be effectively managed:

(a) Test (all types including Unit, Integration and Random).
(b) Release management and coordination.
(c) Security and intellectual property protection.
(d) Continuous improvement and coherent development of specialized and dedicated resources.

In the library, many species of calculation are processed in heterogeneous environments. They include valuation of XVA for front office, VAR and other calculation for risk, capital optimization for treasury. This situation should be managed by Orchestration.

Library

Task framewrok		
serialisation / desrialisation		
Sensitivities		
PNL Explain / Predict		
PV	Exposure	xVAs
payoffs		
trades		
Risk factors models (IR, FX, ...) Analytic / MC		
calibration		
market		
conventions		
Dates	Schedule	static data
Numerical methods		

Processing unit

CPU	GPU	QPU
All	None	None
All	None	None
All	None	None
All	Numerical skeleton	Numerical skeleton
All	Numerical skeleton	Numerical skeleton
All	Numerical skeleton	Numerical skeleton
All	Numerical skeleton	Numerical skeleton
All	None	None
	Numerical skeleton	Numerical skeleton
All	Numerical skeleton	None
All	Numerical skeleton	None
All	Most	optimisation

Fig. 12.18: Grouping of code base in XVA library (Bouayoun, 2018).

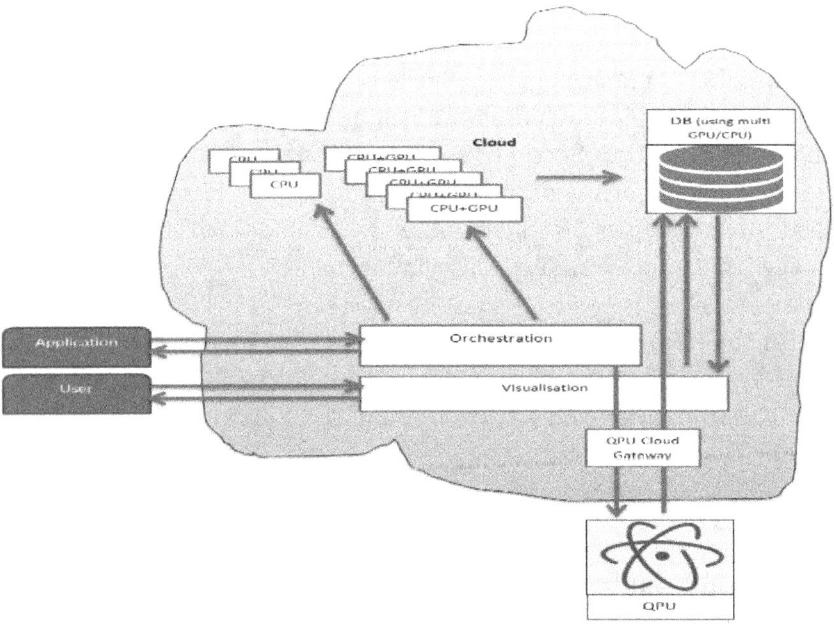

Fig. 12.19: Example of architecture of XVA system (Bouayoun, 2018).

Putting all things together, considering the development of QPU, the future XVA (derivatives valuation library) should be in the form as in Fig. 12.19.

Appendix A

Sample Appendix

A.1. Credit Risk Model in XVA

CVA (and DVA) is the valuation adjustment related to the counterparty default risk. Therefore, treatment of credit risk is an important factor in CVA. In this chapter, systematic account of credit risk in XVA context will be given.

Credit risk is modeled by giving the stochastic distribution of default time. Let us study credit risk of entity A. Let default time of entity A be τ^A, if the probability that default time τ^A is in the period $t \sim t + dt$ is $\gamma^A(t)dt$, we call $\gamma^A(t)$ default intensity. Note that $\gamma^A(t) = E[\delta(t - \tau^A)]$. Now we will introduce hazard rate $\lambda^A(t)$, which is the probability of default happening in the period $t \sim t + dt$ conditional on whether there is no default before t. Survival probability to time $P^A(0, t)$, which is the probability that A does not default till time t, is represented as

$$P^A(0,t) = \lim_{n\to\infty} \prod_j^{\infty} (1 - \lambda^A(u_j)) = \exp\left(-\int_0^t \lambda^A(u)du\right)$$

Therefore, default intensity is related to hazard rate with the following relationship

$$\gamma^A(t)=\lambda^A(t)P^A(0,t)=\lambda^A(t)\exp\left(-\int_0^t \lambda^A(u)du\right)$$

Let us explain the relationship between hazard rate and survival probability in discrete setting in this section. Let us analyze on discrete time grids

$$[0 = t_0, t_1, \ldots, t_M]$$

Let us imagine a coin toss corresponding to period $[t_j, t_{j+1}]$. For each coin toss, the probability of head is λ_j and that of tail is $1 - \lambda_j$. We can assume first appearance of head corresponds to default. The probability that default event happens in the period $[t_j, t_{j+1}]$ is $(1-\lambda_0)(1 - \lambda_1)\cdots(1 - \lambda_{j-1})\lambda_j$.

Here, λ_j is a probability of default conditional on no default before time t_{j-1} and corresponds to hazard rate. On the other hand, default intensity (probability of default in the period $[t_j, t_{j+1}]$) corresponds to $(1-\lambda_0)(1-\lambda_1)\cdots(1-\lambda_{j-1})\lambda_j$. In the continuous limit $dt \to 0$, the relationship between hazard rate and default intensity is given by

$$\gamma^A(t)=\lambda^A(t)\exp\left(-\int_0^t \lambda^A(u)\,du\right)$$

In this book, default time τ^A and hazard rate $\lambda^A(t)$ are assumed to be independent stochastic processes.

Note that the definition of default intensity and hazard rate in this book is not general.

A.2. Interest Rate and Fx Models in XVA

In XVA calculation, we need to simulate many market factors (including interest rate, Fx, equity and commodity) simultaneously. That is, XVA model is an (high-dimensional) FX hybrid model. In this hybrid model, interest rate and Fx dynamics work as a base of all of the asset dynamics. Furthermore, in the derivatives market, interest rate derivatives occupy a significantly important part. Considering this situation, in this chapter, interest rate and Fx hybrid (cross-currency) model will be investigated. Cross-currency model is well investigated for the powered reverse dual currency

(PRDC) pricing, and the techniques developed for it will be used in XVA modeling.

In interest rate derivatives pricing, sometimes multifactor models which can control skew are used. But in the FX hybrid (cross-currency) model, usually a simpler model which has limited capability of volatility skew is used.

A.2.1. *Hull–White model*

In this section, Hull–White model (Andreasen (2014), Hunt (2004)) will be explained as an interest rate part in the cross-currency model. Because interest rate dynamics is the domestic interest rate part, we add suffix d to all the variables. (Foreign rate dynamics is equivalent to the domestic one except for the measure change from foreign to domestic measure.)

In the Hull–White model, short rate $r_d(t)$ follows:

$$dr_d(t) = (\theta_d(t) - a_d(t)r_d(t))dt + \sigma_d(t)dW_d(t)$$

where $\sigma_d(t)$ is the volatility, $\theta_d(t)/a_d(t)$ is the mean reversion level and $a_d(t)$ is the strength of mean reversion. Here, short rate is written as

$$r_d(t) = \phi_d(t) + x_d(t)$$

where $x_d(t)$ satisfies the following equation:

$$\begin{aligned} dx_d(t) &= -a_d(t)x_d(t)dt + \sigma_d(t)dW_d(t) \\ x_d(0) &= 0 \end{aligned}$$

Here, the effect of $\theta_d(t)$ is included in $\phi_d(t)$ and stochastic dynamics is represented in $x_d(t)$. Now we introduce $X_d(t)$ as follows:

$$X_d(t) = \exp\left(\int_0^t a_d(u)du\right) x_d(t)$$

It satisfies

$$dX_d(t) = \tilde{\sigma}_d(t)dW_d(t)$$
$$\tilde{\sigma}_d(t) = \sigma_d(t)\exp\left(\int_0^t a_d(u)du\right)$$

That is, short-rate $r_d(t)$ is represented by the driftless Markov process as

$$r_d(t)=\phi_d(t)+\exp\left(\int_0^t a_d(u)du\right)X_d(t)$$

Next we will investigate the dynamics of discount factor in the Hull–White model. Discount factor of maturity T observed at t is represented in risk-neutral measure as

$$D_d(t,T)=E^Q\left[\exp\left(-\int_t^T r_d(u)du\right)|F_t\right]$$

Here $\int_t^T r_d(u)du$ is an integral of the variable which follows normal distribution. We can easily prove that the integral is represented as

$$\int_t^T r_d(u)du = B_d(t,T)X_d(t) + (\text{deterministic part})$$
$$+ (\text{stochastic part from } t \text{ to } T)$$

where

$$B_d(t,T) = \int_t^T \exp\left(-\int_0^u a_d(s)ds\right)du$$

Therefore, the discount factor has the following form:

$$D_d(t,T) = A_d(t,T)\exp(-B_d(t,T)X_d(t))$$

Here, $A_d(t,T)$ can be calculated directly but can be calculated easily in forward measure as we will show shortly.

From the above form of discount factor, it is clear that the Libor rate follows the displaced diffusion

$$L_n(t) = \left(\frac{1}{\delta}\right)\left(\frac{D(t,T_n)}{D(t,T_{n+1})} - 1\right) \sim \left(\frac{1}{\delta}\right)(C\exp(DX(t)) - 1)$$

Actually, its distribution is close to normal rather than log-normal.

From here on we use the S-forward measure where numeraire is

$$N(t) = D_d(t,S)$$

In the S-forward measure, numeraire is a functional of Markov process $X_d(t)$ and we adopt $X_d(t)$ as a fundamental variable of our model.

In this measure change, only drift term $\theta_d(t)$ in short rate is changed and $A_d(t,T)$ in representation of discount factor is adjusted.

Even more in the S-forward measure, from the arbitrage-free condition

$$\frac{D_d(t,T)}{D_d(t,S)} = E^S\left[\frac{1}{D_d(T,S)}|F_t\right]$$

The form of numeraire-rebased discount factor is determined as

$$\frac{D_d(t,T)}{D_d(t,S)} = \frac{D_d(0,T)}{D_d(0,S)} \qquad \text{(RebasedDF)}$$
$$\exp\left(-\frac{\Xi(0,t)}{2}(B_d^2(T,S)) + (B_d(T,S)), X_d(t)\right)$$

and discount factor is given by

$$D_d(t,T) = \frac{D_d(0,T)}{D_d(0,t)}$$
$$\exp\left(\frac{\Xi(t)}{2}(B_d^2(t,S) - B_d^2(T,S)) - B_d(t,T)X_d(t)\right)$$

where $\Xi(s,t) = \int_s^t \tilde{\sigma}_d^2(u)du$. Note that in this formulation, information about drift term $\theta_d(t)$ is not necessary and calibration to yield curve is trivial. That is, in our formulation, we do not need to treat drift of the stochastic differential equation and we need to simulate stochastic variable only on discrete time step and numerical calculation can be done much more efficient than in the traditional formulation. The parameters which control our model are initial discount factor, volatility of Markov process $\tilde{\sigma}_d(t)$ and strength of mean reversion $a_d(t)$, which give discount factor as a function of Markov process as will be stated afterwards.

A.2.2. *Swaption volatility in the Hull–White model*

In the XVA model, generally speaking, rates volatilities should be calibrated to swaption market. In the Hull–White model, exact solution using the Jamashidian technique is available in calibration. However, simpler (faster) approximation (Tan, 2012) for swaption volatility representation is available. This gives the simple relationship between Hull–White volatility and swaption volatility, which is useful in KVA (Market Risk) when the sensitivity method is used and SIMM MVA where sensitivity with swaption volatility is necessary.

Now let there be a tenor structure $[T_0, T_1, \ldots, T_N, T_{N+1}]$, and let swap rate which starts at T_n and has interest exchanges at $[T_{n+1}, \ldots, T_{m+1}]$ be $S_{nm}(t)$. Swap rate is given by

$$S_{nm}(t) = \frac{(D_d(t, T_n) - D_d(t, T_{m+1}))}{\sum_{j=n}^{m} \delta_j D_d(t, T_{j+1})}$$

The stochastic dynamics of it is given by

$$dS_{nm}(t) = \frac{(dD_d(t, T_n) - dD_d(t, T_{m+1}))}{\sum_{j=n}^{m} \delta_j D_d(t, T_{j+1})} - \frac{(D_d(t, T_n) - D_d(t, T_{m+1}))}{\left(\sum_{j=n}^{m} \delta_j D_d(t, T_{j+1})\right)^2} \times \left(\sum_{j=n}^{m} \delta_j dD_d(t, T_{j+1})\right)$$

Here, the dynamics of discount factor is given by

$$\begin{aligned} dD_d(t, T) &= -B_d(t, T) D_d(t, T) dX_d(t) \\ &= -B_d(t, T) D_d(t, T) \tilde{\sigma}_d(t) dW_d(t) \end{aligned}$$

And swap rate dynamics is given by

$$dS_{nm}(t) = \left(\frac{1}{A_{nm}(t)}\right)\Bigg\{-B(t,T_n)D(t,T_n) + B(t,T_{m\times 1})D(t,T_{m+1})$$
$$+ S_{nm}(t)\sum_{j=n}^{m}\delta_j B_d(t,T_{j+1})D_d(t,T_{j+1})\Bigg\}\tilde{\sigma}(t)dW_d(t)$$

where $A_{nm}(t) = \sum_{j=n}^{m}\delta_j D_d(t,T_{j+1})$.

Here discount factor $D_d(t,T)$ is of course a stochastic variable, but if we approximate it as

$$D_d(t,T) = \frac{D(0,T)}{D(0,t)}$$

we will have the following swap rate dynamics:

$$dS_{nm}(t) = \left(\frac{1}{A_{nm}(0)}\right)\Bigg\{-B(t,T_n)D(0,T_n) + B(t,T_{m\times 1})D(0,T_{m+1})$$
$$+ S_{nm}(0)\sum_{j=n}^{m}\delta_j B_d(t,T_{j+1})D_d(0,T_{j+1})\Bigg\}\tilde{\sigma}(t)dW_d(t)$$

In this situation, swap rate follows normal distribution with volatility

$$\sigma^2_{\text{Normal}}(n,m) = \left(\frac{1}{A_{nm}(0)}\right)^2\int_0^{T_n}\Bigg\{-B(t,T_n)D(0,T_n) + B(t,T_{m\times 1})$$
$$\times D(0,T_{m+1}) + S_{nm}(0)\sum_{j=n}^{m}\delta_j B_d(t,T_{j+1})$$
$$\times D_d(0,T_{j+1})\Bigg\}^2\sigma_d^2(t)dt$$

And the price of payers swaption is given by

$$\text{Normal B}\ \ (K,T_n,S(0),A(0),\sigma_{\text{Normal}}(n,m))$$
$$= A(0)\left[(S(0)-K)N(d_1) + \sigma_{\text{Normal}}(n,m)\sqrt{T}_n\exp\frac{(-\frac{d_1^2}{2})}{\sqrt{2\pi}}\right]$$

where

$$d_1 = \frac{S(0) - K}{\sigma_{\text{Normal}}\sqrt{T_n}}$$

Note that in the Hull–White model, rates follow (approximately) displaced diffusion but in our approximation, they follow normal. However, actually rates distribution is close to normal and our approximation is quite good.

A.2.3. *Two-factor Hull–White model*

As is emphasized in Chapter 9, the interest rate part of an XVA model should have at least two factors. In this section, two-factor Hull–White model will be summarized (Tsuchiya, 2019a).

In the two-factor Hull–White model, short rate is given by

$$r(t) = x_1(t) + x_2(t) + \phi(t)$$

where

$$x_i(t) = -a_i(t)x_i(t)dt + \sigma_i(t)dW_i(t)$$
$$dW_i(t)dW_j(t) = \rho(t)dt$$

with $(i,\ j = 1,\ 2)$.

Here, by converting the Markov process $x_i(t)$ to a driftless one

$$X_i(t) = \exp\left(\int_0^t a_i(u)du\right) x_i(t)$$
$$dX_i(t) = \tilde{\sigma}_i(t)dW_i(t)$$

where $\tilde{\sigma}_i(t) = \exp\left(\left(\int_0^t a_i(u)du\right)\right)\sigma_i(t)$, discount factors are given by

$$D(t,T) = A(t,T)\exp(-B_1(t,T)X_1(t) - B_2(t,T)X_2(t))$$

where

$$A(t,T) = \frac{D(0,T)}{D(0,t)} \exp\left\{\frac{1}{2}[B_1^2(t,S) - B_1^2(T,S)]\Xi_1(t)\right.$$
$$+ \frac{1}{2}[B_2^2(t,S) - B_2^2(T,S)]\Xi_2(t)$$
$$\left. + [B_1(t,S)B_2(t,S) - B_1(T,S)B_2(T,S)]\Xi_{12}(t)\right\}$$
$$B_i(t,T) = \int_t^T \exp\left(-\int_0^s a_i(v)dv\right) ds$$
$$\Xi_i(t) = \int_0^T \tilde{\sigma}_i^2(u)du$$
$$\Xi_{12}(t) = \int_0^T \tilde{\sigma}_1(u)\tilde{\sigma}_2(u)\rho_{12}(u)du$$

A.2.4. *Correlation structure of two-factor Hull–White model*

We will analyze the correlation between coinitial swap rates in the Hull–White model in this section. Here, interest exchanges of swaps are on the tenor structure $[0 = T_0, T_1, \ldots, T_{N+1}]$ where all the tenors are $\delta = T_{j+1} - T_j$. Swap rate with interest exchanges at $[T_{n+1}, T_{n+2}, \ldots, T_{m+1}]$ is written as $S_{nm}(t)$.

Here, we will discuss the issues about calibration of the Hull–White model to the spread option market.

For the expiry T_n, the calibration instruments are volatilities (σ_{nm} and σ_{nl}) and correlation ($\rho_{\text{Swap};ml}$) of the two coinitial swap rates $S_{nm}(t)$ and $S_{nl}(t)$. Here, $T_m < T_l$ is assumed. For example, T_m is 2 years and T_l is 10–20 years.

We assume mean reversion parameters are constant and assumed to be $a_1 > a_2$. So

$$B_1(t,T) = \frac{e^{-a_1 t} - e^{-a_1 T}}{a_1}$$
$$B_2(t,T) = \frac{e^{-a_2 t} - e^{-a_2 T}}{a_2}$$

Now we will introduce the (terminal) correlation of Markov process $\rho_M(T_n)$ such that

$$\Xi_{12}(T_n) = \rho_M(T_n)\sqrt{\Xi_1(T_n)\Xi_2(T_n)}$$

We will approximate swap rate by forward rate with the same tenor structure as the swap rate

$$\frac{D(t,T_{m+1})}{D(t,T_n)} = \frac{1}{(1+\delta S_{nm}(t))^{(T_{m+1}-T_n)/\delta}}$$

In this approximation, stochastic process of swap rate is given by

$$\begin{aligned} dS_{nm}(T_n) = \left(\frac{1+\delta S_{nm}(0)}{\delta_{nm}}\right) &\{-B_1(T_n,T_{m+1})dX_1(t) \\ &-B_2(T_n,T_{m+1})dX_2(t)\} \end{aligned}$$

where $\delta_{nm} = T_{m+1} - T_n$.

We have an approximate formula for covariance between swap rates

$$\begin{aligned} \mathrm{Cov}(S_{nm}(T_n)S_{nl}(T_n)) = &\left(\frac{1+\delta S_{nm}(0)}{\delta_{nm}}\right)\left(\frac{1+\delta S_{nl}(0)}{\delta_{nl}}\right) \\ &\times \{B_1(T_n,T_m)B_1(T_n,T_l)\Xi_1(T_n) \\ &+ B_2(T_n,T_m)B_2(T_n,T_l)\Xi_2(T_n) \\ &+ [B_1(T_n,T_m)B_2(T_n,T_l)+B_2(T_n,T_m) \\ &\times B_1(T_n,T_l)]\,\Xi_{12}(T_n)\} \end{aligned}$$

The swap rate (terminal) correlation is given by

$$\begin{aligned} \rho_{\mathrm{Swap}} &= \mathrm{Corr}(S_{nm}(T_n)S_{nl}(T_n)) \\ &= \frac{\mathrm{Cov}(S_{nm}(T_n)S_{nl}(T_n))}{\sqrt{\mathrm{Cov}(S_{nm}(T_n)S_{nm}(T_n))\mathrm{Cov}(S_{nl}(T_n)S_{nl}(T_n))}} \end{aligned}$$

Now we will investigate the correlation structure between swap rates using this formula.

In the limit of $\rho_M(T_n) \to -1$ (perfect decorrelation of Markov process), the correlation of swap rate is simplified and given by

$$\mathrm{Corr}(S_{nm}(T_n)S_{nl}(T_n)) = \frac{\left\{ \begin{array}{l} \left(B_1(T_n,T_m)\sqrt{\Xi_1(T_n)} - B_2(T_n,T_m)\sqrt{\Xi_2(T_n)}\right) \\ \quad \times \left(B_1(T_n,T_l)\sqrt{\Xi_1(T_n)} - B_2(T_n,T_l)\sqrt{\Xi_2(T_n)}\right) \end{array} \right\}}{\sqrt{\begin{array}{l} \left(B_1(T_n,T_m)\sqrt{\Xi_1(T_n)} - B_2(T_n,T_m)\sqrt{\Xi_2(T_n)}\right)^2 \\ \quad \times \left(B_1(T_n,T_l)\sqrt{\Xi_1(T_n)} - B_2(T_n,T_l)\sqrt{\Xi_2(T_n)}\right)^2 \end{array}}}$$

That is, correlation between swap rates can be +1 or −1 depending on the parameters (strength of mean reversion and volatilities (variances) of Markov processes).

Actually, because $\frac{B_1(T_n,T_m)}{B_2(T_n,T_m)} > \frac{B_1(T_n,T_l)}{B_2(T_n,T_l)}$, we divide the region of the square of ratio of variances $\sqrt{\frac{\Xi_2(T_n)}{\Xi_1(T_n)}}$ into the following three cases:

(I) $\sqrt{\frac{\Xi_2(T_n)}{\Xi_1(T_n)}} > \frac{B_1(T_n,T_m)}{B_2(T_n,T_m)} > \frac{B_1(T_n,T_l)}{B_2(T_n,T_l)}$

(II) $\frac{B_1(T_n,T_m)}{B_2(T_n,T_m)} \geq \sqrt{\frac{\Xi_2(T_n)}{\Xi_1(T_n)}} > \frac{B_1(T_n,T_l)}{B_2(T_n,T_l)}$

(III) $\frac{B_1(T_n,T_m)}{B_2(T_n,T_m)} > \frac{B_1(T_n,T_l)}{B_2(T_n,T_l)} \geq \sqrt{\frac{\Xi_2(T_n)}{\Xi_1(T_n)}}$

In region (II), if the correlation of Markov process $\rho_M(T_n)$ approaches −1, swap rate correlation ρ_{Swap} converges to −1.

On the other hand, if the parameters are in region (I) or (III), when $\rho_M(T_n) \to -1$, swap rate correlation ρ_{Swap} converges to +1.

Actually, when the correlation of Markov process moves from −1 to +1, the correlation of swap rate moves according to the graphs in Figs. A.1 and A.2. If variances are in region (I) or (III), when the Markov process correlation moves from +1 to −1, the swap rate correlation decreases once and again increases to +1.

Therefore, if variances are in region (I) or (III), the model does not explain decorrelation of a swap rate sufficiently.

On the other hand, if the variances pair is in region (II), in the limit $\rho_M(T_n) \to -1$, swap rate correlation converges to −1 and swap rate decorrelation is well explained.

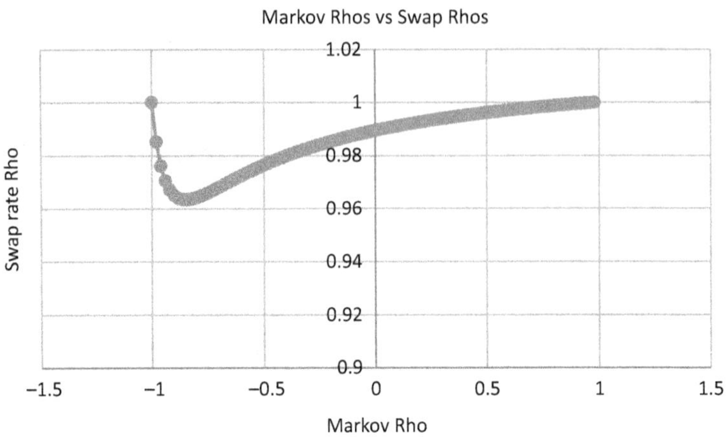

Fig. A.1: Region (I) or (III).

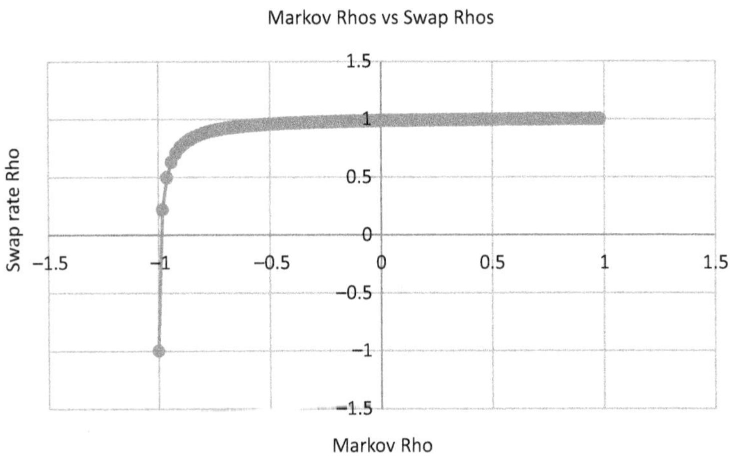

Fig. A.2: Region (II).

At the first glance, it looks strange that even when parameters (or length of longer swap) change continuously, the convergence point of correlation jump from −1 to +1, but it is not.

Actually, in the Monte Carlo simulation, in the limit of $\rho_M(T_n) \to -1$, the scatter plot between the short swap rate $S_{nm}(T_n)$ and long swap rate $S_{nl}(T_n)$ changes as the length of long swap rate changes as per the graph given in Figs. A.3–A.5 when parameters are in region [III], the scatter plot has a positive slope and as they reach to the boundary to region [II], the slope becomes close to flat and when

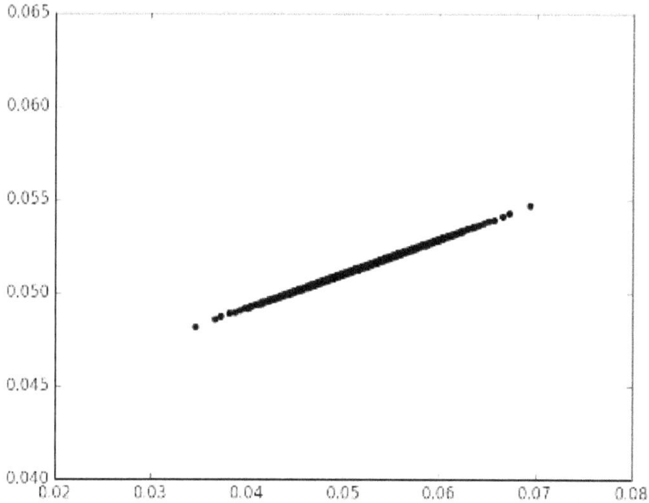

Fig. A.3: Scatter plot of 2-year swap rate vs 7-year swap rate.

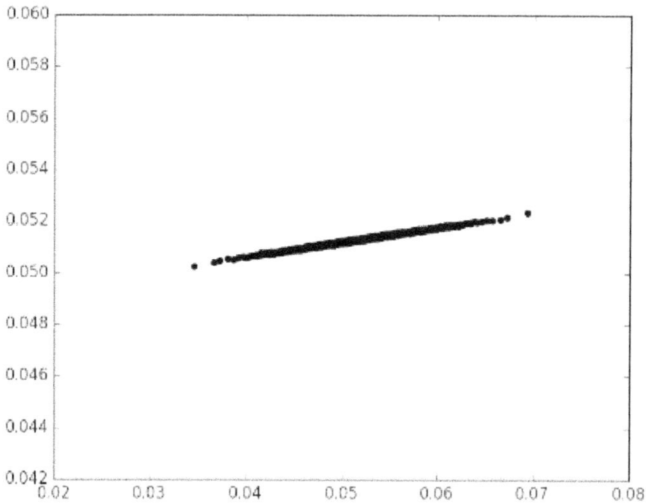

Fig. A.4: Scatter plot of 2-year swap rate vs 8-year swap rate.

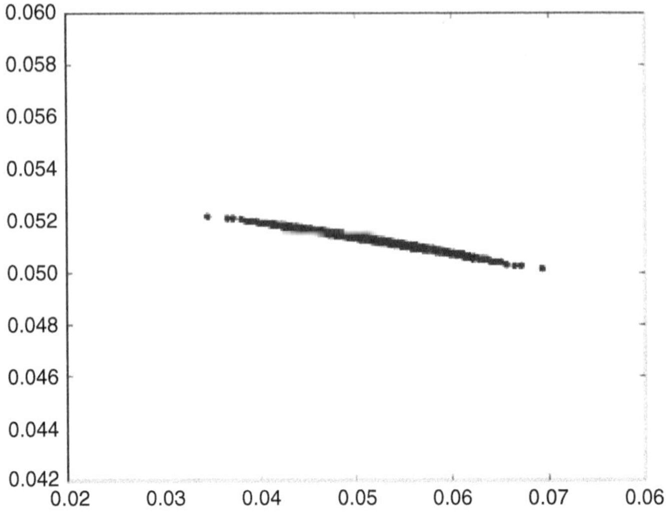

Fig. A.5: Scatter plot of 2-year swap rate vs 9-year swap rate.

they go into region [II], the slope becomes negative. The movement of the scatter plot is continuous, but the correlation changes from +1 to −1 discontinuously.

Note that for the given $\frac{B_1(T_n,T_m)}{B_2(T_n,T_m)} \geq \sqrt{\frac{\Xi_2(T_n)}{\Xi_1(T_n)}}$, as maturity of the long swap T_l moves from T_m to ∞, because $\frac{B_1(T_n,T_l)}{B_2(T_n,T_l)}$ is a decreasing function, the situation moves from region (III) to region (II) and the swap rates correlation decreases as it should.

Based on the above observation, the calibration of two-factor Hull–White model can be done as follows. (Here shorter swap is short enough (typically 2 years) and longer swap is long enough (typically 10 years))

(a) For the given mean reversion parameters, determine variance ratio $\sqrt{\frac{\Xi_2(T_n)}{\Xi_1(T_n)}}$ in region (II).
(b) Fit volatility $\tilde{\sigma}_2(t)$ (with $\sqrt{\frac{\Xi_2(T_n)}{\Xi_1(T_n)}}$ fixed) and correlation $\rho_M(T_n)$ such that volatility of one of the swap rate (for example, σ_{nl}) and correlation of swap rates $\rho_{\text{Swap};ml}$ fit to the market.

Note that in this scheme, the model can be calibrated to only one of the swap volatilities of the spread option. By introducing the term structure of mean reversion, it would be possible to calibrate to the volatilities of both of the swap for spread option.

A.2.4.1. *Better approximation*

The approximation formula in the previous section is enough accurate to analyze the nature of the two-factor Hull–White model. However, it uses discount factor at the start and end of the swap, and there are some errors in the approximation formula of correlation. In this section, more accurate approximation will be discussed. (Note that as is stated in Chapter 1, spread option market has dried up after the crisis and to use rough approximation is also the choice.)

Let us express swap rate as a basket of forward Libors

$$S_{nm}(t) = \sum_{j=n}^{m} \omega_j(t) L_j(t)$$

$$\omega_j(t) = \frac{\delta_j D(t, T_{j+1})}{\sum_{k=n}^{m} \delta_k D_d(t, T_{k+1})}$$

By assuming discount part can be frozen to time 0 value, we have the following stochastic differential equation:

$$dS_{nm}(t) = \sum_{j=n}^{m} \omega_j(0) dL_j(t)$$

Here, if we approximate Libor process as

$$\begin{aligned} dL_j(t) &= \frac{1}{\delta_j} \frac{D(t, T_j)}{D(t, T_j)} \{B_1(T_j, T_{j+1}) dX_1(t) + B_2(T_j, T_{j+1}) dX_2(t)\} \\ &\sim \left(L_j(0) + \frac{1}{\delta_j}\right) \{B_1(T_j, T_{j+1}) dX_1(t) + B_2(T_j, T_{j+1}) \\ &\times dX_2(t)\} \end{aligned}$$

Covariance between Libors is given by

$$\begin{aligned}\operatorname{cov}(L_i(T_n), L_j(T_n)) = &\left(L_i(0)+\frac{1}{i}\right)\left(L_j(0)+\frac{1}{\delta_j}\right)\\ &\times\{B_1(T_i,T_{i+1})B_1(T_j,T_{j+1})\Xi_1\\ &+B_2(T_i,T_{i+1})B_2(T_j,T_{j+1})\Xi_2\\ &+[B_1(T_i,T_{i+1})B_2(T_j,T_{j+1})\\ &+B_1(T_j,T_{j+1})B_2(T_j,T_{j+1})]\,\Xi_{12}\}\end{aligned}$$

With this approximation, the covariance between swap rates is given by

$$\operatorname{Cov}(S_{nm}(T_n)S_{nl}(T_n)) = \sum_{ij}\omega_i(0)\omega_j(0)\operatorname{cov}(L_i(T_n), L_j(T_n))$$

This approximation has a better fitting than the one presented earlier.

A.2.5. *Interest rate skew in XVA*

As is emphasized in Chapter 9, XVA adds optionality. Therefore, even if there are only swaps in the netting set (or portfolio), the adjustments depend on swaption volatility. Depending on the situation, it depends on the volatility of far Out-of-the-Money (OTM) volatilities. So it is desirable to use the interest rate model which can control volatility skew in XVA calculation. With many interest rate models which have control of volatility skew, the Markov Functional Model can be implemented with a high-speed numerical method and is flexible enough for the calculation of XVA (including KVA).

The multifactor Markov functional model was introduced by Hunt and Kennedy (2005) via a pre-model. The pre-model should have a desired correlation structure for the derivatives valued. It does not need to be arbitrage-free, and they suggested to use a Markovian approximation of the Libor Market Model. The Markov functional sweep makes the model to fit to the market and arbitrage-free. However, we will adopt a different approach. We already have the two-factor Hull–White model which is based on the two-factor

Markov process and fit to the spread option market. Therefore, we will use the two-factor Hull–White model as a pre-model of Markov functional model.

Markov functional sweep is done for the coterminal swaptions with maturity T_N. For two-factor Markov processes $X(t) = (X_1(t), X_2(t))$, coterminal swap rate in Hull–White model $S_{mN}(X(t))$ is given as an analytic functional and adopted as a pre-model. We assume swap rate in the Markov functional model is a function of it, $Y_{mN}(S_{mN}(X(t)))$. The swap rate is fitted to the displaced diffusion distribution of market swap rate such that it can capture skew of the market. This fitting of pre-model to market swap rate distribution is called Markov functional sweep. The sweep is done as follows.[1]

Let us calculate the following digital swaption of pre-model:

$$J_m(x^*)= D(0,S)E^S\left[\widetilde{\text{pvbp}}_m(X(t))1\left\{S_{mN}(X(t))>x^*\right\}|F_0\right]$$

where $\widetilde{\text{pvbp}}(X(t))$ is a present value of basis point for swap $S_{mN}(X(t))$.

Let us also consider a digital swaption valuation

$$V_m(K) = D(0,S)E^S\left[\widetilde{\text{pvbp}}_m(X(t))1\left\{Y_{mN}(S_{mN}(X(t))) > K\right\}|F_0\right]$$

If $Y_m(x^*) = K$, the above two equations should have the same value and

$$J_m(x^*) = V_m(K)$$

should be satisfied and functional form is given by

$$Y_{mN}(x^*) = K = V_m^{-1}(J_m(x^*))$$

The swap rate functional derived above $Y_{mN}(S_{mN}(X(t)))$, follows displaced diffusion, T.

[1]In two-factor Markov Functional model, the numerical integration should be done with great care to have a stable result.

A.2.6. *Cross-currency Hull–White Model*

As has been explained before, XVA model is based on the cross-currency model. In this section, cross-currency Hull–White model is explained. The Hull–White model established in Section A.2.5 is a domestic part of the cross-currency model. In the cross-currency Hull–White model, domestic S forward measure is used. In the model, suffix d means domestic currency, f means foreign currency and x means exchange rate.

As is explained in Section A.2.5, domestic currency in the cross-currency Hull–White model is described by the Markov process $X_d(t)$ and numeraire $N_d(t, X_d(t)) = D_d(t, S, X_d(t))$. Next we will introduce driftless Markov process $X_f(t)$ and numeraire in foreign measure $N_f(t, X_f(t)) = D_f(t, S, X_f(t))$. *In foreign measure, functional form of numeraire $N_f(t,X_f(t))$ is the same as the one in domestic measure and it is martingale. Note that in domestic measure $X_f(t)$, is not driftless from the effect of measure change.* Volatility of Markov process $X_f(t)$ is calibrated to swaption volatility in foreign currency market. Exchange rate is not matingale in domestic S forward measure but forward exchange rate $F(t, S) = Fx(t)D_f(t, S)/D_d(t, S)$ is martingale. Therefore, forward exchange rate is given by

$$F(t, S) = F(0, S) \exp\left(X_x(t) - \frac{1}{2}\Xi_x^2(t)\right)$$

for driftless Markov process $X_x(t)$ and the variance of it, $\Xi_x(t)$

Summarizing them the cross-currency Hull–White model is constructed as follows.

There are three Markov processes

$$dX_d(t) = \tilde{\sigma}_d(t)dW_d(t)$$

$$dX_f(t) = \mu_f(t)dt + \tilde{\sigma}_f(t)dW_f(t)$$

$$dX_x(t) = \tilde{\sigma}_x(t)dW_x(t)$$

where drift term in foreign rate process $\mu_f(t)$ is called quanto adjustment and comes from measure change.

Here volatilities of both domestic and foreign rates $\tilde{\sigma}_d(t)$ and $\tilde{\sigma}_f(t)$ are calibrated to swaption volatilities market. (Mean reversions, which determine functional form of discount factor are also determined as is explained before.) All we need to determine is drift term of foreign Markov process $\mu_f(t)$ and volatility of exchange rate process $\tilde{\sigma}_x(t)$.

A.2.6.1. *Quanto adjustment*

In this section, we will derive quanto adjustment $\mu_f(t)$. Let us consider derivative security which pays $V(T)$ at time T. The value of it at time 0, $V(0)$ is the same when calculated in foreign measure and domestic measure. Therefore, the following relationship is satisfied:

$$D_d(0,S)E_d^S\left[\frac{V(T)Fx(t)}{D_d(T,S)}|F_0\right] = D_f(0,T)Fx(0)E_f^S\left[\frac{V(T)}{D_f(T,S)}|F_0\right]$$

Accordingly

$$E_d^S\left[\frac{Y(t)F(T,S)}{F(0,S)}|F_0\right] = E_f^S\left[Y(t)|F_0\right]$$

It means that by multiplying $F(t,S)/F(0,S)$, we can change expectation value in foreign measure to that in domestic measure. That is, Radon–Nikodym derivative is given by

$$\frac{dQ_f}{dQ_d}(t) = \frac{F(t,S)}{F(0,S)}$$

Because $X_f(t)$ is martingale in foreign measure, $X_f(t)F(t,S)/F(0,S)$ is martingale in domestic measure. As Fx forward is given by $F(t,S) = F(0,S)\exp(X_x(t) - \frac{1}{2}\Xi_x^2(t))$, by calculating drift term of $X_f(t)F(t,S)$ in domestic measure, we have

$$\begin{aligned} d(X_f(t)F(t,S)) &= F(t,S)dX_f(t) + X_f(t)dF(t,S) + dX_f(t)dF(t,S) \\ &= F(t,S)(\mu_f(t)dt + \tilde{\sigma}_f(t)dW_f(t)) \\ &\quad + F(t,S)dX_x(t)dX_f(t) + (\text{not drift term}) \\ &= F(t,S)\mu_f(t)dt + F(t,S)\tilde{\sigma}_f(t)\tilde{\sigma}_x(t)\rho_{xf}(t)dt \\ &\quad + (\text{not drift term}) = 0dt + \text{not drift term}) \end{aligned}$$

Therefore, we have derived quanto adjustment as

$$\mu_f = -\tilde{\sigma}_f(t)\tilde{\sigma}_x(t)\rho_{xf}(t)$$

Appendix B

A Brief Outline of Regulatory Capital Charges for Financial Institutions

Regulatory capital is a complex subject and this book cannot attempt to do justice to the treatment of regulatory capital charges. However, we attempt to outline the framework as regards OTC derivatives because of two main reasons (Tan, private communication):

(1) Regulatory capital for Counterparty Credit Risk (CCR) and Credit Valuation Adjustment (CVA) is one of the primary considerations in a model for CVA.
(2) Regulatory capital charges for both counterparty risk (CCR and CVA) and other risk (e.g. market risk, operational risk, leverage ratio) give rise to Capital Valuation Adjustment (KVA), and an understanding of the framework is essential to understanding KVA.

We seek here not to give the precise rules for implementing a regulatory capital framework that satisfies regulatory requirements, but only to present the framework in a way that allows the reader to understand the implications for fully costed derivatives valuation and to appreciate the calculations and modeling subtleties required. For the framework of the Basel III, [Hellmich (2015)]. The web page https://www.modval.org/home/ is also a good resource (Tan, private communication).

B.1. The Latest Prescribed Regulatory Framework

The latest prescribed regulatory framework, as agreed by the Basel Committee for Banking Supervision[1] in December 2017, is due to be phased in over the years from 2022 to 2027. This framework is referred to as Basel III.

The rough outline is that banks must hold capital in the form of fully paid up equities or other instruments where the investor is not contractually entitled to repayment. These different instruments compromise different tiers of capital with regulatory stipulations on what percentage has to be in terms of different qualities of capital.

Components of Capital

Capital requirements are defined based on risk-weighted assets (RWAs), i.e. exposures are converted to the "equivalent" exposures corresponding to standard assets, multiplied by some weights taking account of the risk of these assets. The components of capital are:

- Market Risk RWA
- Credit Risk RWA
- Operational Risk RWA

Summing these up, we then have a total amount of RWAs, that defines capital requirements.

Standardized methods are prescribed for calculating RWAs for each of these categories. Alternatively, sophisticated banks which have obtained regulatory approval from their national supervisors may use internal models to calculate Market Risk RWA and Credit Risk RWA.

Output Floor when Internal Model Used

Any bank seeking to use internal models for calculating capital will be subject to an output floor, i.e.

[1]This committee comprises central banks and regulatory supervisory authorities in major economies (including developing economies) and collectively sets the framework for regulatory capital, with national supervisors given further discretion on details of implementation.

Capital = max(Internal Model Capital, Output Floor × Standardized Model Capital).

Floor on Capital based on Leverage Ratio

Capital requirements is defined as the amount necessary to cover
max(Computed Capital, Floor from Leverage Ratio)

It is the purpose of this appendix to discuss these concepts, but not to provide the necessary level of detail for actual implementation.

B.1.1. *Leverage ratio*

The concept is that leverage ratio is defined as

$$\text{Leverage Ratio} = \frac{\text{Capital}}{\text{On and off balance sheet exposure}}$$

The leverage ratio is a non-risk-based backstop to the risk-based capital rules and aims to limit excessive build-up of leverage. The concept came about in response to the 2008 financial crisis where banks had extremely large amounts of assets in relation to their capital, because their portfolios were designed to be well hedged leading to risk-based measures like Value at Risk (VAR), showing much less capital requirements. The problem with large leverage however is that it only requires a small relative change in the value of the assets (e.g. due to any inaccuracy from modeling or where stressed markets lead to some assets having far greater drop in market values than their hedges) to wipe out the bank's capital in a crisis. Thus, the regulators' desire for a non-risk-based floor.

Banks are required to hold enough capital such that the leverage ratio remains larger than the regulatory prescribed minimum, where there are separate prescribed levels for Tier 1 Capital and Common Equity Tier 1 Capital — the highest quality of capital in terms of permanence. There is an additional buffer for Globally Systematically Important Banks (G-SIBs).

Banks that do not meet the leverage ratio requirements will have constraints on their ability to distribute capital, as defined based on minimum capital conservation ratios.

Specifically, Table B.1 applies.

Table B.1: Leverage ratio.

CET risk-weighted ratio	Tier 1 leverage ratio	Minimum capital conservation ratios (% of earnings)
4.5–5.375%	3–3.125%	100%
>5.375–6.25%	>3.125–3.25%	80%
>6.25–7.125%	>3.25–3.375%	60%
7.125–8%	>3.375–3.5%	40%
>8%	>3.5%	0%

Note: G-SIBs are subjected to an additional 1% risk-weighted buffer and 0.5% leverage ratio buffer.

Given that the leverage ratio is meant to be non-risk-based, for exposure for purposes of this leverage ratio, the standardized method must be used, with some modifications on multiplier and netting of exposures, to be conservative. The details of the standardized method will be discussed with respect to the different calculations in Section B.1.2.

B.1.2. *Output floor*

The output floor applies to any bank seeking to use internal models to compute capital requirement. It has the following effect on capital requirements:

Capital = max(Internal Model Capital, Output Floor × Standardized Model Capital)

This output floor is to be phased in between 2022 and 2027, with a step up each year until the final target floor is reached in 2027.

Year	2022	2023	2024	2025	2026	2027
Output floor	50%	55%	60%	65%	70%	72.5%

The origins of the output floor also lay in the 2008 financial crisis, where there was a crisis of confidence in many financial institutions following large losses from subprime CDOs and related derivatives. There was concern on the suitability of many banks' internal models, given the failure to predict the capital requirements that would have been adequate to sustain the banks over the losses from the crisis — indeed, a vast majority of banks required bailouts. One concern were whether all relevant risks were captured — for this, there was a massive expansion of the type of risk measures included. There was further concern of excessive variability in the RWAs computed by banks' internal models, as discovered by various Quantitative Impact Studies following the 2008 crisis, with this variability not easily explained by genuine differences in the risk profiles of these banks. There is some concern that some banks are too aggressive in their internal models and not allocating adequate risk capital for the exposures they are subject to.

Consequently, the regulators have opted for standardization, seeking to floor aggregate risk capital computed from internal models, in relation to the use of the standardized model. This naturally sacrifices accuracy and efficiency, in the name of simplicity and comparability across different institutions.

B.2. Operational Risk Capital

Operational risk is defined as risk of loss due to inadequate or failed internal processes, people and systems or from external events. It can include losses from legal failures, but not from poor business decisions.

Whereas prior to Basel III, banks were permitted to use internal models to calculate operational risk, regulators have now decided that losses from operational risk are too hard to predict reliably from banks' internal models and have imposed a standardized approach based on the following:

Operational Risk Capital = Business Indicator Component × Internal Loss Multiplier.

The business indicator (BI) is a sum of three components:

- Interest, leases and dividend component
- Services component
- Financial component

This BI is further multiplied by marginal coefficients α_i, which is defined per bucket.

Bucket	BI range (in € billion)	BI marginal coefficients α_i
1	≤ 1	12%
2	$1 < \text{BI} \leq 30$	15%
3	> 30	18%

The Internal Loss Multiplier (ILM) is defined as

$$\text{ILM} = \text{Ln}\left(\exp(1) - 1 + \left(\frac{\text{LC}}{\text{BIC}}\right)^{0.8}\right)$$

where LC is the Loss Component, which is defined as 15 times the average annual operational risk losses incurred over the previous 10 years and BIC is the Business Indicator Component.

Considering the quantities involved, operational risk capital is related to income and size of business, but does not bear a direct relation to market values of the bank's positions.

B.3. Credit Risk, Market Risk and the Various Components of Capital

Credit risk comprises the risk of loss due to default and/or change of credit quality of the counterparty. This can be a party to a direct lending relation (e.g. in a corporate loan) or a counterparty to a bilateral Over-the-counter (OTC) derivatives transaction. The latter means that CCR is a special case of credit risk. Thus, we have the credit risk RWA, including CCR RWA.

Market risk is the risk of loss due to change in values of risk factors (e.g. interest rates, foreign exchange, equities) that affect the valuation of the security. However, as noted earlier and in much of this book, the performance of a derivative depends on the counterparty being solvent if the derivative turns out to be valuable due to market conditions — this is of course CVA. Naturally, CVA also changes in value with changes in market conditions. In fact, during the 2008 financial crisis, banks suffered far greater losses from change in CVA than in actual defaults. Thus, CVA risk can be seen as part of market risk. Hence, we have market risk RWA, including CVA RWA as a special case.

In addition, following the 2008 financial crisis, regulators have found the capital charges set aside to be inadequate and have thus sought additional capital charges for two sets of securities. Generally, they relate to losses due to credit events well beyond what is expected under normal market conditions and the same losses for Credit Correlation Trading, i.e. CDO tranches. These had initially led to Basel 2.5 defining Incremental Risk Charge (i.e. amount of loss on credit products at 99.9% over 1 year horizon due to default or credit rating migration) and Comprehensive Risk Measure (i.e. amount of loss at 99.9% over 1 year horizon applicable to Credit Correlation Trading). The Basel III reincarnations of these charges are:

- Default Risk Charge for Non-securitization — Applicable to equities (default is assumed to cause stock price to go to zero) and debt instruments, but where only default is captured.
- Default Risk Charge under Securitization Framework — Where only standardized approach is allowed for Credit Correlation Trading.

As this is not a regulatory manual, we do not attempt to formally classify the above under credit or market risk components, but rather we seek to present an outline of the calculations, so that the reader can understand the methodology requirements for time 0 calculation, as well as the implications for computation of KVA.

For this reason, we shall present them in a different manner as befits the calculation framework.

B.4. Counterparty Risk

Whereas regulators may officially consider CCR losses to be capitalized under Credit Risk RWA and CVA variability to be capitalized under market risk RWA, the two share a lot of infrastructure. In particular, both are computed at the level of netting sets of counterparties to a bank. Thus, we treat them together in this section.

B.4.1. *CCR element (part of credit risk)*

Credit risk is the risk of loss due to default or deterioration in credit quality of a counterparty to which a bank is exposed in the course of its business. The Basel III framework was designed around financial institutions, with the bulk of credit risk being from direct loans to counterparties. Specifically, these are grouped into asset classes (banks, corporates, specialized lending, corporate purchased receivables, qualifying revolving retail exposures, residential retail mortgages, other retail and retail purchased receivables), with different rules on calculating credit risk.

Derivatives trading is a special case which really comes under exposure to corporates and banks due to off balance sheet activity. For this, the standardized approach to CCR is prescribed or for banks with more advanced models, approval can be sought from national supervisors for the use of the Foundation Internal Ratings-Based method (F-IRB-CCR) or the Advanced Internal Ratings-Based method (A-IRB-CCR).

Standardized Method (SA-CCR)

Under Basel III, the Standardized Approach replaces the old Current Exposure Method and Standardized Method — two alternative approaches to compute CCR. The starting point is the formula

$$\text{Risk-weighted assets (RWA)} = K \times 12.5 \times \text{EAD}$$

where K is risk weight and EAD is Exposure at Default.

Risk Weight

Here different risk weights are assigned to different borrowers and further differentiated according to their credit ratings. Table B.2 shows risk weights assigned to some borrowers, but is not intended to be comprehensive.

Exposure at Default (for a derivative) (Under SA-CCR)

For collateralized OTC derivatives transactions, under the standard approach for CCR (SA-CCR), exposure amount is given by the

Table B.2: Risk weight.

External Rating	AAA to AA−	A+ to A−	BBB+ to BBB−	BB+ to B−	Below B−	Unrated
Sovereign	0%	20%	50%	100%	150%	100%
Public sector entity Option 1: Sovereign rating	20%	50%	100%	100%	150%	100%
Option 2: Own rating	20%	50%	50%	100%	150%	50%
Bank ("Base")	20%	30%	50%	100%	150%	NA
Bank (Short term exposures)	20%	20%	20%	50%	150%	NA
Corporate ("Base")	20%	50%	75%	100%	150%	100%

Note: Short term exposures are those with original maturity of 3 months or less or those arising from movement of goods across national borders with maturity of 6 months or less.

formula below

$$\text{Exposure amount} = \text{alpha} \times (\text{RC} + \text{PFE})$$

where alpha = 1.4 is a regulator-prescribed multiplier, RC is the replacement cost further defined below and PFE is the potential future exposure also defined below.

For unmargined trades,

$$\text{RC} = \max(V - C, 0)$$

where V is the value of the derivative transactions in the netting set and C is the haircut-adjusted value of the net collateral held.

For margined trades,

$$\text{RC} = \max(V - C, \text{TH} + \text{MTA} - \text{NICA}, 0)$$

where TH is the threshold amount (i.e. smallest level of exposure that triggers a margin call), MTA is the minimum transfer amount (i.e. smallest amount that must be transferred as a consequence of a margin call) and NICA is the net independent collateral amount (i.e. segregated or unsegregated collateral posted by counterparty less unsegregated collateral posted by the bank). (Thus, TH + MTA

– NICA represents the largest exposure that would not trigger a variable margin call.)

PFE is defined as

$$\text{PFE} = \text{multiplier} \times \text{AddOn}^{\text{aggregate}}$$

$$\text{where multiplier} = \min\left\{1, \text{Floor} + (1 - \text{Floor}) \times \exp\left(\frac{V - C}{2 \times (1 - \text{Floor}) \times \text{AddOn}^{\text{aggregate}}}\right)\right\}$$

with floor being 5%, and

$$\text{AddOn}^{\text{aggregate}} = \sum_a \text{AddOn}^{(a)}$$

where the sum is taken over each asset class (i.e. diversification benefits across asset classes are not recognized).

The multiplier is meant to take account of negative replacement cost — if so the number is less than 1, with the floor being an attempt to add having a PFE of 0.

The AddOn for Interest Rates and FX asset class is defined as

$$\text{AddOn} = \text{SF} \times \text{Effective Notional}$$

where SF is the supervisory factor (specific to each asset class and calibrated to reflect Effective Expected Positive Exposure (EPE) of a single at-the-money linear trade of unit notional and 1-year maturity) and Effective Notional is as given in Table B.3.

In interest rates, Effective Notional for currency j is defined by combining equivalent quantities for buckets k of the same currency j as follows:

$$\begin{aligned}
&\text{Effective Notional}_j^{(\text{IR})} \\
&= \left[\left(D_{j1}^{(\text{IR})}\right)^2 + \left(D_{j2}^{(\text{IR})}\right)^2 + \left(D_{j3}^{(\text{IR})}\right)^2 + 1.4 \times D_{j1}^{(\text{IR})} \times D_{j2}^{(\text{IR})}\right. \\
&\quad \left. + 1.4 \times D_{j2}^{(\text{IR})} \times D_{j3}^{(\text{IR})} + 0.6 \times D_{j1}^{(\text{IR})} \times D_{j3}^{(\text{IR})}\right]^{1/2}
\end{aligned}$$

Table B.3: Supervisory parameters.

Asset class	Subclass	Supervisory factor(%)	Correlation(%)	Supervisory option volatility(%)
Interest rate		0.50	NA	50
foreign exchange		4.0	NA	15
credit, Single name	AAA	0.38	50	100
	AA	0.38	50	100
	A	0.42	50	100
	BBB	0.54	50	100
	BB	1.06	50	100
	B	1.6	50	100
	CCC	6.0	50	100
Credit, Index	IG	0.38	80	80
	SG	1.06	80	80
Equity, Single name		32	50	120
Equity, Index		20	80	75
commodity	Electricity	40	40	150
	Oil/Gas	18	40	70
	Metals	18	40	70
	Agricultural	18	40	70
	Other	18	40	70

with effective notional for bucket k of currency j defined by

$$D_{jk}^{(\text{IR})} = \sum_{i \in \{\text{Ccy}_j, \text{MB}_k\}} \delta_i \times d_i^{(\text{IR})} \times \text{MF}_i^{(\text{type})}$$

where

(1) $\text{MF}_i^{(\text{type})} = \frac{3}{2}\sqrt{\frac{\text{MPOR}_i}{1y}}$ if margined or $\text{MF}_i^{(\text{type})} = \sqrt{\frac{\min(M,1y)}{1y}}$ if unmargined is the maturity factor (related to Margin Period of Risk if margined or capped at 1 year otherwise).

(2) $d_i^{(\text{IR})} = \frac{\exp(-0.05\times S_i)-\exp(-0.05\times E_i)}{0.05} \times$ Notional being duration-adjusted notional with S_i and E_i being the start and end dates of the underlying (thus, we are assuming 5% interest rates), and

(3) supervisory delta being

$$\delta_i = N\left(\frac{\ln\left(\frac{P_i}{K_i}\right) + 0.5 \times \sigma_i^2 \times T_i}{\sigma_i \sqrt{T_i}}\right)$$

for a bought call or sold put,

$$\delta_i = N\left(-\frac{\ln\left(\frac{P_i}{K_i}\right) + 0.5 \times \sigma_i^2 \times T_i}{\sigma_i\sqrt{T_i}}\right)$$

for a bought put or sold call, with or simply +1 or −1 for linear products, where P_i is underlying price, K_i is strike, σ_i is volatility and T_i is time to maturity. (Note the use of a log-normal delta for options, which does not work too well with negative rates.)

Note that the formula for AddOn aggregation is modified for equities, credit and commodities to account for non-perfect correlation across individual entities as follows:

$$\text{AddOn} = \left[\left(\sum_k \rho \times \text{AddOn}\left(\text{Entity}_k\right)\right)^2 + \sum_k \left(1-\rho^2\right) \times \left(\text{AddOn}\left(\text{Entity}_k\right)\right)^2\right]$$

where the correlation ρ is prescribed by supervisors in Table B.3. as supervisory factor.

Summary of Computational Requirements

Nothing in the above formula requires sophisticated calculations. Thus, any model to produce the above just needs as much computation as necessary to obtain present value for replacement cost calculations.

(F-IRB-CCR or A-IRB-CCR)

Banks using the Internal Rating-Based Model to calculate CCR must use the formula below to calculate risk-weighted assets to corporates or banks:

$$\text{Risk-weighted assets (RWA)} = K \times 12.5 \times \text{EAD}$$

where EAD is exposure at default, K is the capital requirement computed by

$$K = \left[\text{LGD} \times N \left[\frac{N^{-1}(\text{PD})}{\sqrt{1-R}} + \sqrt{\frac{R}{1-R}} N^{-1}(0.999) \right] \right.$$
$$\left. - \text{PD} \times \text{LGD} \right] \times \frac{1 + (M - 2.5) \times b}{1 - 1.5 \times b}$$

with $N(x)$ and $N^{-1}(x)$ being the cumulative normal distribution function and its inverse.

LGD being the loss given default, PD being the 1-year probability of default floored at 0.05%, M being effective maturity and R being correlation given by

$$R = 0.12 \times \frac{1 - \exp(-50 \times \text{PD})}{1 - \exp(-50)}$$
$$+ 0.24 \times \left(1 - \frac{1 - \exp(-50 \times \text{PD})}{1 - \exp(-50)}\right)$$

Further, a multiplier of 1.25 is applied to the correlation parameter of all exposures to regulated financial institutions whose total assets are greater than US$100 billion or unregulated financial institutions regardless of size.

It thus follows that the inputs from the internal model are exposure-at-default EAD, probability of default PD, loss given default LGD and effective maturity M.

Foundation Internal Ratings-Based Method (F-IRB)

Under this method, probability of default PD is calculated by the financial institution.

LGD, M and EAD are however obtained from supervisory estimates under standardized rules.

Advanced Internal Ratings-Based Method (A-IRB)

In this method, banks calculate all four quantities PD, LGD, M and EAD.

It should be noted that probability of default PD and loss given default LGD are attributes of a corporate or bank and apply to all exposures. (It is true that LGD is sometimes used to deal with collateralized exposures and can reflect reduced losses as a consequence. However, banks that use an internal model to compute exposures at netting set levels that take account of collateral are to ignore any effect of collateralized on LGD to avoid double counting.)

Thus, the main specialization in the valuation of derivatives (vs corporate loans) is the need to compute effective maturity M and exposure at default EAD.

EAD is calculated in an approach analogous to computing accounting CVA. Specifically, in the Internal Model Method, EAD is defined as (Basel Committee on Banking Supervision, 2008, Annex 4)

$$\text{EAD} = \alpha \times \text{Effective EPE}$$

where α is a regulatory multiplier set at 1.4, but where banks can seek approval to compute this internally by considering simulated counterparty exposure vs economic capital, subject to a floor of 1.2, and Effective EPE is defined as

$$\text{Effective EPE} = \sum_{k=1}^{\min(1y,\,\text{maturity})} \text{Effective EE}_{t_k} \times \Delta t_k$$

where t_k are future time points (not necessarily evenly spaced), and Effective Expected Exposure (Effective EE) is computed recursively from Expected Exposure (EE) via

$$\text{Effective EE}_{t_k} = \max\left(\text{Effective EE}_{t_{k-1}}, \text{EE}_{t_k}\right)$$

where EE_t is the average exposure at time t, taken over possible future values of relevant market risk factors (e.g. interest rates, foreign exchange, etc.).

Notice here that the definition of EPE is not quite the same as that from CVA, which takes the average exposure of paths that lead to positive PV. Notice further that Effective EPE is only interested in a time horizon no longer than 1 year, whereas in accounting CVA the only limit to time horizon is maturity. The logic here is that it is expected that a bank can unwind a deal with a counterparty in at most one year's time.

The final quantity that needs explanation is the effective maturity M, which is given by

$$M = \frac{\sum_{k=1}^{t_k \leq 1y} \text{Effective EE}_k \times \Delta t_k \times \text{df}_k + \sum_{t_k > 1y}^{\text{maturity}} \text{EE}_k \times \Delta t_k \times \text{df}_k}{\sum_{k=1}^{t_k \leq 1y} \text{Effective EE}_k \times \Delta t_k \times \text{df}_k}$$

where df is the risk-free discount factor up to time point t_k.

Notice here we are taking a weighted average of maturity, where the weight is Effective EE up to 1 year and just EE (i.e. can decrease over time) thereafter.

Summary of Computational Requirements

The calculation of Exposure at Default under A-IRB effectively looks like EPE calculations that we have come across in our discussion of CVA in Chapter 2. Note that if we want capital at a future time t, we need the EPE calculation as seen as of that time. Given this is an expectation (i.e. average quantity) rather than a tail quantity, it is expected to be more stable. However, taking an expectation as of future time t based on realized path of distributions at that time (e.g. for KVA calculation) is like having a Monte Carlo within a Monte Carlo. This definitely requires techniques like Least-Squares Monte-Carlo to predict future values of EPE conditional on realizing some state variables along a path at time t.

B.4.2. *CVA element (part of market risk)*

Accounting CVA is a charge that makes its way into the P&L accounts to reflect the expected losses to a financial institution as a result of counterparties defaulting when they owe money to this institution. Given CVA is part of valuation, CVA risk can be considered part of market risk. But as noted earlier, CVA is calculated at the netting set level, since upon default of a counterparty, a bank's loss is based on the net exposures to the counterparty based on distinct legally recognized netting sets (e.g. by legal entities within different countries). This means the calculation shares a lot of the infrastructure for CCR. And in fact, many components of the calculation are the same or at least related.

Basel III allows banks to use either the standardized "Basic Approach" (based on generic features like maturity of instruments) or the advanced (internal model) "Standardized Approach" (based on sensitivities) when given approval by supervisory authorities. We explore these calculations next.

Standardized "Basic Approach" (BA-CVA)

Institutions using the standardized approach can opt for a reduced version, where hedges are not recognized, or a full version.

Reduced Version

Capital is given by

$$K_{\text{reduced}} = \sqrt{\left(\rho \sum_c \text{SCVA}_c\right)^2 + (1-\rho^2)\sum_c \text{SCVA}_c^2}$$

where $\rho = 50\%$ is a supervisory parameter to give partial recognition that a bank's total CVA risk is less than the sum of CVA risk for each counterparty and SCVA_c is the standalone CVA capital for counterparty c given by

$$\text{SCVA}_c = \frac{1}{\alpha} \times \text{RW}_c \times \sum_{\text{NS}} M_{\text{NS}} \times \text{EAD}_{\text{NS}} \times \text{DF}_{\text{NS}}$$

with RW_c being the supervisory risk weight for counterparty c as per Table B.4, M_{NS} being the effective maturity for the netting set NS calculated as for CCR but without application of the 5-year cap, EAD_{NS} is the exposure at default of the netting set NS calculated as for minimum capital requirements for CCR and DF_{NS} is a supervisory discount factor (set to 1 for banks using IMM and $\frac{1-\exp(-0.05\times M_{\text{NS}})}{0.05\times M_{\text{NS}}}$ for banks not using IMM), and $\alpha = 1.4$ is a supervisory factor (to convert EAD back to Effective EEPE).

Table B.4: Supervisory risk weight.

Sector of counterparty	IG risk weight (%)	HY and NR risk weight (%)
Sovereigns (including central banks, multilateral development banks)	0.5	3.0
Local government, government-backed non-financials, education and public administration	1.0	4.0
Financials including government-backed financials	5.0	12.0
Basic materials, energy, industrials, agriculture, manufacturing, mining and quarrying	3.0	7.0
Consumer goods and services, transportation and storage, administrative and support service activities	3.0	8.5
Technology, telecommunications	2.0	5.5
Health care, utilities, professional and technical activities	1.5	5.0
Other sector	5.0	12.0

Full Version

This recognizes the benefits of CVA hedges, with eligible hedges being single-name CDS, single-name contingent CDS and index CDS.

The full version has a floor that limits the extent to which hedging can reduce capital as given by $\beta = 0.25$ and utilizes the reduced version to achieve this. The capital is

$$K_{\text{full}} = \beta \times K_{\text{reduced}} + (1 - \beta) \times K_{\text{hedged}}$$

where

$$K_{\text{hedged}} = \sqrt{\begin{array}{l}(\rho \sum_c (\text{SCVA}_c - \text{SNH}_c) - \text{IH})^2 \\ \quad + (1 - \rho^2) \sum_c (\text{SCVA}_c - \text{SNH}_c)^2 + \sum_c \text{HMA}_c\end{array}}$$

Table B.5: Supervisory prescribed correlation between counterparty and its hedge.

Single-name hedge h of counterparty c	Value of r_{hc}
References counterparty c directly	100
Has legal relation with counterparty c	80%
Shares sector and region with counterparty c	50%

with

$$\mathrm{SNH}_c = \sum_{h \in c} r_{hc} \times \mathrm{RW}_h \times M_h^{\mathrm{SN}} \times B_h^{\mathrm{SN}} \times \mathrm{DF}_h^{\mathrm{SN}}$$

$$\mathrm{IH} = \sum_{i} \mathrm{RW}_i \times M_i^{\mathrm{ind}} \times B_i^{\mathrm{ind}} \times \mathrm{DF}_i^{\mathrm{ind}}$$

$$\mathrm{HMA}_c = \sum_{h \in c} \left(1 - r_{hc}^2\right) \left(\mathrm{RW}_h \times M_h^{\mathrm{SN}} \times B_h^{\mathrm{SN}} \times \mathrm{DF}_h^{\mathrm{SN}}\right)^2$$

with further M being the remaining maturity (the superscript "SN" referring to single name and "ind" referring to index), B being notional, RW being risk weight of the hedge (subscript h) or index (subscript i), DF being the non-IMM supervisory discount factor as defined when discussing the reduced version and r_{hc} is supervisory prescribed correlations given by Table B.5.

Summary of Computation Requirements

Nothing in the above formula requires sophisticated calculations. Thus, any model to produce the above just needs as much computation as per the standardized approach for CCR.

Advanced (Internal Model) "Standardized Approach" (SA-CVA)

The internal model for CVA risk is actually an adaptation of the standardized approach for market risk (SA-TB), to be discussed in Section B.5.1. It is thus referred to as the Standardized Approach and is sensitivities based. But a bank can only adopt this if approval is granted by national supervisors. In making clear the distinction with CCR charge, the drift of risk factors must be consistent with a risk-neutral probability measure, since CVA is part of valuation.

The capital requirement is given by

$$K = m_{\text{CVA}} \sqrt{\sum_b K_b^2 + \sum_b \sum_{c \neq b} \gamma_{bc} K_b K_c}$$

where m_{CVA} is a regulatory multiplier with default value 1.25 to take account of higher level of model risk compared with sensitivities of market value of trading book instruments and can be further increased by the bank's supervisory authority,

$$K_b = \sqrt{\left[\sum_{k \in b} \text{WS}_k^2 + \sum_{k \in b} \sum_{l \in b; k \neq l} \rho_{kl} \text{WS}_k \text{WS}_l\right] + R \sum_{k \in b} \left[\left(\text{WS}_k^{\text{Hdg}}\right)^2\right]}$$

where R is the hedging disallowance parameter currently set at 0.01 (to prevent perfect hedging), the correlation parameters γ_{bc} and ρ_{kl} applicable to each risk type are prescribed by regulators,

$$\begin{aligned} \text{WS}_k &= \text{WS}_k^{\text{CVA}} + \text{WS}_k^{\text{Hdg}} \\ \text{WS}_k^{\text{CVA}} &= \text{RW}_k s_k^{\text{CVA}} \\ \text{WS}_k^{\text{Hdg}} &= \text{RW}_k s_k^{\text{Hdg}} \end{aligned}$$

where RW_k is the risk weight prescribed by regulators for risk type k, and s_k^{CVA} and s_k^{Hdg} are the net sensitivities of the CVA and its hedge to risk type k.

Sensitivities are computed by bump and revalue of a base quantity, which is regulatory CVA. Regulatory CVA is to be calculated in the same approach as for accounting CVA (including use of the risk-neutral measure in contrast to CCR), with some exceptions: the primary one being that there should be no recognition of DVA (i.e. the effect of the bank's own losses), and there could be adjustments if needed to meet the requirements imposed for regulatory CVA.

Risk Weights and Correlation Parameters for Different Asset Classes

The correlation parameters and risk weights vary according to asset class and even vertices (e.g. IR tenor) within each asset class.

Table B.6: Risk weight for different asset classes.

Risk factor	1y	2y	5y	10y	30y	Inflation
Risk weight	1.59%	1.33%	1.06%	1.06%	1.06%	1.59%

Table B.7: Correlations between pairs of risk factors.

ρ_{kl}	1y (%)	2y (%)	5y (%)	10y (%)	30y (%)	Inflation (%)
1y	100	91	72	55	31	40
2y		100	87	72	45	40
5y			100	91	68	40
10y				100	83	40
30y					100	40
Inflation						100

For interest rates, each currency is considered a bucket, with the cross-bucket correlation parameter being $\gamma_{bc} = 0.5$. For currencies USD, EUR, GBP, AUD, CAD, SEK, JPY and the bank's domestic currency, the following risk weights and correlations given in Tables B.6 and B.7 apply.

For other currencies, there is only one risk factor plus inflation and risk weight is set to 2.25% while correlation with interest rates and inflation is set to 40%.

Delta sensitivities are obtained by a bump and revalue approach where the bump size is 1 bp.

Similarly, vega sensitivities are defined to involve a 1% relative bump in all interest rate and inflation vega risk factors. Here the risk weight is $\text{RW}_k = \text{RW}_\sigma \sqrt{6}$ where $\text{RW}_\sigma = 55\%$ for both interest rate and inflation volatilities.

Similarly, for FX, the buckets are individual currencies with respect to the bank's domestic currency, with $\gamma_{bc} = 0.6$. Risk weights for all currency pairs is $\text{RW}_k = 21\%$, while risk weight for FX volatility is $\text{RW}_k = \text{RW}_\sigma \sqrt{4}$ where $\text{RW}_\sigma = 55\%$.

Counterparty credit spread has buckets based on sector, while risk factors are for 0.5 year, 1 year, 3 years, 5 years and 10 years. In contrast, reference credit spread has buckets based on investment grade vs high-yield/non-rated and each is further subdivided into sectors. Equities on the other hand have buckets based on whether the cap is large or small, then further subdivided into emerging markets vs sectors. Commodity buckets are based on the nature of the commodity.

No sensitivity to curvature or basis risk is required.

Summary of Computation Requirements

The internal model (standardized approach) for market risk capital requires calculation of sensitivities. Since sensitivities are calculated by bump and revalue, each sensitivity requires a separate PV calculation. Thus, calculating 5 delta sensitivities per curve will mean 5 times the computation effort of single valuation for interest rates.

B.5. Market Risk Capital

The three parts of market risk capital we shall consider here are general market risk RWA, Default Risk Charge and the Securitization Framework.

B.5.1. *General market risk RWA*

Here, we consider the capital charges that are to be held by banks as a result of risks in their trading books. These risks come from movements in risk factors such as interest rates, foreign exchange, equities, commodities and credit. Basel III allows for a standardized approach or an Internal Models Approach (IMA) — the latter being available to more sophisticated banks that have obtained supervisory approval.

Standardized Approach (SA-TB)

In contrast to Basel II (which allowed only for broad characteristics such as maturity to be taken into account), the new requirements are for sensitivities to be used in the standardized approach, and there is a limited recognition of offsets from hedging activities. The rationale is to have an approach that is more risk-sensitive but still simple enough for most banks to adopt and also for comparability across different institutions.

Seven risk classes are defined in this approach: general interest rate risk, credit spread risk (non-securitization), credit spread risk (securitization, non-correlation trading), credit spread risk (securitization, correlation trading), equity risk commodity risk and foreign exchange risk.

Institutions are required to compute delta, vega and curvature risk. Further, they are required to compute risk charges for each risk class based on three different scenarios for correlation. Some diversification benefit is recognized within each risk class, but not between risk classes. And a residual risk add-on is introduced to capture risk of exotic products that the standardized model is likely not to capture.

Delta and Vega Risks

The formula is

$$\text{Delta (respectively, Vega)} = \sqrt{\sum_b K_b^2 + \sum_b \sum_{c \neq b} \gamma_{bc} S_b S_c}$$

where

$$K_b = \sqrt{\sum_k \text{WS}_k^2 + \sum_k \sum_{k \neq l} \rho_{kl} \text{WS}_k \text{WS}_l}$$

with all quantities within square roots floored by zero, and

$$\text{WS}_k = \text{RW}_k s_k$$

with s_k being the net sensitivity to a risk factor and RW_k the corresponding risk weight.

Sensitivities and risk weights are defined for each risk factor. For example, under general interest rate risk, sensitivities are defined with respect to each currency, curve (separate curve for OIS and each Libor tenor) and the following vertices in Table B.8.

For selected currencies by the Basel Committee (EUR, USD, GBP, AUD, JPY, SEK, CAD and domestic currency of a bank), the risk weights may be divided by 2.

Table B.8: Risk weight for SA-TB.

Vertex	0.25y	0.5y	1y	2y	3y	5y	10y	15y	20y	30y
Risk weight	2.4%	2.4%	2.25%	1.88%	1.73%	1.5%	1.5%	1.5%	1.5%	1.5%

Further, there is one vertex for inflation risk factor with risk weight 2.25% and cross-currency basis risk factor also has a risk weight of 2.25%.

For interest rates, the delta risk correlation ρ_{kl} is set to 99.90% between sensitivities WS_k and WS_l within the same bucket (i.e. same currency), same vertex but different curve. If within different vertex but same bucket and curve, correlation is set to $\max\left(\exp\left(-\theta\frac{|T_k-T_l|}{\min(T_k-,)}\right), 40\%\right)$ where θ is set to 3%. Where different curves are involved, we further multiply by 99.90% the correlation from different vertices.

Correlation between sensitivity to inflation and a vertex of the curve is set to 40%. There is 0% correlation assumed between interest rate sensitivities and cross-currency basis sensitivities. The parameter $\gamma_{bc} = 50\%$ is used for aggregating between different buckets (i.e. currencies).

Note that the use of non-zero correlation is meant to recognize the benefits of diversification and hedging, but the prescribed correlation parameters were chosen to be conservative, except where the same bucket, curve and vertex is involved, i.e. limited recognition of portfolio benefits.

For foreign exchange, a relative risk weight equal to 30% is used. And correlation of $\gamma_{bc} = 60\%$ is used to aggregate FX sensitivity — note FX sensitivity is defined with respect to a bank's reporting currency.

Similarly, buckets are defined for credit (non-securitization) based on whether Investment Grade or High Yield, further subdivided by sector. Credit (non-securitization) further uses maturity buckets of 0.5 year, 1 year, 3 years, 5 years and 10 years. And buckets are defined for equities based on whether Large (≥USD 2 billion market capitalization) or Small, further subdivided into emerging market or advanced economy, and then into sector. And buckets are defined based on nature of underlying commodity. Similar recognition of portfolio effect from diversification and hedging is attained by use of prescribed non-zero correlations.

Sensitivities are computed as per bump and revalue, as per typical sensitivities used in risk management. For general interest rate risk, credit risk and equity repo risk, the prescription is for a 1 bp bump, i.e.

$$s_k = \frac{V(r_k + 0.0001) - V(r_k)}{0.0001}$$

For FX, equities and commodities, a 1% bump is used, i.e.

$$s_k = \frac{V(1.01R_k) - V(R_k)}{0.01}$$

Vega for GIRR is defined based on maturity vertices of 0.5 year, 1 year, 3 years, 5 years and 10 years and residual underlying maturity of the same.

Curvature Risk

Curvature is a simple attempt to capture the impact of nonlinear price moves (e.g. of options or long-dated products showing nonlinear sensitivity to rates).

$$\text{Curvature risk} = \sqrt{\sum_b K_b^2 + \sum_b \sum_{c \neq b} \gamma_{bc} S_b S_c \psi(S_b, S_c)}$$

where $S_b = \sum_k \mathrm{CVR}_k$ for all risk factors in bucket b, and

$$\psi(S_b, S_c) = \begin{cases} 0 & \text{if } S_b < 0 \text{ and } S_c < 0 \\ 1 & \text{otherwise} \end{cases}$$

$$K_b = \sqrt{\begin{aligned} &\max\Big(0, \textstyle\sum_k \max(\mathrm{CVR}_k, 0)^2 \\ &\quad + \textstyle\sum_k \sum_{k \neq l} \rho_{kl} \mathrm{CVR}_k \mathrm{CVR}_l \psi(\mathrm{CVR}_k, \mathrm{CVR}_l)\Big) \end{aligned}}$$

$$\mathrm{CVR}_k = -\min\left[\sum_i \left\{V_i\left(x_k^{\mathrm{RW}^{(\mathrm{curvature})}+}\right) - V_i\left(x_k\right) - \mathrm{RW}_k^{(\mathrm{curvature})} s_{ik}\right\}, \sum_i \left\{V_i\left(x_k^{\mathrm{RW}^{(\mathrm{curvature})}-}\right) - V_i\left(x_k\right) - \mathrm{RW}_k^{(\mathrm{curvature})} s_{ik}\right\}\right]$$

with i being an instrument subject to curvature risk with respect to risk factor k, $x_k^{\mathrm{RW}^{(\mathrm{curvature})}+}$ and $x_k^{\mathrm{RW}^{(\mathrm{curvature})}-}$ being the positive and negative curvature shocks, and $V_i(x)$ the value of the instrument i when risk factor k takes value x, and $\mathrm{RW}_k^{(\mathrm{curvature})}$ being the curvature risk weight.

For interest rates, curvature shocks are applied to all vertices and curves at the same time. There is no curvature shock applied to inflation or cross-currency basis.

A similar approach is taken for the other risk classes.

For FX and equities, the curvature risk weights are equal to the delta risk weights. For GIRR, CSR and commodities, the curvature risk weight is the parallel shift of all vertices for each curve based on the highest prescribed delta risk weight (e.g. this is based in the 0.25 year of vertex for GIRR).

Correlation Scenarios

In order to assess the impact of correlation under periods of financial stress, the risk charges must be calculated for each risk class based on "high", "medium" and "low" correlations. The "medium" correlations are as defined earlier. "High" correlations are defined by multiplying "medium" correlations by 1.25, subject to a cap of 100%. "Low" correlations are defined by multiplying "medium" correlations by 0.75. The ultimate portfolio level risk charge is obtained as the highest of the three scenario-related portfolio level risk capital charges.

Residual Risk

The residual risk add-on is to be calculated for relevant instruments in addition to other charges above under the standardized approach.

This is defined as the sum of gross notional amounts of instruments bearing residual risks, multiplied by 1% for instruments with an exotic underlying or 0.1% for other instruments with other residual risks.

Examples of exotic underlying exposures include: longevity risk, weather, natural disasters, future realized volatility.

Instruments bearing other residual risks are those subject to vega or curvature risk, with payoffs that cannot be perfectly replicated by a linear combination of vanilla options and instruments in the Correlation Trading Portfolio (except if recognized as eligible hedges). Such residual risk types can include gap risk (e.g. barrier options, Asian options and digital options), correlation risk (e.g. basket options, best-of options, spread options, basis options, Bermudan options and quanto options) and behavioral risk (e.g. callable bond held by retail clients).

Summary of Computation Requirements

The new standardized approach for market risk capital requires calculation of sensitivities. Since sensitivities are calculated by bump and revalue, each sensitivity requires a separate PV calculation. Thus, calculating 10 delta sensitivities per curve, say on 3 curves (OIS, Libor 3 months, Libor 6 months) will mean 30 times the computation effort of single valuation for GIRR.

Internal Models Approach (IMA)

The main changes from Basel II are as follows:

- VAR at 99% level will be replaced by Expected Shortfall at 97.5% level.
- Rather than a uniform 10 days horizon for market risk metrics, liquidity horizon will depend on the asset class.
- Internal models approval will be at trading desk level rather than legal entity level, where each desk seeking approval must separately satisfy criteria on backtesting and quality of P&L explains.

- A new concept of non-modelable risk factors (where there is lack of liquid observable data), which requires separate capitalization (replacing the previous framework of Risk Not in VAR).

Implications of Desk Level Approval

To be clear on the implications, it means that a bank will quite possibly have approval for the Internal Models Approach for some desks but not others (e.g. harder to satisfy criteria for desks with exotic risk or illiquid products).

Aggregate Capital Charge

Aggregate capital charge is defined as

$$\mathrm{ACC} = \mathrm{CA} + \mathrm{DRC} + \mathrm{CU}$$

where CA is capital charge from desks using internal model, DRC is default risk charge (discussed in Sections A.7.2 and A.7.3) and CU is capital charge from desks not approved for internal model (hence using standardized model).

Further, define

$$\mathrm{CA} = \max\left(\mathrm{IMCC}_{t-1} + \mathrm{SES}_{t-1}, m_c \mathrm{IMCC}_{\mathrm{avg}} + \mathrm{SES}_{\mathrm{avg}}\right)$$

where m_c will be 1.5 or the multiplier set by individual supervisory authorities, the quantities with subscript "avg" are based on a weighted average of the previous 60 days,

$$\mathrm{SES} = \sqrt{\sum_{i=1}^{L} \mathrm{ISES}_{\mathrm{NM},i}^2 + \sum_{j=1}^{K} \mathrm{SES}_{\mathrm{NM},j}}$$

with $\mathrm{ISES}_{\mathrm{NM},i}$ being the stress scenario capital charge for idiosyncratic credit spread non-modelable risk i from the L risk factors aggregated with zero correlation and $\mathrm{SES}_{\mathrm{NM},j}$ being the stress scenario capital charge for non-modelable risk j,

$$\mathrm{IMCC} = \rho\mathrm{IMCC}\left(C\right) + \left(1-\rho\right)\sum_{i=1}^{R}\mathrm{IMCC}\left(C_i\right)$$

with $\mathrm{IMCC}\left(C\right) = \mathrm{ES}_{R,S} \times \frac{\mathrm{ES}_{F,C}}{\mathrm{ES}_{R,C}}$, $\mathrm{ES}_{R,S}$ being the expected shortfall under stress based on a reduced set of risk factors captured by the internal model, $\mathrm{ES}_{R,C}$ being the expected shortfall under current (past 12 months) markets based on the reduced set of risk factors, $\mathrm{ES}_{F,C}$ being the expected shortfall under current markets based on the full set of risk factors, the "i" subscript denoting partial expected shortfall charges (i.e. all other risk factors held constant) and $\rho = 0.5$ is the relative weight assigned by regulators to the firm's internal model, to enforce a certain amount of non-diversifiable risk.

$\mathrm{ES}_{R,C}$ is computed in the 12-month period by the bank, which it identifies to be when its portfolio experiences the largest loss, where the data must go back to and include 2007. The reduced set of risk factors takes into account the practical compromise that it might be difficult to obtain sufficient history for the full set of risk factors.

We should remark that for the internal model to be approved, the quality of explains of the modelable risk factors must be satisfactory. It is beyond the scope of this book to discuss the computation of capital for non-modelable risk factors. But to a first order, it is expected the bulk of capital will come from IMCC instead.

Liquidity Horizons

The new liquidity horizons applicable to different risk factor categories is as per Table B.9.

Based on a given liquidity horizon, expected shortfall is calculated as

$$\mathrm{ES} = \sqrt{\left(\mathrm{ES}_T\left(P\right)\right)^2 + \sum_{j\geq 2}\left(\mathrm{ES}_T\left(P,j\right)\sqrt{\frac{\mathrm{LH}_j - \mathrm{LH}_{j-1}}{T}}\right)^2}$$

where T is the base horizon (10 days), $\mathrm{ES}_T\left(P\right)$ is the expected shortfall at horizon T of a portfolio with position $P = \left(p_i\right)$ with respect to shocks to all risk factors and the index "j" for expected shortfall denotes shocks based on the subset of risk factors denoted by

Table B.9: Liquidity horizon.

Risk factor category	Horizon (days)
Interest rate (EUR, USD, GBP, AUD, JPY, SEK, CAD and bank's domestic currency)	10
Interest rate (other currencies)	20
Interest rate: volatility	60
Interest rate: other types	60
Credit spread: sovereign (IG)	20
Credit spread: sovereign (HY)	40
Credit spread: corporate (IG)	40
Credit spread: corporate (HY)	60
Credit spread: volatility	120
Credit spread: other types	120
Equity price (large cap)	10
Equity price (small cap)	20
Equity price (large cap): volatility	20
Equity price (small cap): volatility	60
Equity: other types	60
FX rate (EURUSD, USDJPY, GBPUSD, AUDUSD, USDCAD, USDCHF, USDMXN, USDCNY, NZDUSD, USDRUB, USDHKD, USDSGD, USDTRY, USDKRW, USDSEK, USDZAR, USDINR, USDNOK, USDBRL, EURJPY, EURGBP, EURCHF, AUDJPY)	10
FX rate: other currency pairs	20
FX: volatility	40
FX: other types	40
Energy and carbon emissions trading price	20
Precious metals and non-ferrous metals price	20
Other commodities price	60
Energy and carbon emissions trading price: volatility	60
Precious metals and non-ferrous metals price: volatility	60
Other commodities price: volatility	120
Commodity: other types	120

$Q(p_i, j)$ — the set of risk factors for the desk where p_i is booked with liquidity horizons at least as long as LH_j.

The time series of changes in risk factors over the base interval T may be determined by overlapping observations.

Note that the above calculation of expected shortfall just involves scaling the base horizon expected shortfalls $\mathrm{ES}_T(P)$ and $\mathrm{ES}_T(P, j)$ suitably, so these are really the quantities that need to be computed.

Expected Shortfall

Expected shortfall was chosen by regulators partly due to what is perceived as some deficiencies in VAR, e.g. non-subadditivity: a more diversified portfolio does not always have lower VAR than a lesser portfolio because VAR only measures the amount of loss, the occurrence of which should not exceed the frequency threshold (1%), but not the expected amount of loss under such circumstances.

In contrast, expected shortfall measures how much one expects to lose on average if loss exceeds a threshold. Formally, define expected shortfall as

$$\mathrm{ES}_T(\alpha) = -E\left[V(T) - V(0) \,|V(T) - V(0) < Z(\alpha, T)\right]$$

where $E[\,]$ is an expectation, $V(t)$ is the value of the portfolio at time t and $Z(\alpha, T)$ satisfies $P(V(T) - V(0) < Z(\alpha, T)) = 1 - \alpha$.

Basel III requires expected shortfall to be based on a base horizon of $T = 10$ days and at confidence level of $\alpha = 97.5\%$. Thus, it measures the expected loss conditional on reaching the worse 2.5% of cases. The choice of 97.5% (vs 99%) for VAR is a compromise because of the difficulty of getting accurate tail numbers and also as this change was not intended to directly increase capital requirements.

Summary of Computational Requirements

As expected shortfall is a tail quantity, it requires a certain amount of accuracy in modeling, and hence can be computationally expensive. As discussed in Chapter 5 on MVA, VAR is typically modeled either by a parametric approach or by historical simulation, and approximations can be of the form such as using a sensitivities-based approximation (Taylor expansion) for value at future time. Certainly, the need to capture further ends of the tail (to get the average of all values less than 2.5% probability) may make it harder to achieve the same accuracy as VAR with existing methods, and so does the 10-day horizon (whereas VAR was traditionally calculated based on a 1-day horizon and multiplied by $\sqrt{10}$).

B.5.2. *Default risk charge for non-securitization*

Default Risk Charge (DRC) is intended to replace the current Incremental Risk Charge (IRC). The main differences are that

- DRC only considers default while IRC considers credit migration for instance.
- DFC covers bonds and equities, with the assumption that stock price drops to zero on default.

DRC can be treated via a standardized approach or internal models where approved by national supervisors. This is a complex topic to which we can do little justice in this book, except to introduce the framework to give the reader some idea of computational requirements.

Standardized Approach

For non-securitization, there is a table of risk weights by credit quality.

Credit quality	AAA	AA	A	BBB	BB	B	CCC	Unrated	Defaulted
Default risk weight	0.5%	2%	3%	6%	15%	30%	50%	15%	100%

We consider gross jump-to-default (JTD) risk, exposure by exposure.

$$\text{JTD (long)} = \max(\text{LGD} \times \text{notional} + \text{P\&L}, 0)$$
$$\text{JTD (short)} = \min(\text{LGD} \times \text{notional} + \text{P\&L}, 0)$$

where notional is bond-equivalent notional, P&L is cumulative mark-to-market loss (or gain) already taken on the exposure and LGD is loss given default.

This is set to 100% for non-senior debt, 75% to senior debt and 25% to covered bonds.

To account for defaults within the one-year horizon, the JTD for all exposures of maturity less than one-year and their hedges are scaled by a fraction of a year.

We can then write the default risk capital charge as

$$\mathrm{DRC}_b = \max\left[\left(\sum_{i\in\mathrm{Long}} \mathrm{RW}_i \mathrm{netJTD}_i\right) - \mathrm{WtS}\left(\sum_{i\in\mathrm{Short}} \mathrm{RW}_i \left|\mathrm{netJTD}_i\right|\right), 0\right]$$

where $\mathrm{WtS} = \frac{\sum \mathrm{netJTD_{Long}}}{\sum \mathrm{netJTD_{Long}} + \sum |\mathrm{netJTD_{Short}}|}$ is the hedge benefit ratio.

Summary of Computational Requirements

Nothing in the above formula requires sophisticated calculations. Thus, any model to produce the above just needs as much computation as per the standardized approach for CCR.

Internal Model

This is calculated for a one-year horizon at a confidence level of 99.9%, i.e. DRC is given by $Z(\alpha = 99.9\%, T = 1 \text{ year})$ which satisfies

$$P(V(T) - V(0) < Z(\alpha, T)) = 1 - \alpha$$

where $V(t)$ is the value of the portfolio at time t.

The simulation must consist of two types of systemic risk factors. Default correlations are to be based on credit spreads or equity prices and based on 10 years of data covering a period of stress.

Under DRC, an index is looked through to its constituent. So for DRC, it is necessary to treat a default of an index constituent by applying default to that constituent and reconstituting the value of the index. This can be very computationally expensive. For example, the iTraxx has 125 constituent underlying CDS, whereas the S&P 500 comprises 500 stocks.

DRC is taken as the greater of average DRC over previous 12 weeks and most recent DRC.

Note that probabilities of default have to be floored at 0.03%.

Summary of Computational Requirements

DRC is an extreme tail quantity and thus requires high accuracy in modeling, which is very computationally expensive. The extreme tail (0.1%) and long horizon will make it harder to achieve the same accuracy as VAR with existing methods. Further, if we consider the large number of calculations needed to deal with an index (by looking through the default of its constituents individually), then this method does lend itself to Adjoint Algorithmic Differentiation (assuming we approximate with sensitivities to risk factors — harder to justify given default will correspond to very large shock, but maybe OK given large number of constituents in indices and lack of better solution to such a complex problem).

B.5.3. *Securitization framework*

The framework for securitization is a specialized topic. There are separate arrangements for banks that have approval for internal models vs those that will use the standardized approach for credit risk, as pertains securitized products that satisfy the criteria of "simplicity, transparency and comparability" (STC), but all correlation trading portfolios will be subject to the standardized approach. Even the internal approach for STC products involve a heavy element of application of prescribed rules on top of internal estimates of PD (for foundation-internal rating-based approach) or additionally LGD (for advanced-internal ratings-based approach). Suffice to say, this means there is not a lot of computational requirements for exposures once these quantities are obtained. However, it is beyond the scope of this book to discuss this topic any further.

B.5.4. *Relevant calculations*

To summarize the computation requirements, we note the following:

- Standardized method requires sensitivities calculation for Market Risk RWA (excluding CVA RWA), but otherwise no calculation more complex than PV is required.
- Banks will always have to compute capital charge under standardized method, due to leverage ratio and output floor if using internal method.
- Banks using internal method need an Expected Shortfall (tail) calculation for market risk RWA, EEPE (a CVA-like calculation

of Exposure at Default) for CCR RWA, a sensitivities calculation for CVA RWA and an extreme tail calculation for DRC, with no other charges being subject to internal calculations.

In short, banks attempting to build a KVA framework will require the following:

- Ability to calculate sensitivities at a future time (can utilize Green–Kenyon Shocked-States Augmentation or Adjoint Algorithmic Differentiation if many bump and revalue calculations will be too slow).

If internal method are used, additionally:

- Ability to compute Expected Shortfall (tail) at a future time for market risk RWA (likely need Green–Kenyon Shocked-States Augmentation to deal with big shocks).
- Ability to compute EEPE (i.e. something akin to CVA) at future time (likely to need Least-Squares Monte Carlo to obtain future values based on state variables).
- Ability to compute extreme tail for DRC — this time quality of GKSSA may be harder to ascertain due to small number of samples far in the tail.

Conclusion

In this book, the practical approach to XVA has been discussed. The word practical means the model and the algorithm which make the calculation of XVA with practical calculation burden. In the conclusion, we will summarize the points to be considered in the development of the XVA model in practice.

The ultimate question we will consider is why we need a sophisticated pricing model. For the derivatives valuation, especially for the exotic interest rate or hybrid derivatives, many banks are developing sophisticated pricing models. Basically, the banks hedge their exotic derivatives position by the plain vanilla derivatives. For the hedge operation to be effective, they need an accurate pricing model which gives stable sensitivities.

The reasons the pricing models should have the above features are the following:

(1) If the sensitivities are not sufficiently stable and correct, the hedge is not effective.
(2) If the price is wrong, the hedge cost does not compensate the derivatives value.

With this observation, we would like to categorize the XVA into the following four categories:

From the above categorization, we need a reasonably sophisticated model for CVA because it is hedged though it does not need to be as sophisticated as risk-free valuation. On the other hand, for the FVA and MVA, the valuations are important because these are

(a)	Risk free value (Non-defaultable value)	The position is hedged and the market moves basically following the model.
(b)	CVA	Basically the position is hedged, but the hedge operation can be different from the model. (Usually, the credit spread is hedged by Index or Proxy.)
(c)	FVA (and DVA) and MVA	Basically not hedged. These are the actual cost related to the derivatives trade.
(d)	KVA	Not hedged. This is the cost for the shareholders. The actual rate is not clear.

the actual cost of the derivatives trade. However, because it is not hedged practically, the stability of the same level as risk-free price is not required. Here, the calculation burden of FVA is higher than CVA because it should be calculated in the funding set level rather than the netting set level in CVA. The calculation cost of MVA is much higher than CVA and FVA because the calculation of VAR is necessary for MVA.

Regarding KVA, we are not yet sure what the cost of capital is. In this situation, even if we calculate future capital accurately, we are not sure whether KVA is accurate or not.

The development of the valuation library for XVA started from that of CVA. MVA and KVA were introduced quite recently. So many banks developed MVA, KVA and other adjustments by enhancing CVA library. It is also a constraint to the XVA library because CVA calculation boils down to the calculation of exposure, where MVA and KVA need sensitivities (in the sensitivity VAR) of the exposure.

In summary, in the above list of valuations, the necessary granularity is in descending order, while the calculation burden is in ascending order. With this situation, we need to be considerate how much calculation and development cost can be spent for the calculation of the XVA. For the CVA, we should have reasonably sophisticated models, but for the KVA, we should consider whether we need to develop sophisticated models like exotic interest rate derivatives. That is, we need a balance between sophistication and the calculation burden.

I hope this book gives one of the benchmarks in the practice of XVA.

The development of XVA started, similar to derivatives valuations, by the global investment banks. However, the necessity of it is growing in many financial institutions. This book will be useful not only for the quant in global investment banks but also people who are willing to develop or manage XVA models in any financial institutions or consulting firms.

I believe all the necessary ingredients of XVA are discussed in this book but the development of the field is rather fast and there are some newly developed topics which are not discussed. One of the most significant ones is a relationship to machine learning. As is briefly stated in Chapter 9, application of LSM to the CVA of plain vanilla derivatives corresponds to regression to training set in supervised learning. The LSM in callable exotic derivatives corresponds to deep learning. The interactions between these two fields are beneficial for XVA calculation. Especially in machine learning, regression in high dimensional space is extensively used, where in the derivatives valuation, regression is used in rather smaller dimensional space. The details of this relationship will be published elsewhere.

Thank you for reading this book to the end!

References

Albanese, C. and Andersen, B. G. (2014). Accounting for OTC Derivatives: Funding Adjustments and the Re-Hypothecation Option, Working paper.

Albanese, C., Andersen, L. and Iabichino, S. (2014). The FVA Puzzle: Accounting, Risk Management and Collateral Trading, Working paper.

Andersen, L. B. and Piterbarg, V. V. (2010). *Interest Rate Modeling*, Vol. 1–3, Atlantic Financial Press.

Andreasen, J. (2014). CVA on an iPad Mini.

Antonov, A. and Brecher, D. (2012). Exposure & CVA for Large Portfolios of Vanilla Swaps: The Thin-Out Optimization.

Antonov, A., Issakov, S. and McClellaud, A. (2017a). Efficient SIMM-MVA Calculation for Callable Exotics, Working paper.

Antonov, A., Issakov, S., Konikov, M., McClelland, A. and Mechkov, S. (2017b). PV and XVA Greeks for Callable Exotics by Algorithmic Differentiation. Working paper.

Basel Committee on Banking Supervision. (2008). International Convergence of Capital Measurement and Capital Standards (Basel II).

Basel Committee on Banking Supervision. (2010). Basel III: A Global Regulatory Framework for More Resilient Banks and Banking Systems.

Basel Committee on Banking Supervision. (2012). Application of Own Credit Risk Adjustments to Derivatives.

Basel Committee on Banking Supervision. (2013a). Fundamental Review of the Trading Book: A Revised Market Risk Framework.

Basel Committee on Banking Supervision. (2013b). Margin Requirements for Non-centrally Cleared Derivatives.

Basel Committee on Banking Supervision. (2014). The Standardized Approach for Measuring Counterparty Credit Risk Exposures (SA-CCR).

Basel Committee on Banking Supervision. (2015). Review of the Credit Valuation Adjustment Risk Framework (FRTB CVA).

Basel Committee on Banking Supervision. (2016a). Minimum Capital Requirements for Market Risk (Standard Approach of Market Risk in FRTB).

Basel Committee on Banking Supervision. (2016b). Revisions to the Securitisation Framework.

Basel Committee on Banking Supervision. (2017). Basel III: Finalising Post-Crisis Reforms (Basel III Final).

Baxter, M. and Rennie, A. (1996). *Financial Calculus: An Introduction to Derivative Pricing*, Cambridge University Press.

Bianchetti, M. (2010). Two Curves, One Price: Pricing and Hedging Interest Rates Derivatives Decoupling Forwarding and Discounting Yield Curves, Risk, SSRN working paper.

Bishop, C. M. (2006). *Pattern Recognition and Machine Learning*, Springer.

Bouayoun, A. (2018). New Developments and Advances in HPC (High performance Computing) for Credit Risk and Exposure Analytics.

Brace, A. (2013). Primer: Curve Stripping with Full Collateralisation.

Brigo, D., Morini, M. and Pallavicini, A. (2013). *Counterparty Credit Risk, Collateral and Funding*, Wiley.

Burgard, C. and Kjaer, M. (2011a). In the Balance, *Risk*, 24(11), pp. 72–75.

Burgard, C. and Kjaer, M. (2011b). Partial Differential Equation Representations of Derivatives with Bilateral Counterparty Risk and Funding Costs, *The Journal of Credit Risk*, 7, pp. 75–93.

Burgard, C. and Kjaer, M. (2013). Funding Strategies, Funding Costs, *Risk*, 26(12).

Chourdakis, K., Epperlein, E., Jeannin, M. and Mcewen, J. (2013). A Cross-Section across CVA.

Clark, I. (2011). *Foreign Exchange Option Pricing: A Practitioner's Guide*, Wiley.

Clark, I. (2014). *Commodity Option Pricing: A Practitioner's Guide*, Wiley.

Dermon, E., Miller, M. B. and Park, D. (2016). *The Volatility Smile*, Wiley.

Fujii, M., Shimada, Y. and Takahashi, A. (2010). A Note on Construction of Multiple Swap Curves with and without Collateral, CARF Working Paper Series No. CARF-F-154.

Görg, A. (2014). SA-CCR: The Standardised Approach for Measuring Counterparty Credit Risk Exposures.

Goodfellow, I., Bengio, Y. and Courvile A. (2016). *Deep Learning*, The MIT Press.

Green, A. (2016). *XVA Credit, Funding and Capital Valuation Adjustments*, Wiley.

Green, A. D. and Kenyon, C. (2015). MVA: Initial Margin Valuation Adjustment by Replication and Regression.

Green, A., Kenyon, C. and Dennis, C. (2014). KVA: Capital Valuation Adjustment.

Gregory, J. (2009). Being two-faced over counterparty credit risk? Working Paper.

Gregory, J. (2012a). Closing out DVA? Working paper.

Gregory, J. (2012b). *Counterparty Credit Risk and Credit Valuation Adjustment: A Continuing Challenge for Global Financial Markets*, Wiley.

Gregory, J. (2016). *The XVA Challenge: Counterparty, Credit Risk, Funding, Collateral and Capital*, Wiley.

Hellmich, M. (2015). Counterparty Credit Risk (CCR) and Collateral Management in the light of Basel III, Basel III.5 and EMIR.

Hull, J. and White, A. (2012a). The FVA Debate.
Hull, J. and White, A. (2012b). Is FVA a cost for derivatives desks? Working paper. Available at www.defaultrisk.com.
Hull, J. and White, A. (2013). Valuing derivatives: Funding value adjustments and fair value.
Hunt, P. (2004). *Financial Derivatives in Theory and Practice*, Wiley.
Hunt, P. and Kennedy, J. (2005). Longstaff-Schwartz, Effective Model Dimensionality and Reducible Markov-Functional Models.
Morgan/Reuters, J. P. (1996). RiskMetrics — Technical Document.
Ji, B. (2017). Impact of Skew for CVA at Portfolio Level.
Kenyon, C. and Green, A. (2014). Efficient XVA Management: Pricing Hedging, and Allocation using Trade-Level Regression and Global Conditioning, Working paper.
Kenyon, C. and Green, A. (2016). Warehousing Credit (CVA) Risk, Capital (KVA) and Tax (TVA) Consequences, Working paper.
Kjaer, M. (2017a). Consistent XVA Metrics Part I: Single-currency.
Kjaer, M. (2017b). Consistent XVA Metrics Part II: Multi-currency.
Lee, J. (2010). Credit Valuation Adjustment (CVA).
Luca, C. and Giles, M. (2012). Algorithmic Differentiation: Adjoint Greeks Made Easy.
Naumann, U. (2012). The art of differentiating computer programs (software, environments and tools). *Society for Industrial and Applied Mathematics.*
Pelsser, A. (2000). *Efficient Methods for Valuing Interest Rate* Derivatives, Springer.
Piterbarg, V. V. (2003). A Practitioner's Guide to Pricing and Hedging Callable Libor Exotics in Forward Libor Models.
Piterbarg, V. V. (2010). Funding Beyond Discounting Collateral Agreements and Derivatives Pricing, Risk.
Piterbarg, V. V. (2012). Cooking with Collateral, Risk, p. 58.
Rebonato, R. (2004). *Volatility and Correlation: The Perfect Hedger and the Fox*, John Wiley & Sons Ltd.
Tan, C. C. (2012). *Market Practice in Financial Modelling*, World Scientific.
Tan, C. C. (2013). New Practical Techniques for Pricing Cross-Currency Swaps with Multi-Currency Collateral, *Global Derivatives Conference.*
Tan, C. C. (2014). A Practical Approach to CVA, DVA and FVA.
Tan, C. C. and Tsuchiya, O. (2016). Unveiling FVA: Simple Cash Flows Analysis with Counterparty and Own Default for Funding Value Adjustment.
Tsuchiya, O. (2019a). Two-Factor Hull-White Model Revisited: Correlation Structure for Two-Factor Interest Rate Model in CVA Calculation.
Tsuchiya, O. (2019b). Correlation in MVA, The 8th XVA Conference London from WBS Citation is include in the body of the book.
Zinn-Justin, J. (2002). Quantum Field Theory and Critical Phenomena. Clarendon Press Oxford.

Index

N

O

P

Q

R

www.ingramcontent.com/pod-product-compliance
Lightning Source LLC
LaVergne TN
LVHW052034200926
848481LV00005B/1677
* 9 7 8 9 8 1 1 2 2 1 4 2 2 *